CREATING THE WELFARE STATE

CREATING THE WELFARE STATE

The Political Economy of Twentieth-Century Reform

Edward Berkowitz
Kim McQuaid

Second Edition—Revised and Expanded

PRAEGER

New York
Westport, Connecticut
London

Copyright Acknowledgments

The authors wish to thank the following journals for permission to reprint materials that have previously appeared in different form: The Business History Review, The American Journal of Economics and Sociology, The Historian, *and* The Journal of Economic History. *Thanks are also owed to JAI Press of Greenwich, Connecticut, the publishers of* Research in Economic History.

Library of Congress Cataloging-in-Publication Data

Berkowitz, Edward D.
    Creating the welfare state: the political economy of twentieth-century reform / Edward Berkowitz, Kim McQuaid.
       p.   cm.
    Bibliography: p.
    Includes index.
    ISBN 0-275-92747-4 (alk. paper)
       1. Social service—United States—History.   2. Public welfare—United States—History.   3. Welfare state—Case studies.
    I. McQuaid, Kim.   II. Title.
    HV91.B39   1988
    361'.973—dc19   87-25871

Library of Congress Catalog Card Number: 87-25871

ISBN: 0-275-92747-4

First published in 1988

Praeger Publishers, One Madison Avenue, New York, NY 10010
A division of Greenwood Press, Inc.

Printed in the United States of America

The paper used in this book complies with the
Permanent Paper Standard issued by the National
Information Standards Organization (Z39.48-1984).

10 9 8 7 6 5 4 3 2 1

For Sarah Elizabeth Berkowitz
and
Francis Walter and Margaret Fitzgerald Phelan McQuaid

CONTENTS

ACKNOWLEDGMENTS

This collaboration has more than doubled its authors' debts. Two individuals deserve special mention. Jonathan Hughes of Northwestern University encouraged us to develop our ideas in seminars and private conversations. We owe him a great deal. Robert Wiebe of Northwestern, for his part, has read more of our prose over the years than either of us cares to mention. Any stylistic grace or analytic clarity this book contains results largely from his efforts.

Each of the authors has more personal debts. Edward Berkowitz would like to thank his parents, Emily Frank, Mary Walsh, Amy Kahn and Eleanor Sachs for their help and support. Kim McQuaid pays his respects to Joel Mokyr and Lou Cain (for editorial advice), Terry and Bonnie Byrnes, Sid and Helene Amster, Marc Gaynes, Stanley Pozdziak, George Farrell, and Dave French (for being worthy friends), and his parents.

We hasten to add the traditional disclaimer that all errors are our own, and are not the fault of the people who have helped us. This volume is the work of two people, however. So, we can add one further note: most of the mistakes in this book are the fault of the other author.

PREFACE TO THE
SECOND EDITION

Doing a second edition, like taping a television show, gives the authors a chance to correct their old mistakes and to make new ones.

This book has enjoyed what might be described as modest success in the world of academia. We began the book as very young assistant professors, just out of graduate school, where we had studied with Robert Wiebe and Jonathan Hughes. One year it happened that, when Jonathan Hughes and Joel Mokyr were put in charge of an academic meeting, they asked us to write a paper. We pooled our resources and ideas. One of us knew about the world of business and the other had done work on the federal bureaucracy. We decided to collaborate on a paper that discussed businessmen and bureaucrats and their respective roles in the creation of modern social welfare programs. After the presentation of this paper, an editor approached us and asked us if we "had a book." No, we didn't, but we were young, energetic, and eager to see our names in print. "Give us a few weeks," we said, "and you will have your book."

We did the book in a particular way and for particular reasons. We emphasized what the academy has dubbed the "new institutionalism." That meant we highlighted corporate and governmental programs. Although businessmen and bureaucrats figured prominently in the resulting narrative, we did not present them as spiders at the center of every web. We looked at their interactions to determine how each influenced the other and how both were affected by wider events. We believe that businessmen and bureaucrats were major actors but not the only actors. Nor were they the dominant actors during each and every phase of the lengthy creation of the American version of a welfare state. Our belief was and is that during the *formative* stages of the American welfare state the private sector provided the conceptual models and the administrative capacities upon which the public sector programs were based. The influence of private actors on public actions lessened over time, as the private sector accommodated its activities to the existence of a central government that did more than fight an occasional Indian war, care for the victim of these and other wars, and deliver the mail to everyone. Similarly, public actors gained the self-confidence and the ability to undertake important social welfare responsibilities, such as providing a pension to nearly everyone over the age of 65.

As we tossed ideas around, the weeks became months, during which we were repeatedly advised against collaboration: it was not the way to get ahead in the profession, we were told. Instead, one published his dissertation as a tight little monograph with a good university press and, having become known to a small audience, wrote a larger book that made slightly less restricted points to this same small audience. To do otherwise invited disaster in a more and more limited job market. These facts became painfully clear to us as we attended to the business of getting jobs and teaching courses. We persisted, in part because the project provided reassurance in a profession that, viewed from our perspective, lacked assurances. Collaboration reduced the sense of isolation that seemed, but we believed did not have to be, the inevitable environment in which historians worked. We traded chapters back and forth, and we endured the process of peer review from people who were puzzled by what we were attempting to do.

Praeger published the book in 1980. Some reviewers were quick to spot our debt to Robert Wiebe, Louis Galambos, and Alfred Chandler. "This is as pure a statement of the organizational interpretation of recent American history as any available today," wrote Stuart Brandes in the *Journal of American History*. Or as Theda Skocpol put it in a recent paper on "The Politics of American Social Provision," our account is "sophisticated" because it makes a "structural point, rather than . . . assertions about capitalists as policy actors (or controllers of other policy actors). According to this view, the growth of large scale bureaucratic organization has been the master tendency in twentieth-century America as in other industrial nations; yet in the U.S. case big business preceded big government in undergoing bureaucratic transformation. In turn, as laggards in the bureaucratization process, government units and actors have often relied upon prior business models or coopted the existing organizational capacities of large-scale corporations to implement public policies, with the result that such policies had to be especially closely tailored to certain business needs."

Other, less sympathetic reviewers lamented the absence of any sort of theory in the book and decried its "strident empiricism." As Larry Griffin of the University of Indiana wrote in *Contemporary Sociology*, "General social theory of any perspective is completely eschewed, and even limited generalizations are conspicuously absent."

Still others complained that the book was too short and too limited; it hardly justified its grandiose title. The book, these critics properly pointed out, failed to explain the creation of the welfare state as a whole. Much lay beyond the book's reach; education was hardly mentioned and even (means-tested) welfare took second place to social insurance. Just as the book did not cover all the relevant subjects, so it omitted many of the important characters. Writing in the *American Historical Review*, Vaughn Davis Bornet supplied a virtual roster of people who failed to make the book including Norman Thomas, Robert M. LaFollette, Abraham Epstein, Hubert Humphrey and Lyndon Johnson. Abe Bortz, the former chief historian at the Social Security Administration, pointed out in *The Public Historian* that even when we named names, we sometimes forgot to check the titles. In a particularly memorable "howler," to use Jonathan Hughes's phrase, we made Robert Ball of the Social Security Administration into an actuary, no doubt to the horror of former Chief Actuary Robert Myers. Bortz also had more telling criticism: Why does the study stop in 1956? he asked. "What about Medicare and Medicaid and the other significant social welfare programs of the 1960s and 1970s?"

At the time, we might have responded to Bortz by saying that Medicare and Medicaid were worthy subjects but they were not *our* subjects. Now, from a distance of seven years, we see his point and those of the other reviewers. What about Medicare and Medicaid? Where do they and the other recent social welfare programs fit into the story of the welfare state? Has the public sector triumphed over the private sector?

As a result, our second edition will at least mention Medicare, even if education fails to make an appearance. You will still not find Norman Thomas in the index, however.

The first edition had gaps. We were encouraged, however, by the way in which the book showed up in studies of social welfare history, such as those by James Patterson and Michael Katz, and in debates about the development of the American welfare state conducted by Jill Quadagno, Theda Skocpol, Bill Domhoff, Andy Achenbaum, Clarke Chambers and Walter Trattner.

We are a bit dismayed to find ourselves consigned to the camp that holds that businessmen were always and inevitably the dominant influence over social welfare policies and programs at all times. But that may be the price of even limited fame. Our own view of our view is that no single explanation works for all cases.

In the years separating the two editions, our perspectives on social welfare history have matured. Edward Berkowitz has spent the seven years in and out of academia, including one stint on the staff of a presidential commission, another in academic administration, and still another trying to blend history and public policy in a university. These experiences have led to his writing policy papers on welfare reform, essays on social security, articles on the relationship between history and public policy, a book on disability policy, and a book on the market for health care. These experi-

ences have undoubtedly brought him a little closer to the federal bureaucracy and given him a greater appreciation for the constraints under which
federal bureaucrats have operated, particularly in the era of Jimmy Carter.

Kim McQuaid, meanwhile, has moved around less and enjoyed it more.
In 1985 and 1986, he had an opportunity to gain some international perspective on his work when he was appointed the Mary Ball Washington
Professor of U.S. History at the University College Dublin. *Big Business
and Presidential Power from Roosevelt to Reagan*, published in 1982, summarized a decade of trying to understand how big business has influenced a
wide variety of federal policies over the course of the last half-century.
Extramural political involvements and essays written for nonacademic
journals gave him a better understanding of how the real world works.

When Praeger offered a chance to do another version of the book, therefore, Berkowitz agreed to put aside his longer study of the American social
welfare system, and McQuaid decided to take a break from writing a history of contemporary America to undertake this second edition of *Creating
the Welfare State*.

In this second edition, we intend to fatten up what one reviewer called a
"slender monograph" by incorporating some of the recent literature and by
applying some of the insights we have gained from our later work.

Specifically, we have lengthened the introduction to reflect our new
understanding of what Morton Keller has called the nineteenth-century
"polity." We have thoroughly revamped the discussion of social security in
Chapter 6, and we have added a new chapter that summarizes
developments after 1956. We hope in this manner to convince others that
collaboration pays dividends and that Professors Hughes and Mokyr did
the world a service by creating *Creating the Welfare State*.

CREATING THE WELFARE STATE

INTRODUCTION

Between 1900 and 1950, private businessmen and public bureaucrats operating on both the state and federal levels created the modern American social welfare system. Never well organized or well administered, the system nonetheless marked America's response to a world in which most people worked for someone else and enjoyed long life expectancies at birth. In formulating this system, private employers and public officials interacted and produced strategies for maintaining people's incomes in times of unemployment and disability, providing access to health care, and delivering social services.

Traditionally, accounts of America's path from poor law to welfare state or of its struggle for social security portray the process as one in which the public sector assumes responsibilities and the private sector, often quite reluctantly, yields them. Social welfare concerns bureaucrats and reformers a lot more than it involves businessmen. If businessmen appear at all they become clichés: Babbitts mouthing Gilded Age slogans; Social Darwinians denying bread to the disabled and hungry; gray eminences conspiring to thwart the people. When businessmen receive a more three-dimensional portrayal, they are often penned within the Progressive Era or the 1920s and left to die with the New Deal.[1]

Such established methods of analysis obscure important historical facts. The American social welfare system was not created by public officials *de novo*. It evolved from concrete experiences with the social challenges of an industrializing society. Because the federal government did not exist as a social welfare entity throughout much of the twentieth century, the nation relied on other groups for both the creation and the implementation of welfare procedures. Although local and state governments were a factor here, so, too, were businessmen. Corporations, in fact, were the first organizational entities to face modern problems of providing income supports and welfare services for national occupational constituencies. It is, therefore, important to understand how they went about the process and to analyze how businessmen's experiences affected the ways in which public officials established their own priorities and programs.

In what follows, we attempt a synthesis between the "private" and "public" approaches in twentieth-century America. Our inquiry alters the established terms of social welfare and business history. Social welfare becomes more impersonal and analytic: less the story of the struggles of individual reformers and more a reflection of the federal government's bureaucratic abilities. Business history, for which Alfred D. Chandler, among others, has provided an impressive analytic structure, moves away from a primary emphasis upon production, distribution, and command techniques toward an increased concern for the human dimension of industrial development.[2]

In such an inquiry, we must of necessity be selective. We focus on the labor market, for that has been the major arena for social welfare innovation in this century. Business and government have together changed the terms of employment. Today, for example, most employers pay a minimum wage determined by the state and federal governments and also meet government-established safety standards. In addition, many employers assume the obligation of protecting workers against the risk of industrial accidents and ill health and also set aside money that will help to fund a worker's retirement.

The basic point of our book is quite simple. There was a time when employers established and maintained the terms of minimum wages, retirement plans, and other social welfare amenities by themselves, with minimal help or hindrance from the government. Businessmen preceded government into many social welfare fields. Early in the twentieth century, the federal government began to complement these efforts. Later, it began to get more involved and to provide social welfare services directly. It would be foolish to think that the government simply entered into the picture without consulting private businessmen and learning from the business experience or, to put it more plainly, that private sector precedents did not influence public sector activities.

As historians, we want to understand *when* the federal government became a significant force in social welfare policy. Here we are aided by the analytic work of political scientists like Stephen Skowronek as well as by Alfred Chandler and other business historians. In an important work published after this book first appeared, Skowronek introduced the concept of "administrative capacity" into discussions of public administration. He surrounded this concept with elegant yet delicate jargon that reflected current theories and concerns in political science.[3]

Theories come and go, of course. Our more vulgar sense of Skowronek's term is summed up by the notion that in the nineteenth and early twentieth centuries, a large public sector could not simply be commanded into existence. Until well into the twentieth century, the U.S. government lacked the administrative capacity to undertake elaborate social welfare programs. By way of contrast, private employers had achieved this capacity much earlier. In the case of railroads, such capacity was an established fact well before 1890.

That brings us to a point advanced by Alfred Chandler in *The Visible Hand*. Chandler makes the point about comparative administrative advantage quite directly: "No public enterprise," he writes, "came close to the railroad in size and complexity of operations. In the 1890s, a single railroad system managed more men and handled more funds and used more capital than the most complex of American governmental and miltary operations." To clinch his point, Chandler notes that the Pennsylvania Railroad employed over 110,000 workers in 1891, while the Postal Service, the largest federal agency, had 95,440 workers, scattered across 64,000 post offices. The postal workers earned their jobs as political favors; the railroad workers managed one of the first modern corporate enterprises. Chandler concludes it ws the "railroad, not government or the military, [that] provided training in modern large-scale administration."[4]

It took the federal government several decades to catch up with the railroads, for, like the larger private companies, it evolved from a relatively simple structure that regulated the action of external entities, into a complex organization whose parts performed specialized actions and served specialized functions. The analyses of Chandler, Fritz Redlich and others can be broadened to demonstrate how this process occurred in both business and government.[5]

As late as 1900, the internal administrative structure of large American businesses, outside of the railroad industry, remained relatively simple. It resembled a long, vertical "chain" of command. As this image suggests, management was loosely based upon hierarchical models customary to the lower levels in the military. At the top a central executive, often an owner-capitalist, exercised final authority over every stage in the production and distribution process. Below him came a descending series of subexecutives who reported directly and informally to the chief executive. At the bottom of the chain dangled the foremen, the platoon leaders of industrial capitalism. These lower-level administrators enjoyed a wide range of powers, including the right to provide such welfare services as existed. It was primarily the foremen who set the intimate and ultimate terms of the employment contract. Therefore, such welfare services that the masses of workers received depended upon the *ad hoc* decisions of tens of thousands of foremen.

Between 1880 and 1920, changes in industrial strategy altered this decentralized bureaucratic structure. Many companies, particularly those in the electrical manufacturing, chemical, rubber, automobile, petroleum, steel, copper, business machines, and agricultural implements industries, expanded their operations through vertical integration and geographic dispersal. Such consolidated enterprises increasingly "came to do their own marketing, their own purchasing from primary sources, and often their own producing of the raw materials." Substantive structural reorganizations were necessary to fulfill these augmented administrative responsibilities. Managerial capitalists replaced all-purpose autocrats. These new administrators substituted departmental or regional units that performed specialized functions such as marketing, research and development, or "welfare work" for the old undifferentiated bureaucracy. In this new bureaucratic structure, specialized experts gradually assumed responsibilities for hiring, firing, safety, and overall employee well-being.[6]

The evolution of the federal government's social welfare programs involved many of the same changes in organizational strategy and structure as the development of company welfare services. Between the American Revolution and the late nineteenth century, the executive branch of the federal government provided few social welfare services. Those that it did provide either took place on the periphery of American development or reflected the rudimentary administrative style of what Skowronek calls the state of "courts and parties." Wards of the state, such as Indians, former slaves, and veterans of the nation's wars, received welfare services from the federal government. Even this rudimentary activity, however, occurred primarily at the state or local level. Washington, as Robert Wiebe has noted, served as a "clearing house for a quite limited range of problems."[7]

Such federal welfare work as did occur was temporary in nature and administered by flexible, multipurpose bureaucratic agencies. Typically, nineteenth-century federal social welfare activity consisted of a single, short-term transaction between Congress and groups of local representatives often unconnected with government. Congress gave these groups land, the one commodity it had in abundance. The groups sold or used the land without further federal interference. As a result, there was no need for a large federal social welfare bureaucracy. As just one example, the Connecticut Asylum for the Deaf and Dumb asked for and received a federal grant of 23,000 acres of land and promptly sold it in 1819 for $300,000.[8]

Expanding nineteenth-century boundaries of settlement nearly always involved encounters with Indians. They posed long-term problems for the federal government, rather than sporadic or incidental ones. In quite a literal way, the Indians paid the price of expanding American settlement. They were also among the first groups in America to trade in their traditional independence for the benefits of a loosely organized and indifferently administered welfare state. This welfare state, if such it was, came complete with cash payments, the provision of education at federal expense, and even federally subsidized health care. Although wide-ranging, the Indians' benefits were not financed from general revenues. Instead, the federal government sold to railroads and settlers the land it had taken from the

Indians—and gave the Indians some of the proceeds. The federal bureaucracy involved was so vestigial that military officers often served as Indian agents; priests and other religious figures doubled as teachers. As a result, implementation of welfare services for Indians was often poor, as suggested by the location of the Bureau of Indian Affairs first in the War Department and later in the Interior Department.

Beginning in 1889, for example, the Red Lake Band of the Chippewa Indians of Minnesota received payments, education, and health services from a fund created by the sale of lands that had previously been reserved for this tribe. The Red Lake Indians did not deal with professional social workers. Instead, they took what they could get from party regulars, local residents, or others who happened to find themselves in the remote sectons of the country where the Indians lived.[9]

During and after the Civil War, displaced southern blacks became wards of the state, except that their period of federal largess lasted only a short time. Antislavery congressmen sought to provide freedmen with food, clothing, education, medical attention, and land. Even this effort to insure that freedom would have real meaning failed to lead to the creation of new federal bureaucatic structures or permanent responsibilities. Instead of creating a new executive department to house the Freedmen's Bureau designated to carry out these tasks, Congress placed it within the War Department. Within ten years of the new bureau's creation, congressional conservatives had destroyed it altogether. During the Freedmen's Bureau short life, it operated through institutions that had been in existence since the era of George Washington: Congress, the armed forces, and the courts.[10]

In a sense, these flexible, all-purpose governmental institutions were the organizational equivalents of foremen within the industrial order. Foremen, judges, soldiers, and Congressmen worked on the same informal and unspecialized basis.

Veterans turned this rudimentary welfare state to their advantage. They enjoyed a significant edge over the other groups: they were white, for the most part, and respectable. Alone among the groups, they had unquestioned rights, not the least of which was the right to vote. Politicians tended to treat them with a certain degree of respect, one that often translated into pensions and other favors.

In 1862, for example, Congress passed a law, traditional in form and content, that provided pensions to Union soldiers who were wounded, or, if they had died in battle, to their survivors. In the last quarter of the nineteenth century, Congress, bidding for votes, made the pensions more liberal, raising the benefit level and making the benefits easier to get. Congress also passed an inordinate number of special acts granting pensions to people whose requests had been denied by the Pension Bureau, which had been created to oversee the process. In this way, Congress became personally involved in the administration of the program and extended its boundaries. Veterans' pensions resembled expenditures for rivers and harbors: programs of direct benefit to local constituents for which individual congressmen could take personal credit—and in which the wide distribution of benefits took precedence over their careful administration.

With the passage of time, expenditures for veterans' pensions mounted. In 1890 veterans' pensions consumed 34 percent of the federal budget, and veterans' pensions became the largest single item (with the exception of debt service) in the federal budget every year between 1885 and 1897. Over time, as well, Congress loosened the relationship between a disability pension and wartime injury until, by 1906, any Union veteran over 62 automatically qualified for a pension.[11]

Veterans' pensions were the only nineteenth-century social welfare program that could be described as large or significant or anything close to universal. Despite their size, however, they were administered in a very loose manner and reached relatively few of those in need. Civil War pensions, for example, excluded by definition those who fought on the wrong side or those who arrived in America after the war. That meant that Southerners, eastern European immigrants and other immigrants, for example, were beyond the program's selective reach. If they wanted help from the government, they would have to look elsewhere. Some Southerners received pensions from the former Confederate states; some immigrants received welfare of one sort or another from city governments or local machines. Northern veterans depended on Uncle Sam's more certain generosity.

Only at the end of the nineteenth century did this traditional system change. In part, this change reflected dismay over the high costs of veterans' pensions and the administrative scandals in the Bureau of Indian Affairs. In part, the change related to a political realignment that assured the Republicans supremacy over the Democrats and eliminated the need to bid for votes through veterans' pensions and other "giveaways." In part, also, the change marked a response to a series of unsettling changes in nineteenth-century society.

Viewed dispassionately, the evolution in federal strategies came about because of the same forces that altered the strategies of individual corporations. These forces could be summarized in a word: industrialism. As business firms widened their geographic and product ranges and created national markets for important goods and services, political and administrative patterns that put primary emphasis on locality or region became more and more inappropriate. Interest groups increasingly needed to petition the government not as representatives of localities but as spokesmen for wider, more inclusive national constituencies.

Professional and occupational groups met the need. After the 1890s, the federal government responded to a growing number of nationally organized professions and occupations: farmers represented by the National Grange; craftsmen organized in unions; employers organized by industrial trade associations; civic activists grouped in associations such as the General Federation of Women's Clubs, National Consumer's League, National Child Labor Committee, and National Conference of Charities and Corrections; and professionals represented by such organizations as the American Medical Association. To bargain with these groups new bureaucratic structures evolved.[12]

These new bureaucratic structures took the form of occupational departments that regulated and served occupational constituencies. By 1913 the executive branch of the federal government included departments of agriculture, commerce, and labor. Each of these new departments supplied some form of welfare service to its respective groups, although most of their activities strained the modern conception of welfare. Farmers received packets of improved seed strains and free scientific advice; businessmen received industrial statistics or information about the welfare programs of important companies; laborers received treatises on the incidence of industrial accidents.[13]

Although other occupational groups—farmers in particular—posed political problems, contemporaries believed that industrial workers had the most potential for creating general social disorder, even revolution. They were right. The strike waves of 1877, 1886, and 1894 reinforced their beliefs. These conditions gave particular urgency to the creation of a federal bureau that would respond to these problems.

Despite this urgency, the Department of Labor and its bureaucratic predecessors relied upon nonspecialized officials to deal with the workers' welfare. Federal officials did not see their task as involving the direct provision to industrial laborers of welfare services that would quiet industrial unrest. Instead, indirect, largely advisory assistance was provided to nongovernmental organizations, and a small number of minimum standards—like the hours and conditions for those few industrial employees in federal establishments, including government arsenals—were enforced.

In this initial stage of its twentieth-century development, the federal government resembled those business corporations that had not yet attempted to rationalize their bureaucratic operations. Functions that could have been coordinated among departments and bureaus were not. This condition contrasted with the state of bureaucratic development in large corporations that were evolving strategies and structures to handle diversified product markets. Simply put, large corporations provided more welfare services to more people in more places than did the federal government.

By 1920, however, the federal government haltingly began to realize its possibilities and to undergo a process of structural change. It moved from advising, subsidizing, and regulating special groups, like veterans and farmers, to supplying welfare services to *all* citizens. First, it used local and professional intermediaries in this process; then, beginning in the 1940s, it began to supply the services itself. The structure that followed these changed strategies resembled that of a mature, consolidated corporation.

In its present form, the federal government consists of a collection of specialized departments increasingly organized by function. The Department of Health and Human Services, organized between 1939 and 1953, supplies social welfare services to all citizens, regardless of region or occupation. All other cabinet-level departments created since the end of World War II have, likewise, been organized by function. These include Housing and Urban Development (1965), Energy (1977), and Education (1980). Older general departments—such as the Department of the Interior and occupationally defined departments, such as the Department of Labor—have undergone a painful process of finding niches for themselves in the new administrative format. In so doing, they have attempted to sound functional themes, as when the Secretary of the Interior pleaded with Congress throughout the 1930s to change the name of his department to the Department of Conservation.[14]

We do not mean to suggest that there is an inevitability in the transformation of the federal bureaucracy. Individuals make their world as well as being made by it. Politics has always played a role in bureaucratic structure. Since policymakers tend to retain old departments, bureaucratic fossils litter the landscape. Congress often hesitates to change the location of bureaus that confer benefits on their constituents. Program administrators fight against changes in their powers, programs, and operations.

For all of these political deviations, the direction of change remained clear. The federal government moved from all-purpose departments doing little for anyone, to an occupationally oriented bureaucracy providing benefits to particular groups, to a functional bureaucracy supplying benefits to everyone. No one seriously suggested, for example, that a cabinet-level department be created to serve the interests of black Americans, even at the height of the agitation over civil rights. To do so would have been to return to an earlier time when most people looked after themselves.

Changing from an occupational to a functional form of administration, the federal government has retraced many of the organizational steps taken by major American corporations. In so doing, its bureaucracy has perceived the necessity of advisory contact and institutional collaboration with corporate managers at many points—particularly those relating to the creation of social welfare legislation. The combined efforts of these businessmen and bureaucrats have produced the structure of the "welfare state" as we know it.

This brief analysis of organizational change suggests an agenda for the analysis of the American social welfare system. This agenda can be stated as a sequence of five questions:

1. How did businessmen begin to supply welfare services in the early twentieth century, and how did these strategies evolve over time?
2. How and why did the federal government enter the welfare field in the early twentieth century?
3. What motivated the transformation of the federal government from indirect regulator, subsidizer, and adviser to direct-service provider in the decade after the end of World War I?
4. How did businessmen in the private sector (particularly those in the corporations most active in providing welfare services) react and readjust to this transformation?
5. How has this process of interaction between businessman and bureaucrat shaped the creation of the contemporary American social welfare system, particularly with regard to the social security program?

In the chapters that follow, we shall attempt to answer these questions. The chapters tell the story of the development of the public and private social welfare systems in the United States and of the uneasy process of merging the two.

NOTES

1. Walter Trattner, *From Poor Law to Welfare State* (New York: Free Press, 1974); Roy Lubove, *The Struggle for Social Security* (Cambridge: Harvard University Press, 1968); Robert H. Wiebe, *Businessmen and Reform* (Cambridge: Harvard University Press, 1962).

2. Alfred D. Chandler, *Strategy and Structure* (Cambridge: MIT Press, 1962) and *The Visible Hand: The Managerial Revolution in American Business* (Cambridge: Harvard University Press, 1977).

3. Stephen Skowronek, *Building a New American State: The Expansion of National Administrative Capacities, 1877–1920* (New York: Cambridge University Press, 1981).

4. Chandler, *Visible Hand*, pp. 204-05.

5. Chandler and Fritz Redlich, "Recent Developments in American Business Administration and their Conceptualization," in *American Economic History: Essays in Interpretation*, ed. S. Coben et al. (Philadelphia: Lippincott, 1966), pp. 546-49.

6. Daniel Nelson, "The New Factory System and the Unions: The National Cash Register Dispute of 1901," *Labor History* 15 (Spring 1974): 163-78; Nelson, *Managers and Workers: Origins of the New Factory System in the United States, 1880-1920* (Madison: University of Wisconsin Press, 1975).

7. Robert H. Wiebe, *The Segmented Society: An Historical Preface to the Meaning of America* (New York: Oxford University Press, 1975), p. 36.

8. Walter I. Trattner, "The Federal Government and Social Welfare in Early Nineteenth Century America," *Social Service Review* 50 (June 1976): 243-55; Trattner, *From Poor Law to Welfare State: A History of Social Welfare in America*, 3rd ed. (New York: The Free Press, 1984), pp. 47-76.

9. William H. Becker and Edward Berkowitz, "Relief and Civilization: Nelson Act Dis-

bursements and the Red Lake Band," unpublished paper.

10. Kenneth M. Stampp, *The Era of Reconstruction* (New York: Random House, 1967), pp. 131-35.

11. More than any other scholar, Theda Skocpol is responsible for the rediscovery of this nineteenth-century version of a welfare state. See Theda Skocpol and John Ikenberry, "The Political Formation of the American Welfare State in Historical and Comparative Perspective," in *Comparative Social Research: An Annual Publication, The Welfare State, 1883-1893, Volume Six, 1983,* ed. Richard Tomasson (JAI Press: Greenwich, Connecticut, 1983), pp. 94-97.

12. Samuel P. Hays, *The Response to Industrialism, 1885-1914* (Chicago: University of Chicago Press, 1957); Robert H. Wiebe, *The Search for Order* (New York: Hill and Wang, 1967), pp. 44-110.

13. *First Report of the Secretary of Agriculture* (Washington, D.C.: G.P.O., 1889), p. 7; *First Annual Report of the Secretary of Commerce and Labor* (Washington, D.C.: G.P.O., 1903), p. 27; "A Brief History of the U.S. Department of Labor," *Labor Information Bulletin*, February 1948, Records of the Department of Labor, Record Group 174, S 195, National Archives, Washington, D.C.

14. *Annual Report of the Secretary of the Interior* (Washington, D.C.: G.P.O., 1936), p. vii.

1

A NEWLY OUTRAGEOUS FORTUNE: A PRIVATE SOCIAL WELFARE SYSTEM EMERGES IN THE UNITED STATES, 1880–1910

During the final quarter of the nineteenth century America became a nationally-integrated industrial society, and this experience changed the terms of the social welfare system. No longer could business enterprises rely on informal mechanisms to solve welfare problems; instead, companies needed to create new institutions able to function over expanding market spaces. The story of the search for these institutions was not the story of an inevitable process beyond human control; instead, it was a story of individuals limited by the perspectives of their times who struggled to solve problems within specific markets and firms. After reviewing the late nineteenth-century social and political scene this chapter deals with the careers of three welfare innovators, and attempts to use these businessmen as indicators of more general social welfare trends.

In late nineteenth-century America the pace of industrial change had outdistanced American social attitudes and institutions. The balanced, self-regulatory economic order hypothesized by Jeffersonian Republican, Jacksonian Democrat, and classical economist alike increasingly appeared to conflict with the realities of a new period in the nation's affairs. Americans faced challenges in understanding the tone and direction of their times.[1]

Beginning in the 1880s articulate members of professional groups attempted to deal with workers' welfare in a changing world. Reintegration of community through settlement houses became the passion of social workers such as Jane Addams, Lillian Wald, and Graham Taylor. Economists such as Richard T. Ely favored cooperative economic institutions based on the ideology of the Social Gospel. College-educated municipal reformers such as Frederic C. Howe and Albert

Shaw focused on less idealistic models of social uplift, advocating control based "on order, on plans on doing things the way business men did them in their own shops and factories." Varieties of reform were endless; only the feeling that an era of free security had passed insofar as the social welfare of the nation was concerned united these reform efforts.[2]

Businessmen were a major factor in reform hopes, for private entrepreneurs possessed the primary responsibility for establishing norms to govern the conduct of the institutions at the center of an industrializing society. The fraternal relations that workers enjoyed— or did not enjoy—with their employers would result from the decisions that businessmen made.

Despite the central role that circumstances forced businessmen to play, however, they had their own difficulties seeing the late nineteenth-century world clearly. Their difficulties stemmed from the fact that between 1880 and 1910 the established patterns of American business underwent marked changes. In particular, firms became larger and more complex and businessmen became more ambitious in defining the limits of their markets. Corporate leaders were discovering the nation—considered as an interdependent industrial entity—and this discovery made the provision of social welfare services difficult.

At the same time local and state governments—the traditional guarantors of mass welfare—were equally ill-equipped to deal with welfare problems. Since early colonial times village and county authorities had provided emergency employment, kept the peace, overseen relief for the poor, and enforced minimum standards regarding the quality, price, and provision of basic goods and services. Between 1830 and 1850 their efforts had been joined by those of the states, particularly those of the industrial Northeast and Middle Atlantic. Education and factory laws, institutions for the care of the mentally retarded and insane, and efforts to regulate railroads and banks gave state governments responsibilities previously confined to local governments.[3] National welfare and employment problems, however, were not amenable to these local or state solutions.

As for national government, the central government did not exist as a social welfare entity in the early twentieth century. In 1900 the national government's civilian bureaucracy totaled 256,000 men and women, most of whom were occupied in the prosaic tasks of delivering the mails, overseeing federal lands, forests, and parks, collecting customs duties, or processing immigrants. Federal officials could not compete with the aggregations of administrative and technical expertise possessed by private corporations. Few people inside or outside Washington entertained the idea that the federal government should assume *direct* responsibilities for maintaining general welfare programs. Although modest survivors' and disability benefits were paid by the Treasury Department to veterans, these awards were temporary and specific in nature. So, too, those Indians living on tribal reserves might obtain occasional direct health and welfare services from the Bureau of Indian Affairs. The passage of the Dawes Act in 1887, however, put Washington well on the way toward a hoped-for abolition of the special status of the national government's aboriginal wards. In time, it was hoped, the federal government would cease to distribute charity entirely, except to veterans who had engaged in patriotic activities in wartime.[4]

Businessmen could not so easily ignore growing problems of work and welfare. In 1886 the emergence of the "labor problem" gave a special urgency to businessmen's social welfare efforts. After a short but severe depression during which unemployment levels climbed and wage rates plummeted an average of 15 percent a wave of industrial unrest occurred. Strikes idled over 10,000 plants throughout the country—three times as many as in any of the preceding five years. A newly-formed American Federation of Labor attempted to formulate national strike strategies for skilled crafts laborers, and the Knights of Labor attempted to speak for close to a million semi- and unskilled workers. In the popular mind strikes were closely linked with alien radicalism and with such events as the Haymarket Riot of 1886. Even so resolutely phlegmatic a President as Grover Cleveland contended that "[t]he gulf between employers and the employed is constantly widening, and classes are rapidly forming, one comprising the very rich and powerful, while in the other are found the toiling poor."[5]

Businessmen needed to lower the temperature of industrial debate. Strikes destroyed their property, disrupted their production schedules, and lowered their profit margins. The first modern social welfare plans, therefore, were efforts to conduct peaceful labor relations. The earliest pioneers were not normal men, nor were they rational bureaucratic actors dispassionately analyzing the columns of profit and loss. An age of experts would come and bring with it fundamental changes in the concepts of articulate business leaders. The last decades of the nineteenth century were, instead, a time of beginning, and the earliest American employers to recognize the necessity for enhancing mass industrial welfare were concerned men. In attempting to transcend the boundaries of their times such men began to create foundations for the corporate welfare system of twentieth-century America. To their stories we now turn.

THE RISE AND DECLINE OF THE
COMMUNITARIAN IMPULSE

The first notable employer-initiated welfare measures followed longstanding traditions in a segmented American society. Throughout earlier American history groups or individuals that deemed a particular local social order to be uncongenial to their welfare had often moved elsewhere and created their own. Businessmen, like the members of various religious, ethnic, and political groups, shared this tradition. In the 1820s and 1830s, for example, the Lowell Associates, a group of Boston entrepreneurs, had met the nation's first industrial spurt by using techniques familiar to Puritans, Mormons, and Utopian Socialists. At Lowell, Massachusetts, they created a miniaturized industrial world, a local society that paralleled the social structure of preindustrial New England without either changing it or being changed by it. In the late nineteenth century businessmen attempted, often unconsciously, to extend the Lowell tradition.

The industrial suburb of Pullman, Illinois, exemplified their efforts. Between 1881 and 1884 railroad car manufacturer George M. Pullman constructed one of the most ambitiously planned settlements ever created in the United States—a company town complete with hotel, markets, landscaped parks, factories, and residences for over 8,000 people. During the next twenty years large firms including Colorado Fuel and Iron, Carnegie Steel, Pelzer Manufacturing, Westinghouse Air Brake, Maryland Steel, and American Waltham Watch Company instituted their own versions of Pullman. Geographically-isolated mining and textile firms joined in. Company-supplied housing, recreation, and educational facilities dotted the American industrial landscape. Although such innovation later became notorious in labor relations annals, the fact remained that businessmen were for the first time in a century accepting wider responsibilities for the health and comfort of employees.[6]

Although the existence of these earliest benevolent "feudalisms" owed little to philanthropy and even less to ideology there were men who managed to operate within this tradition and orient it toward the future. Such men thought in terms of systems. Far more than the *spirit* of contemporary industrialism needed to be changed; instead, new *institutions* and *institutional relationships* had to bridge the widening gap between those who owned and those who labored.

Among those men who managed to be innovators within this old tradition was Nelson Olsen Nelson. His story traced a curve of acceptability regarding welfare procedure and concept.

In 1886 Nelson, a 42-year-old Norwegian immigrant who had become a millionaire in the St. Louis plumbing hardware business, began his search for community. First, he was selected to serve on a three-man board organized by the "better elements" of St. Louis' commercial community to mediate between strikers organized by the Knights of Labor and the managers of Jay Gould's railroad empire. Gould and the strikers' leaders seemed to Nelson equally unwilling to forswear "sheer buncombe and class pride." The mediation failed resoundingly, so Nelson began to search for other means of restoring a community of interest between employer and employed.[7]

The techniques he selected owed much to a marriage of a European program and a preindustrial American communitarian ethic. First, Nelson introduced himself to books explaining new doctrines of profit sharing recently developed in France, Germany, and England. At base, profit sharing was a means by which the interests of owner and worker might be mutualized, a kind of half-way house toward the abolition of a wage system under which the many were dependent laborers and the few were independent owners of the means of production, distribution, and exchange. The system guaranteed workers within individual companies a fixed (and sometimes preannounced) percentage of the net profits that their labor had helped to create. Dividends would be prorated among all employees, managerial and nonmanagerial, on the basis of salaries or wages. The higher the wage or salary, the higher the profit-sharing dividend the worker received; the higher the total firm's profits, the more money distributed to the workers. Here was a means to restore an identity of interest between employers and employed. Worker incomes over and above wages or salaries might escalate as fast as the overall profit of a company's operations. As a result, both workers and employers retained an incentive to maximize their total incomes. Using profit-sharing programs they could cooperate in a fashion so that both could gain simultaneously, and neither was required to increase their total revenue at the expense of the other.

To perfect his scheme Nelson traveled to Europe in August 1886. There he was introduced to the work of a French businessman that changed the course of his life and enabled him to marry his vision of a mutualism through profit sharing to the vision of the ordered community of a New England township.

Although forgotten today, J. B. A. Godin, a wealthy follower of the French, utopian socialist Charles Fourier, enjoyed considerable repute in the nineteenth century. Godin's large factory community in Guise, France, was one of the most successful examples of industrial communitarianism in Europe; a French equivalent to Pullman, Illinois. At Guise, workers lived in multistoried apartment complexes called "Familisteres" (after Fourier); shopped in cooperative stores; sent their children to daycare centers; and enjoyed the amenities of parks, theaters, schools, community washrooms, and laundries. Further, workers were the beneficiaries of profit-sharing programs that allowed them to invest their dividends in the voting stock of the firm. This allowed a gradual version of workers' control to evolve should employees desire it.[8]

Guise entranced Nelson. Not only was Godin a "philanthropist of the broadest and most practical views," and the world's "most conspicuous example" of a successful profit-sharing employer, he was also a man who was trying to unite the factory system of the industrial present with the preindustrial past. Nelson returned to America, sought the assistance of Social Gospel churchmen such as Edward Everett Hale, traveled throughout New England investigating the structure and operation of the Yankee village, and then made another trip to Europe to consult with French profit-sharing employers and leaders of the British cooperative movement.[9]

In 1890 Nelson secured a 250-acre tract of land in rural Illinois about 30 miles from St. Louis and relocated the workshops of the Nelson Company on the site. Construction began on single-family houses for the employees. Nelson moved his own family from a fashionable home in St. Louis to a two-story wooden dwelling in "Leclaire." In this new village named after a prominent French profit-sharing pioneer, gardens, walkways, and a school soon appeared. Workers were encouraged to purchase or construct homes. People who wished to leave Leclaire could sell their homes without sacrifice. Others who wished to live in the neighboring town of Edwardsville were free to do so. All employees who had worked for Nelson's firm more than six months were granted a preannounced percentage of total company profits, paid annually. Within a few years the N. O. Nelson Manufacturing Company had become one of the half-dozen firms in the United States to experiment with a program of labor-capital partnership through profit sharing. Nelson had established his cooperative world-in-miniature, a world that was inside an industrializing society in terms of dollars and cents, but outside of it in terms of internal social and economic organization.[10]

The question remaining was whether he could broaden his following. He began in 1892 when he helped found the Association for the Promotion of Profit Sharing with Social Gospeler Nicholas Paine Gilman, U.S. Commissioner of Labor Carroll D. Wright, economist Francis Amasa Walker, and fellow employer H. R. Towne of the Yale and Towne Lock Company. The association worked to spread its model of industrial cooperation through profit sharing beyond individual companies and into the mainstream of corporate America. A small quarterly entitled *Employer and Employed* covered European and American developments, particularly Nelson's Leclaire Plan. *Harper's Weekly, North American Review*, the *Forum*, and the newly-established *American Journal of Sociology* gave sympathetic coverage to Nelson's experiments, and other journals such as the *Independent* and the *Review of Reviews* covered profit sharing more generally. These early writings argued for profit sharing in what later generations would dismiss as highly moralistic terms. Nelson invoked the Golden Rule and images of moral regeneration in explaining the importance of his reform efforts.

Depression soon altered the terms of the discussion. Until 1893 Nelson's profit-sharing programs worked well. Dividends averaging 8 to 10 percent of annual wages were regularly paid. After 1890 Nelson had taken the additional step of making these dividends payable in the stock of the company. This practice enabled those workers who chose not to sell their certificates back to the firm for cash to begin owning a larger and larger portion of the firm's total capital and to put aside a reserve for use in hard times.[11]

By 1893, 400 of the 500 employees in the firm held stock in the company. Additional percentages of the firm's annual profits were reserved for employee sickness, death, and retirement programs. At a time when the normal working day in the metal trades was ten hours, Nelson's employees worked a nine-hour day. In 1892 the annual dividend on wages was raised. That December Nelson informed his employees that those of them who had invested their profit-sharing dividends in the stock of the company from the beginning had then received a return of "72 per cent on your wages, or $449.28 on $12 a week." The advantages of partnership appeared obvious.

By 1895, however, a widespread depression had forced the annual profit-sharing dividend down to 4 percent. For the next eight years the Nelson Manufacturing Company paid no dividends at all. A ten-hour day was restored to help the firm meet competitive pressures. Finally, in 1894 Nelson ruled that only those workers who invested 10 percent of their annual wages in the stock of the Nelson Company could participate in the profit-sharing program. He defended this emergency savings plan as a means by which each member of the firm might be thrown upon his own responsibility to "save and support, by his own exertions, the system which gave him a return." Partnership, however, was now a matter of mutual losses, as well as mutual gains. This fact was not inclined to lead employees to uncritical admiration for Nelson's program.[12]

By 1903 the company regained its fiscal composure and the profit-sharing programs at Leclaire began to be restored. First, the nine-hour day was revived. A year later Nelson announced the payment of a retroactive 4 percent dividend on total employee earnings during the 1896–1904 period.

Finally, in 1905 Nelson formulated what he hoped to be the capstone of his firm's profit-sharing plan—a means by which a fully cooperative restructuring of ownership might be achieved. Nelson stopped taking any profit or interest on his own majority stockholding in his company over and above 6 percent per annum. Remaining profits were, in Nelson's words,

> divided between the employees, the customers, philanthropy, and the [one-fifth of the] stock held by others than myself. . . . The employees get about one-third of the profits, the customers one-third, and the employee stockholders and philanthropy the other third. The employees get dividends in relation to their wages, the customers in proportion to the profitability of their purchases, . . . Philanthropy gets about one-fourth of the whole . . . and such a portion of my capital as can conveniently be withdrawn from the business.
>
> The dividends will be paid in my stock, thus giving me the money, and the employees and customers the ownership of the business. It will take no great length of time to make them the complete owners and the company a completely cooperative concern. This has been my objective for many years past, awaiting only the proper conditions.[13]

Nelson's cooperative community, in short, would become a cooperatively owned firm. Workers in the little world of Leclaire would collectively control (in conjunction with the customers) the capital and tools necessary to their labor. Distinctions between owning capital and selling labor would be abolished. Leclaire would serve as a beacon into the future, a functioning model of what progressives and many socialists of the period termed a "cooperative commonwealth."

Despite these considerable achievements Nelson never succeeded in making Leclaire a blueprint for the development of an American industrial welfare system. His failure stemmed from three causes. First, workers often failed to understand the logic of the economic concepts behind profit sharing. Second, Nelson's success in the product market undercut the success of his experiment. Company expansion in the decade after 1897 highlighted the problem. As did many businesses operating in national markets the Nelson Manufacturing Company built branch plants and set up sales offices in distant regions. By 1910 the works at Leclaire were joined by others in Indiana and Alabama. The 200 workers of 1886 had grown to a total of 1200 by 1918. Providing the same services for the workers in the branch plants as for the core labor force in Leclaire proved difficult. The problems were complicated by the fact that a large percentage of the firm's southern laborers were blacks. The concept of an equality of rights proved difficult for many workers (though not for Nelson) to understand. The numbers of workers in the branch plants who retained their stock dividends remained small, in part because senior employees who were the best-established participants in the stock ownership and profit-sharing plans wanted to restrict the cooperative plan to themselves.[14]

The organized labor movement presented the third barrier to the effective spread of Nelson's cooperative ideas. Nelson tolerated unions during his early years at Leclaire, but he believed that unionism was no substitute for the "organic relief" for the welfare problems of an industrial society provided by cooperation. The gradual evolution of a cooperative industrial system, Nelson believed, provided a means by which all workers, not just a privileged few, could obtain long-term financial security. Accordingly, Samuel Gompers' American Federation of Labor (AFL), the first trade union alliance to solve the riddles of national labor organization, exemplified in Nelson's view all that was wrong with the labor movement. The AFL abandoned the nonskilled in favor of the "talented tenth" of skilled craftsmen—and then forced the consumers to pay the final bill. Although Nelson was not about to champion free enterprise and institute popular antiunion strategies of the period such as labor spies, yellow dog contracts, and punitive firings, neither did he want craft unions to gain a dominant position in the affairs of his industrial world.

The watershed for trade unionism came in 1907. At that time one-sixth (the highest paid foundrymen) of the Leclaire work force went on strike for a 10 percent pay raise. Angered by what he termed "this attempt to subvert the Leclaire idea of the rights of all," Nelson refused to hire any more union men. For those employees who were already union members Nelson offered a choice: remain unionists and forfeit future profit-sharing dividends or cease being unionists and continue to take part in the firm's cooperative programs. All but twenty-three men turned in their union cards. Those who did not continued to work for the company.[15]

Nelson's inability to merge an expanded labor force and organized labor into his firm's welfare system underscored his failure to come to grips with the forces that increasingly defined the twentieth century and distinguished it from the nineteenth. Between 1910 and 1922 Nelson's interests diverged further and further from company affairs. With growing insistency Nelson championed rural regeneration, agricultural cooperatives, and integrated "new towns" or "garden cities" such as those begun in England by urban reformers. Nelson's own rural background and communitarian loyalties made him unable to understand the shifting emphasis of reform, and he drifted further and further away from mainstream opinion regarding welfare matters.[16]

In the end, Nelson was drawn to the city himself. De facto control over company operations was given to subordinates and the aging businessman moved to New Orleans. There, between 1910 and 1920, he created an ambitious chain of cooperative retail food stores to serve the city's poor. Business and idealism refused to merge. War-related inflation of agricultural prices, competition from other businesses, and dishonest employees caused losses for which Nelson tried to compensate by withdrawing funds from his plumbing supply firm. Between 1916 and 1918 top management of the Nelson Company grew restive and in February of 1918 deposed the founder. Stock distributions were speedily stopped and the chain of New Orleans cooperative stores was forced into the bankruptcy courts. Nelson lived on for a few years as a bitter, disillusioned old man. In 1922 he died in Los Angeles shortly after visiting long-time socialist acquaintance Upton Sinclair.[17]

Irrespective of the failure of Nelson's dreams, he represents an important late nineteenth-century reform tradition. As had many of his contemporaries, he came from rural, small-town America, and he sought to continue traditions of decentralization and voluntarism within the confines of a centralized national industrial system. "Community" was the key element in this reform process. When introduced to the problems of tuberculosis sufferers in southern California on a visit in the early 1900s Nelson did what came most naturally—he purchased lands in an arid climate and helped create a self-sufficient agricultural settlement where the ill could achieve recovery.[18] As many of his contemporaries had, Nelson sought to create a more humane industrial order by ignoring the realities of the industrial process. His ideas, like those of many of the most influential figures of Populism and Progressivism, came from Europe and received a typically American treatment. As had others who felt the necessity of creating blueprints for a more just society, Nelson set out upon an errand into the wilderness. His relocation to rural Illinois represented a longstanding tradition in America's segmented society: If local society is not congenial, move away from it and create your own. Nelson's failure was in fleeing when it was no longer possible to flee. Getting away from the competitive market and replacing it with a cooperative world-in-miniature was a difficult task in late nineteenth- and early twentieth-century America. Although a handful of especially devout religious groups succeeded, the communitarian hopes of Socialist, businessman, and single-taxer were dashed. The market destroyed Nelson's welfare schemes by not permitting the relatively homogenous and unspecialized economic order upon which preindustrial ideals of cooperation depended.

Nelson's ultimate failure lay in the fact that he never came to terms with the progressive movement that swept the United States in the first decade of the twentieth century. He concluded in 1912 that reformers attempting to preserve fair competition through governmental agencies such as the Interstate Commerce Commission were "merely tinkerers who will stop no leak in the roof, plug no hole in the bottomless pit of poverty." Much like modern revisionist scholars, Nelson believed that state or federal regulatory commissions perpetuated unethical business practices and worker exploitation. In this regard he once remarked that government regulation had "minimized restraints of trade to trade's advantage." Nelson, therefore, thought that progressive reform was moving in an unprogressive direction; solving social welfare problems demanded uncoerced cooperation, not government stipulation.[19]

Nelson's proposals for cooperative community were not persuasive to middle-class Americans in general or businessmen in particular. Still, the spirit of his reforms survived to influence the next generation of social welfare innovators, men who made lasting impressions on America's modern social welfare system.

TOWARD AN URBAN COMMUNITY: EDWARD A. FILENE

The career of Boston merchant Edward Albert Filene exemplified the problems involved in translating older reform, community, and welfare norms into an increasingly urbanized, technological, and occupationally specialized industrial system. Filene, like Nelson, was an unusual capitalist, a man whose welfare efforts put him on a liberal fringe of his peers. His stature as an enlightened entrepreneur gained him impressive measures of reform support throughout the Progressive Era.[20]

In essential respects Filene viewed the welfare questions of American society in the same manner as Nelson. He realized, however, that reform was not a matter of escape from the city into a rural past; instead, businessmen must fashion their betterment programs to exist within an urban society. In Filene's personal efforts to accomplish this end he marked an important transition between the communitarianism of the late nineteenth century and the "efficiency management" approach of the 1920s and beyond.

Like Nelson, Filene sprang from immigrant stock. Nelson's fore-bearers were immigrant Norwegian farmers, but Filene's parents were representatives of a highly urbanized and professionalized German Judaism. Nelson, in addition, was a first-generation capitalist, a man who could quite naturally look back to the preindustrial aspects of his youth for conceptual guidance. Filene, on the other hand, was born to a family of Massachusetts storekeepers in 1860. He lived in the workaday world of retail clothing shops in and around Boston. Not for him the legends of the self-sufficient Jeffersonian yeoman.

Early in his career Filene was moved by many of the same impressions and reform desires as was Nelson. As Nelson did, Filene realized that the growing differentiation between owners of capital and sellers of labor had destroyed the world of the village artisan. Popular welfare had suffered accordingly. He wished somehow to reintegrate the economic roles of employer and employed. The cooperative movement was a logical answer. Aided by cooperative distribution agencies this movement might help America "control the threatening dangers of combinations and trusts" by training citizens to collectively understand and operate their commercial institutions.[21]

Formulating institutional means to achieve these cooperative ends proved difficult. At first Filene attempted to create a modified version of Nelson's Leclaire within the city. Filene's world-in-miniature was different from Nelson's, and these differences illustrated the decline of cooperative ideals within Progressive Era America.

Basically Filene attempted to create in an urban department store what Nelson had attempted in a rural, industrial community. Although Filene's welfare betterments were initially informal, he and his younger brother Lincoln pressed to formalize an overall program as the business grew. Between 1891 and 1900 the two brothers, with Edward in the lead, created an employee thrift plan and loan fund, a free medical program, a mutual insurance fund, an at-cost cafeteria, and a recreation program. Employee representatives received full control over the day-to-day administration of these programs. These institutions were not substitutes for adequate pay. Union members were hired without prejudice. In an industry characterized by long hours, harsh conditions, and low wage scales the Filene store accumulated national repute as a "good place to work."[22]

Filene's good start was not enough. As did every employer, Filene had to deal with labor relations, which in the 1890s and 1900s were less than cordial. Panic and depression in these years swelled unemployment rolls and led to bloody strikes. Membership in trade unions increased from 470,000 in 1898 to almost two million only six years later. The

AFL, although still struggling, now accounted for a respectable ten per cent of the industrial labor force.

A product of his times, Filene wanted to make his store into a labor relations laboratory. An idealist, Filene hoped other, more troubled, employers would copy his experiments and replicate what Filene hoped would be his successful results. After receiving advice from lawyer Louis D. Brandeis, philosopher William James, Harvard president Charles W. Eliot, and muckraker Lincoln Steffens, Filene instituted additional company welfare programs. His elaborations produced the first "company union" plan in the United States.[23]

By 1903 the major outlines of the resulting Filene Cooperative Association (FCA) were clear. Under the terms of the FCA's written constitution all full-time employees were allowed to vote annually for their company union's officers. These officials, in turn, appointed representatives to administer ongoing welfare activities. A Cooperative Association Council also existed to serve as a legislative decision-making body. The FCA officials, welfare administrators, and employee-elected delegates to the council were able to initiate, modify, or cancel store regulations concerning hours of labor, working conditions, pro-motions, transfers, fines, wage rates, discipline, and employee dismissal by a two-thirds vote of the membership. Management might veto any council decision. The council, however, could then appeal the issue to the employees as a whole. If two-thirds of the firm's total work force supported the council its decisions were binding; if not, management's veto stood. In this scheme company managers represented the indus-trial executive, but they ruled only with the advice and consent of the legislative branch, represented by the FCA council.

Attached to this legislative branch was an FCA Arbitration Com-mittee that served as the judicial wing of the Filene store's industrial welfare system. It was elected by a full employee electorate. No representative of the managerial executive oversaw its decisions, which were arrived at by simple majority rule. No administrator, however powerful, could compel the board not to consider any case appealed to it, and the board regularly adjudicated cases of discipline or dismissal involving employees. Board decisions were final. Over a twenty-year period for which data were kept 46 percent of the total decisions went against management.

Finally, employees who became dissatisfied with their elected representatives could recall them. They were also granted powers to initiate new store rules through petition campaigns. If as few as 4 percent of the workers expressed a desire for a vote on a disputed regulation a referendum of the total work force was mandatory.

Filene had, in effect, attempted to recreate progressive reform within the confines of his Boston department store. Like the citizens of a state such as Robert LaFollette's Wisconsin, Filene employees could govern their industrial welfare with elected representatives, secure judicial and legislative review of management decisions, and stage initiative, referendum, and recall campaigns in the best traditions of Progressive Era "direct legislation."[24]

Here was the main difference between the reform generations that Filene and Nelson represented. Nelson separated his factory from the world, placing it within an isolated "island community;" Filene, on the other hand, attempted to blend the most democratic elements of the surrounding society within his personalized business environment. Nelson fled, but Filene selectively incorporated. In doing so he based his efforts on the belief that social welfare and justice were possible within the existing structures of business enterprise and industrial organization, rather than in re-creations of the villages of an agrarian past. Thereby he insured for himself the appreciative notice of eminent capitalists, including Andrew Carnegie, and middle-class reform spokesmen such as Louis Brandeis, Lincoln Steffens, economist John Rogers Commons, municipal ownership advocate Frank Parsons, and *Collier's* magazine editor Norman Hapgood. Men such as these had ignored Nelson's presence and programs; but Filene was speaking for— and speaking to—the world they knew and in which they lived.

Filene was also using idioms that businessmen and urban professionals understood. Nelson had spoken of the Golden Rule and moral regeneration. Filene, in contrast, justified his firm's version of a welfare state in economic, rather than spiritual or political terms. Moreover, he addressed his appeals for expansion of corporate welfare systems to businessmen, rather than to society at large. Filene belittled the value of philanthropy. In his view, employers should pay high wages, provide decent working conditions, and create welfare systems as part and parcel of an "intelligently selfish" approach to profit maximization and industrial stability. High wages, for example, led to greater employee efficiency, higher productivity, and, ultimately, higher profits. This decided shift in the fundamental rationale for the provision of welfare services made the idea more palatable to the members of the one group in society with the most direct interest in securing labor peace— businessmen.[25]

The arguments of Nelson and others of his generation appealed to all elements in society to end class warfare. Their search for the cooperative commonwealth was at base a search for a classless industrial society. Filene and his generation recognized, however slowly and reluctantly, the permanent separation of employers and employees and the importance of appealing to businessmen as the primary providers of welfare services in a society divided along occupational lines.

Despite this adjustment to some of the realities of twentieth-century America, Filene's programs encountered many of the same difficulties as had Nelson's. Rapid growth brought four new partners into the firm in 1912. Although Filene and his younger brother Lincoln controlled just over half the voting stock, frictions between the elder Filene and the other partners grew steadily. Fledgling moves to guarantee future collective ownership of the business by the FCA were speedily quashed. Finally, in 1928 the division reached a crisis point over the issue of whether the company should merge itself into a loose federation of department store firms. Anxious to retain as much managerial independence as possible to broaden the base of his welfare system Filene opposed the merger; but Lincoln allied himself against his brother, helped depose him from the presidency of the store, and assisted in the slow hobbling of the firm's cooperative plan. Although he retained his title and the returns from his portion of the stock, Edward Filene was denied any effective authority.[26]

Although Filene's welfare plans eventually failed within his firm, the concepts upon which they were based survived among other employers. From 1910 until his death in 1937 Filene worked to create forums through which ideas and practical programs regarding industrial welfare and labor relations could be spread from one employer to another. Filene helped create the United States Chamber of Commerce in 1912. He supported the American Association for Labor Legislation and the National Consumer's League, two important Progressive Era organizations that fought for the passage of workmen's compensation, minimum wage, and child labor laws. In 1919 Filene founded and generously endowed the independently controlled Twentieth Century Fund. This organization served as a research center to open the way to what Filene hoped would be the next steps in a liberalized social and economic development. After World War I Filene was also an officer of the National Economic League and a member of the elite Council on Foreign Relations. His career, in short, epitomized the Progressive Era urge to organize professional forums, join professional societies, and use these agencies to spread reform ideas across the nation.[27]

It was a mark of Filene's effectiveness that true radicals thought him dangerous. In July 1913, for example, V. I. Lenin attacked this "advanced capitalist" in an article that Lenin's wife Krupskaya later termed "of especial interest" in influencing his analysis of the immediate prewar period. Filene, Lenin wrote, urged businessmen to grant paltry wage and welfare concessions to the masses in order to guarantee the "natural leadership" of international finance capital. The workers, Lenin concluded, were not "such simpletons" as to allow such efforts to blunt their developing revolutionary awareness.[28]

For all his stature, Filene remained rather an exotic among his business peers, much as Nelson had been. Other men would come to best represent the generation of employers that brought the first stage of the modern welfare system to its conclusion.

THE TRIUMPH OF AN EFFICIENCY-MANAGEMENT SYNTHESIS: HENRY S. DENNISON

Henry S. Dennison, born in Boston in 1877, represented the generation that brought corporate welfare practice to its culmination. Unlike Nelson and Filene, Dennison never passed through a moralistic and cooperative phase. He never believed that producers' or consumers' cooperatives had essential relevance to the world of twentieth-century industry. From the beginning, Dennison was all business—a firm believer that welfare reform within individual companies "paid."

As was Filene's, Dennison's was a second- to third-generation business career, but his family was old stock and well established. Young Henry attended the Roxbury Latin School. Graduating in 1899 from Harvard he entered his family's paper products firm, the Dennison Manufacturing Company of Framingham, Massachusetts. After spending several years in lower-level jobs Dennison ascended into the managerial hierarchy. His father's alcoholism had caused the elder Dennison's ejection from the firm's presidency in 1892. Private family scandal failed to hamper Henry's advance; in 1906 he became works manager, in line to inherit controlling authority.[29]

Dennison quickly became interested in larger issues. In 1900 he visited Dayton, Ohio, to observe the National Cash Register Company's well-publicized welfare programs. As had other welfare programs of the period, National Cash Register (NCR) schemes had passed through three stages. In the first, welfare arrangements were spasmodic and informally administered. In the second, administrative responsibility was delegated to a "welfare secretary" who operated outside existing authority channels and reported directly to the chief officer of the company. The powers of this specialist remained unspecified and steady opposition from foremen and lower-level administrators hampered company efforts. In response to such infighting NCR initiated a third stage of welfare capitalism. Welfare procedures were coordinated as a bureaucratized staff function within a new Labor Department, created near the time of Dennison's visit.[30]

Impressed with NCR's work Dennison gradually brought its ideas to the Dennison Manufacturing Company. In 1901 he instituted a bonus system for employee suggestions used by the company. Between 1903 and 1908 he organized a factory clinic, employee cafeteria, library, social club, and savings bank. These moves corresponded to the first stage of NCR's development.[31]

In 1911 Dennison and his uncle Charles Dennison announced an experimental Management Industrial Partner program. Under its terms the firm's active administrators exercised an independent functional ownership of the company. Absentee stockholders had their shares reclassified as preferred or nonvoting stock. Owners of such certificates could no longer ratify or oppose management decisions at annual stockholders' meetings.

In an untheoretical style Dennison had helped to create an industrial program that closely approximated what a decade later Thorstein Veblen would term a "soviet of technicians." Dennison's dream was to build an expert managerial team to collectively own and operate a self-financing business along the most "scientific" principles of workmanship and personnel relations. This step corresponded to the second stage of NCR's development.[32]

In 1913 Dennison was appointed to serve on a Massachusetts State Pension Commission with fellow businessman Magnus W. Alexander. Alexander, a director of the General Electric works at Lynn, Massachusetts, had gained repute for corporate welfare programs. Increasingly, however, he turned his attentions toward more scientific management research. When Dennison first met Alexander the General Electric official was completing pioneering studies that measured the prevalence of labor turnover in American industry. Alexander's disturbing statistics regarding the dollars-and-cents significance of labor discontent moved Dennison to further action on the welfare front. Dennison promptly improved worker selection, training, and placement standards at his firm. Conversations with trade union leaders during the Pension Committee's hearings caused Dennison to augment management training programs and restrict the powers of foremen over hiring, firing, and grievances. All welfare projects were placed under the control of an employment manager. Strong efforts were made to even out the irregularities in production schedules and thereby avoid layoffs. In 1916 the Dennison Company established the first employer-initiated unemployment insurance system in the United States, and capped a series of moves that corresponded to the third and final stage of NCR's development.[33]

At each stage of his entrepreneurial development Dennison viewed those who supported welfare programs in moral terms with disdain. After he had first visited NCR Dennison decided that, although riddled with faults, its "steady, gradual advance" in welfare capitalist procedure offered the best and most "efficient" means of bettering industrial society. By contrast, American Socialists such as Edward Bellamy were hampered by "stagnant and insipid" outlooks. Refusing to recognize the "imperfections of human nature," Socialists could do nothing more than vainly "jump to their goals and try to pull a heavy public after them." Dennison's skepticism of the concepts of even so unrevolutionary a Socialist as Bellamy contrasted sharply with the views of N. O. Nelson (who had joined both Socialist and single-tax organizations) and Edward Filene (whose contacts with European social-democratic spokesmen remained close throughout his life).[34]

Dennison was also unwilling to support cooperative ideals that aimed at a gradual transcendence of the wage system. In 1915 Dennison, who by this time had become deeply interested in the ideas of scientific management advocate Frederick Winslow Taylor, collaborated with fellow businessmen Henry P. Kendall and A. W. Burritt and Harvard Business School professor Edwin F. Gay on a book concerning profit sharing. After four years of effort the authors concluded that profit-sharing systems such as N. O. Nelson's that had aimed to operate along cooperative lines were idealistic dreams. Although bonus systems confined largely to managers and foremen were useful, the masses of workers were simply not responsible enough to comprehend the spirit or operation of such programs. In H. S. Dennison's view the prevention of absentee control and an unemployment insurance program took a clear and permanent precedence over profit sharing, cooperative ownership, or "workers' control."[35]

Like Filene, Dennison was a joiner and spoke primarily to business audiences. From 1912 to 1916 he was the vice-president of the Boston Chamber of Commerce. He worked with Filene to establish the Twentieth Century Fund. He maintained contacts with the American Association for Labor Legislation and served as president of the Taylor Society from 1919 to 1921. Most important of all, as an indicator of the immediate future, was his participation in the National Civic Federation's Welfare Work Department.

The National Civic Federation, composed of a mixture of nationally-known corporate and labor officials, was perhaps the most important Progressive Era forum for the spread of industrial welfare work. When individual firms such as NCR first developed welfare capitalist systems complete with welfare specialists working in functionally organized welfare departments, they tended to view their achievements as something that saved them money and strengthened their positions in their respective product markets. This view initially limited their desire to spread their ideas. As time passed, however, employers began to see welfare capitalism as something they purchased, rather than produced. This shift in vision created incentives to pool resources among companies to create scale economies and lower the costs of such things as safety programs and insurance against labor radicalism. In early 1904 the formation of the Welfare Department of the NCF demonstrated a growing corporate interest in a national research and development institution. Such a forum could more efficiently formulate new welfare programs and compare old industrial experiences. In 1904 the executive committee of the Welfare Department included Edward A. Filene, John H. Patterson of National Cash Register, N. O. Nelson, and representatives from General Electric, Westinghouse, Studebaker, National Biscuit Company, American Locomotive, H. J. Heinz Co., International Harvester, and R. H. Macy and Company. A significant step had been taken in formulating a nationalized businessmen's welfare strategy. From this point in time businessmen such as Dennison would seek to organize and systematize welfare capitalist programs to span the entire corporate order of twentieth-century America.[36]

In this chapter has been presented a sequence of tendencies among businessmen, concentrating upon the careers of individuals who exemplified an evolution of reform concept and institutional program. Arguments by businessmen in favor of welfare capitalism moved from moral to pragmatic. The moral arguments appealed to society at large. Efficiency-oriented or scientific-management arguments persuaded businessmen, who were best able to operationalize company welfare plans. Welfare arrangements evolved from Nelson's efforts to recreate the structure of preindustrial community, to Filene's efforts to replicate Progressive Era democracy within the confines of an individual company, to Dennison's program of elite bureaucratic administration. Welfare arrangements that had started on an informal and decentralized basis became progressively centralized and organized for particular client groups among both workers and management. Information of the operation of various plans spread at first through the informal efforts of individual businessmen and then through the organizational activities of such national forums as the NCF.

The question of how pervasive these welfare plans in fact were remains. The Progressive Era, after all, was as much the time of the National Association of Manufacturers, and Sears, Roebuck's Julius Rosenwald (who baldly contended that low wages bore "no substantial relation" to the incidence of prostitution among women retail clerks), as it was of Edward Albert Filene. How representative, then, were Filene, Dennison, and the other employers who belonged to the NCF's Welfare Department?

Here we must rely on scattered contemporary statistics. In 1908 a self-styled "social engineer" named William Tolman declared that 1.5 million workers were covered by some form of welfare work or plant safety program. Among the companies involved were giants such as Proctor & Gamble, Eastman Kodak, General Electric, Sherwin Williams, United States Steel, and International Harvester. Initially only 100 firms were represented in the NCF's Welfare Department. Yet, within only seven years, that total had quintupled. By 1914 over 2500 companies were known to the NCF as having incorporated various forms of betterment work. Fragmentary records show that employees of the NCF were making efforts to make the most enlightened procedures known to a national business clientele.[37]

In the end, however, we must move from the quantitative to the qualitative realm. There are precious few numbers left to count. Adoption of company welfare schemes represented a significant trend throughout the Progressive Era. The number of those plans increased most rapidly among large firms that tended to operate in expanding geographic and product markets whose size enabled them—indeed, required them—to undergo the functional bureaucratic structural changes necessary for coordinated programs of welfare work. The resulting corporate plans operated outside the two welfare channels that already existed in late nineteenth- and early twentieth-century America. They differed from traditional local and state welfare systems that covered only fragmented client groups and were administered through a hodgepodge of fundamentally local or regional institutions such as the county poor house and the state mental hospital. They also differed from traditional company welfare systems that, if they existed at all, relied basically on the personal and informal efforts of a boss to provide for a relatively few loyal employees of long service and unrebellious character.

The employers attending the meetings of forums such as the NCF's Welfare Department were engaged in a different exercise—the effort to formulate welfare strategies for widespread worker constituencies whose firms increasingly operated on a national scale. Using segments of the earlier experience of pioneers such as Nelson, Filene, and Dennison, they were engaged in constructing their own versions of the welfare state.[38]

In this account of the origins of the modern American social welfare system, there is no intention to disregard the role of the state and federal governments. As historians have long recognized, the Progressive Era was a time of expansion and innovation in the public sector. This innovation and expansion in government social welfare activity, however, bore a close relation to developments in the private sector, as the next chapter reveals.

NOTES

1. Surveys of the period include Samuel P. Hays, *The Response to Industrialism, 1885-1914*; Robert H. Wiebe, *The Search for Order*; Thomas Cochran and William Miller, *The Age of Enterprise: A Social History of Industrial America*, rev. ed. (New York: Harper and Row, 1961).

2. Frederic C. Howe, *Confessions of a Reformer* (New York: Macmillan, 1925), pp. 5-6; Graham Taylor, *Pioneering on Social Frontiers* (Chicago: University of Chicago Press, 1930), pp. 117-83; Lillian Wald, *The House on Henry Street* (New York: Henry Holt, 1915), p. 202. Edward C. Kirkland, *Dream and Thought in the American Business Community, 1860-1910* (Chicago: Quadrangle, 1964) is useful for mainstream business thinking.

3. J. R. T. Hughes, *The Governmental Habit: Economic Controls from Colonial Times to the Present* (New York: Basic Books, 1977), especially chapters 1-4. In addition to the Trattner article cited earlier, many good sources concerning early governmental efforts take the form of biographies of individual reformers. Among the best are Josephine Goldmark, *Impatient Crusader: The Life of Florence Kelley* (Urbana: University of Chicago Press, 1953), and Harold Schwartz, *Samuel G. Howe: Social Reformer* (Cambridge: Harvard University Press, 1956).

4. *Historical Statistics of the United States: Colonial Times to 1970*, vol. 2 (Washington, D.C.: G.P.O., 1976), pp. 1102-03; *Final Report of the American Indian Policy Review Commission*, vol. 1 (Washington, D.C.: G.P.O. 1977), pp. 65-67.

5. Gerald Grob, *Workers and Utopia: A Study of Ideological Conflict within the American Labor Movement, 1865-1900* (Evanston, Ill.: Northwestern University Press, 1969), p. 138; Richard Hofstadter, *The American Political Tradition and the Men Who Made It* (New York: Vintage, 1978), pp. 236-37.

6. Richard T. Ely, "Pullman: A Social Study," *Harper's Monthly Magazine* 70 (February 1885), pp. 452-66; Thomas Bender, *Toward an Urban Vision* (Lexington, Kentucky: University of Kentucky Press, 1975); G. W. Hanger, *Housing of the Working People in the United States by Employers*, U.S. Department of Labor Bulletin no. 154 (Washington, 1904); John R. Commons et al., *History of Labor in the U.S.*, vol. 1 (New York: Macmillan, 1918), p. 423; Stanley Buder, *Pullman: An Experiment in Industrial Order and Community Planning, 1880-1930* (New York: Oxford University Press, 1967).

7. Nelson's career is covered in Kim McQuaid, "The Businessman as Reformer: N. O. Nelson and Late 19th Century Social Movements in America," *American Journal of Economics and Sociology* 33 (October 1974): 423-35; and "The Businessman as Social Innovator: N. O. Nelson . . . and the Consumer Cooperative Movement," *American Journal of Economics and Sociology* 34 (October 1975): 411-22. N. O. Nelson, "My Business Life—I," *The World's Work* 19 (December 1909): 12390; N. O. Nelson, "Profit Sharing," pamphlet (St. Louis, n.p., 1887); W. E. Barns, ed., *The Labor Problem* (New York: Harper and Brothers, 1886), pp. 87-88.

8. Aneurin Williams, *Twenty Eight Years of Co-partnership at Guise* (Letchworth Garden City, England: Letchworth Cooperative Press, 1908); N. O. Nelson, "Profit Sharing," pp. 32-35.

9. N. O. Nelson, "My Business Life—II," *The World's Work* 19 (January 1910): 12505; Arthur Mann, *Yankee Reformers in the Urban Age: Social Reform in Boston, 1880-1900* (New York: Harper and Row, 1966), p. 18.

10. Edwin Balmer, "The Spirit of Co-operation . . . ," *The Commons* 10 (June 1905): 335–43; G. W. Eads, "N. O. Nelson, Practical Co-operator," *The Arena* 36 (November 1906): 463–80; F. W. Blackmar, "Two Examples of Successful Profit Sharing," *Forum* 19 (March 1895): 62–67; A. R. Kimball, "The Story of Leclaire," *Harper's Weekly* 38 (March 24, 1894), p. 278; Edward Everett Hale, "A Visit to Leclaire," *Employer and Employed*, October 1893, pp. 2–5; "Kindly Caricatures: N. O. Nelson," *The* (St. Louis) *Mirror*, July 1905 (Clipping in the N. O. Nelson Collection, Missouri Historical Society, St. Louis).

11. Nicholas Paine Gilman, *Profit Sharing: A Study in the Evolution of the Wages System* (London: Macmillan, 1890), pp. 386–87; Boris Emmet, *Profit Sharing in the United States*, U.S. Bureau of Labor Statistics Bulletin no. 208 (Washington, D.C.: G.P.O., 1917).

12. *Report of the U.S. Industrial Commission*, vol. 14 (Washington, 1902), p. 359; E. E. Hale, "A Visit to Leclaire," p. 5; Samuel Milton Jones (with N. O. Nelson), *The New Right: A Plea for Fair Play Through a More Just Social Order* (New York: Eastern Book Concern, 1899), p. 353; N. O. Nelson, "My Business Life—II," pp. 12505–06; Blackmar, "Two Examples," p. 64.

13. N. O. Nelson, "Through Profit Sharing to Co-operation," *Employer and Employed*, January 1894, pp. 20–24; Nelson to Henry Demarest Lloyd, March 9, 1896, Henry Demarest Lloyd Collection, State Historical Society of Wisconsin, Madison; W. D. P. Bliss, ed., *The New Encyclopedia of Social Reform* (New York: Funk and Wagnalls, 1897), pp. 1105–06; N. O. Nelson, "Profit Sharing with the Consumer," *Independent* 58 (May 25, 1905): 1180.

14. Emmet, "Profit Sharing in the United States," p. 50; Eltweed Pomeroy, "Nelson O. Nelson: A Man with Enough," *The World To-Day* 9 (December 1905): 1327.

15. N. O. Nelson, "Organized Labor," *New England Magazine* n.s. 13 (November 1895): 340–45; N. O. Nelson, "The Associated Worker's Idea," in *Labor and Capital*, ed. John Peters (New York, 1902), pp. 345–52; Samuel Gompers, *Labor and the Employer* (New York, 1920), pp. 291–94; N. O. Nelson, "Co-partnership with Wage Earners," *Survey* 29 (February 13, 1913): 653; "The Strike in N. O. Nelson's Cooperative Works," *The Arena* 38 (September 1907): 334–35; N. O. Nelson, "Letter to My 1200 Associates in the Plumbing Supply Business," March 28, 1918, N. O. Nelson Collection.

16. N. O. Nelson, "The Farm, A Congestion Cure," *Charities and the Commons* 20 (May 8, 1908): 220–21; N. O. Nelson, "Leclaire, An Existing City of the Future," *Independent* 77 (January 19, 1914): 100; N. O. Nelson, "Leclaire, The Model Town," *Charities and the Commons* 21 (March 27, 1909): 1276.

17. "Memorial Tribute to N. O. Nelson by his daughter . . . ," n.d., N. O. Nelson Collection; N. O. Nelson, "Cooperative Stores," *Outlook* 112 (February 16, 1916): 396; Ray Samuel, "Fired Because He Made a Profit," *Dixie Roto-Magazine* (New Orleans), August 20, 1950, p. 17; Ida M. Tarbell, *New Ideals in Business* (New York: Macmillan, 1916), p. 232; Upton Sinclair, "The Conscience-Stricken Millionaire," *Upton Sinclair's Magazine* 1 (February 1919): 6; National Industrial Conference Board, *Research Report no. 29* (New York: National Industrial Conference Board, 1920), pp. 11–12; St. Louis *Globe-Democrat*, October 7, 1922, p. 2.

18. Charles M. Destler, *Henry Demarest Lloyd and the Empire of Reform* (Philadelphia: University of Pennsylvania Press, 1963), pp. 380–90; N. O. Nelson, "A Baby Community," *New England Magazine* n.s. 17 (October 1897): 166–69; *The Coming Nation* (Ruskin Cooperative Association, Ruskin, Tennessee, May 29, 1897; May 28, 1898; May 20, 1899); N. O. Nelson, "The First American Anarchist," *Charities and the Commons* 18 (April 6, 1907): 670.

19. N. O. Nelson, "The Progressives," *Independent* 73 (July 9, 1912): 123–214.

20. Kim McQuaid, "An American Owenite: Edward A. Filene and the Parameters of Industrial Reform, 1890–1937," *American Journal of Economics and Sociology* 35 (January, 1976): 77–94; Gerald W. Johnson, *Liberal's Progress* (New York: Coward-McCann, 1948).

21. Edward A. Filene to Edwin Mead, March 20, 1893; "E.A.F.—Biography." Filene's

papers are located in the Bergengren Memorial Museum Library, Filene House, Madison, Wisconsin (hereafter cited as BMML).

22. The best source for Filene's programs is Mary LaDame, *The Filene Store* (New York: Russell Sage Foundation, 1930). For a good early summary see Frank Parsons, "An Experiment in Industrial Harmony," *Outlook*, July 15, 1905, pp. 671-76.

23. W. Jett Lauck, *Political and Industrial Democracy, 1776-1926* (New York: Funk and Wagnalls, 1926), pp. 209-12, 288-91; John R. Commons et al., *History of Labor in the U.S.*, vol. 3 (New York: Macmillan, 1935), pp. 337-38.

24. Edward A. Filene, "Speech Before the Filene Cooperative Association, January 1, 1907" and "The New Store, April 26, 1911," in *Collected Speeches*, vol. 1, BMML; LaDame, *Filene Store*, pp. 91-92, 323-24, 157-58, 333-34; R. F. Phelps, "An Experiment in Industrial Democracy," *The Commons* 10 (February 1905): 91-95; Lincoln Steffens, *The Autobiography of Lincoln Steffens* (New York: Harcourt, Brace, 1931), pp. 601-03.

25. *System, The Magazine of Business*, March 20, 1921, p. 478; Edward A. Filene, *Successful Living in This Machine Age* (New York: Simon and Schuster, 1931), pp. 113-14; Edward A. Filene, "Employer's Policies—A Speech before the Economic Club of Boston—February 17, 1904," *Collected Speeches*, vol. 1, BMML; Edward A. Filene, "The Minimum Wage and Efficiency," *American Economic Review* September, 1923, pp. 411-15; Edward A. Filene, "The Truth Can Make Us Free," *Survey* 30 (August 3, 1913): 579; Robert Asher, "Business and Worker's Welfare in the Progressive Era: Workmen's Compensation Reform in Massachusetts, 1880-1911," *Business History Review* 43 (Winter 1969): 462.

26. Filene to Lincoln Steffens, March 27, 1928, Lincoln Steffens Collection, Columbia University, New York; New York *Times*, May 3, 1930, p. 34; Johnson, *Liberal's Progress*, pp. 32-33; Interview with Paul Mazur of Lehman Brothers, Inc., New York City, May 21, 1973.

27. Wiebe, *Businessmen and Reform*, pp. 35-37; "National Council of Commerce" and "Missions—EAF Correspondence with U.S. Chamber of Commerce Officials," BMML; Filene to Colonel Edward M. House, October 25, 1913, Edward M. House Collection, Yale University, New Haven, Conn.

28. V. I. Lenin, "The Ideas of an Advanced Capitalist," in *Collected Works*, vol. 19 (Moscow: Progress Publishers, 1968), pp. 275-76; N. K. Krupskaya, *Reminiscences of Lenin* (New York: International Publishers, 1970), p. 258.

29. Sources for Henry S. Dennison's life and early career include Kim McQuaid, "Henry S. Dennison and the 'Science' of Industrial Reform, 1900-1950," *American Journal of Economics and Sociology* 36 (January 1977): 79-98; J. T. Dennison, "Henry S. Dennison: New England Industrialist Who Served America," (New York, 1953); C. Heath, "History of the Dennison Manufacturing Company—II," *Journal of Economic and Business History* 2 (November 1929); R. W. Hidy, ed., *Individual Enterprise and National Economic Growth* (Boston: D.C. Heath, 1967), p. 7. The Henry S. Dennison Papers have recently been deposited by the Dennison family at the Baker Library, Harvard Graduate School of Business Administration, Cambridge Mass. (Hereafter cited as Dennison Papers.)

30. John H. Patterson, "Altruism and Sympathy as Factors in Works Administration," *Engineering Magazine* 20 (January 1901), pp. 577-602; Samuel Crowther, *John H. Patterson* (New York: Garden City Publishing Company, 1923), p. 196; John H. Patterson, "The Factory as an Element in the Improvement of Society," *Charities Review* 8 (December 1898): 473; D. Nelson, "The New Factory System and the Unions"; Daniel Nelson's *Managers and Workers: Origins of the New Factory System in the United States, 1880-1920* is a good source for overall patterns of managerial change in the period.

31. Herman Krooss, *Executive Opinion: What Business Leaders Said and Thought on Social Issues, 1920's-1960's* (Garden City, New York: Doubleday 1971), p. 351; interview with Elizabeth Dunker (Dennison's daughter) and J. T. Dennison (Dennison's son), Cambridge,

Mass., December 27-28, 1973.

32. R. W. Hidy, *Individual Enterprise*, pp. 7-11; H. S. Dennison, "Mr. Dennison's Recollections," Dennison Papers; Mary Dewhurst, "Something Better Than Philanthropy," *Outlook* 3 (September 1, 1915): 48-51; *National Cyclopaedia of American Biography.*, vol. 34, p. 203.

33. "Mr. Dennison's Recollections," Dennison Papers; John R. Commons, ed., *Trade Unionism and Labor Problems—Second Series* (Boston: Ginn and Company, 1921), pp. 156-64; H. S. Dennison, "Speech to the Employment Manager's Association . . . May 10, 1916." Dennison Papers; *Bulletin of the Taylor Society* 3 (May 1917): 1, and 5 (February 1920): 4; Dennison daybooks, entries for March 4, 1913, December 9, 1916, August 27, 1914, February 26, 1913, Dennison Papers.

34. (H. S. Dennison), untitled memo regarding a trip to the National Cash Register Company (dated 1900), Dennison Papers.

35. *Annals of the American Academy of Political and Social Science* 44 (November 1912): 97-103; *Outlook* 3 (September 1, 1915): 48-51; *Annals of the American Academy* 65 (May 1916): 87-94; A. W. Burritt, E. F. Gay, H. S. Dennison, and H. P. Kendall, *Profit Sharing: The Principles and Practices* (New York: Harper Brothers, 1918); *Century Cyclopaedia of American Biography*, vol. 44, pp. 58-59.

36. National Civic Federation, "Conference on Welfare Work Held . . . March 16, 1904," (New York: National Civic Federation, 1904), pp. xvii-xxiii; Adolph A. Berle, *Leaning Against the Dawn: An Appreciation of the Twentieth Century Fund—1919-1969* (New York: Twentieth Century Fund, 1969); Elizabeth Dunker interview. Concerning the National Civic Federation see Gordon M. Jensen, "The National Civic Federation . . . 1900-1910," (Ph.D. diss., Princeton, 1958), especially pp. 108, 143; James Weinstein, *The Corporate Ideal in the Liberal State* (Boston, 1971); Marguerite Green, *The National Civic Federation and the American Labor Movement, 1900-1925* (Washington, D.C.: Catholic University of America Press, 1956), especially pp. 267-70. The 1904 and 1905 issues of *The National Civic Federation Review* have information concerning the NCF's "Welfare Department."

37. Good sources for welfare capitalist impulses include Donald M. Nelson, *Managers and Workers*; Stuart D. Brandes, *American Welfare Capitalism, 1880-1940* (Chicago: University of Chicago Press, 1976); Robert Ozanne, *A Century of Labor-Management Relations at McCormick and International Harvester* (Madison: University of Wisconsin Press, 1967). Contemporary estimates are found in E. L. Shuey, *Factory People and their Employers* (New York: Lentilhon and Company, 1900); William Tolman, *Social Engineering* (New York: McGraw Publishing Company, 1909); *Welfare Work for Employees in Industrial Establishments*, U.S. Bureau of Labor Statistics Bulletin no. 250 (Washington D.C.: G.P.O., 1919); Norman J. Wood, "Industrial Relations Policies of American Management, 1900-1933," *Business History Review* 34 (Winter 1960); and Donald Nelson and S. Campbell, "Taylorism versus Welfare Work in American Industry: H. L. Gantt and the Bancrofts," *Business History Review* 44 (Spring 1972) are also useful sources.

38. Employers' welfare policies are put in a revisionist historical context by David Noble's *America By Design: Science, Technology, and the Rise of Corporate Capitalism* (New York: Alfred Knopf, 1977). For the traditional view see Reinhard Bendix, *Work and Authority in Industry: Ideologies of Management in the Course of Industrialization* (New York: Harper and Row, 1963).

2

THE ROLE OF GOVERNMENT, 1900–1920

The part that government played in the welfare system between 1900 and 1920 was determined by the conflict between its mission to maintain the general welfare, as defined by a large body of English and American law, and its limited resources. These limited resources distinguished the public from the private sector. More than Eric F. Goldman's "steel chain of ideas" kept reformers from creating a large and active public sector.[1] Low levels of government finances and the small number of government employees made the creation of a welfare system that demanded the expenditure of large amounts of human or monetary resources impossible.

By late twentieth-century standards the public sector was small-time. At the turn of the century the federal establishment contained fewer employees than a single basic industry such as steel. A federal government that did not even possess the right to tax incomes of businesses and individuals until 1914 was hardly capable of expensive experiments in any field. Large private companies employed far more people and spent much more money than the largest and wealthiest state government. One railroad with offices in Boston employed 18,000 people, had gross receipts of about $40 million a year, and paid its highest salaried officer $35,000 annually. At the time, the State of Massachusetts employed only 6,000 people, spent about $7 million, and paid its highest official far less than $35,000. In terms of access to revenue and manpower, the state was no match for the railroad.

In the Progressive Era, therefore, welfare reformers built with what they had available. They proposed programs that conditioned private-sector practices but that required only minimal expenditures of public funds.[2] Working within these constraints early twentieth-century reformers produced policy proposals that permanently altered the American social welfare system. These proposals were not uniformly applied throughout the country. Despite wide regional and state diversities, the twin notions of "social insurance" and "minimum standards" united the many components of government welfare practice in the Progressive Era.

At the heart of the new public system were workers' compensation and minimum wage laws. Reformers did not formulate these laws to replace private control over welfare practice, but to create incentives for what they regarded as moral conduct within industry. The reformers simply suggested that it was in the interest of both businessmen and the general public to adopt the new workers' compensation and minimum standard laws.

UPDATING THE TRADITIONAL WELFARE SYSTEM: THE PRINCIPLES OF MINIMUM STANDARDS AND SOCIAL INSURANCE

The same incongruity between economic forces and administrative systems that motivated the creation of increasingly formalized welfare structures within individual American corporations produced changes in public welfare procedure in the late nineteenth and early twentieth century. The public welfare system, like the corporate, began to replace the reign of men with the reign of rules. Benefit systems were formalized, and bureaucratic oversight made more automatic and less discretionary.

In its most traditional and purest form the public sector relied on local initiative to separate the deserving from the undeserving poor and to maintain the deserving poor at a subsistence level. Beginning in the Jacksonian era institutions that David Rothman calls "asylums" entered this system. State and local authorities delegated the responsibilities for both the custodial and curative care of the welfare population to these new asylums.

By the late nineteenth century many state governments had attempted to standardize and regulate the treatment in these institutions by creating state boards of charity or public welfare. In Massachusetts, for example, this process began as early as 1865 and led in time to the creation of a state board of health, lunacy, and charity. Despite this attempt and similar attempts across the nation, welfare institutions remained highly localized, and as they paid more attention to their custodial than to their curative tasks they became dumping grounds for society's failures.[3]

Because the traditional welfare system and its nineteenth-century institutions appeared to be an anachronism, a group of late nineteenth- and early twentieth-century reformers hoped to modernize this system by substituting cash grants for institutional care. This group needed to frame proposals for such a modernization that maintained incentives for citizens to remain outside the institutional welfare system and that recognized the fiscal limitation of state and local governments. Two innovative ideas first formulated in Europe enabled the group to formulate coherent policy proposals. The first was state legislation of minimum standards and the second was state-supervised insurance programs.

The most influential statement of the minimum standard idea came from Sidney and Beatrice Webb, English Fabian socialists, who published *Industrial Democracy* in 1897. This book made a case for government legislation of industrial standards. Translated into American institutional terms the Webbs' proposals meant that state governments should prohibit employers from conducting business under conditions detrimental to the public welfare and require employers to pay minimum wages, observe maximum hours, and meet safety standards. The various standards defined levels of decency that would eliminate industrial hazards and at the same time preserve and even strengthen industrial benefits. In this way employers themselves would provide for the welfare of employees and their families.

The case for minimum standards relied heavily on contemporary notions of efficiency and racial evolution. In ascending order, minimum standards forced employees, employers, manufacturers of common products, and the entire economy to operate efficiently. As contemporary economist Arthur Holcombe explained, "wages must depend upon efficiency." If a state legislated a minimum standard concerning wages, workers would be forced to increase their output to correspond to the minimum standard. Workers, Holcombe concluded, would meet the challenge, increase their efficiency, and pocket the increased wages.[4] The Webbs believed that minimum standard legislation would provide a "positive stimulus to the entire [working] class to become more and more efficient."[5] Employers also would be stimulated by the increased costs that minimum standard laws imposed upon them to develop a more efficient and consequently more humane production process. Minimum standard laws concerning industrial accidents, for example, forced employers to pay for each accident that occurred in the plant. This fact stimulated them to develop safer, but equally efficient, production processes. More efficient production processes would in time produce lower product costs and expand the size of the economy. In the long run, therefore, forcing employers to meet minimum standards saved the country money.

In addition, because of the nature of evolutionary processes, legislation of minimum standards would prevent what the Webbs called degeneracy. Without government-imposed minimum standards, conditions allowed employers to produce cheap goods by exploiting employees, underpaying them, and robbing them of their health and vitality. Acting as parasites these unscrupulous employers stole valuable human capital from society and contributed to society's degeneration. Sidney Webb explained that degeneracy was the result of a malevolent evolutionary process that could as easily foster degenerates capable of living on inadequate wages and in unsanitary surroundings, as the superior types who moved society forward.[6] The new system eliminated the parasitic employer by outlawing the practices that enabled him to flourish.

Although minimum standard laws helped prevent welfare problems and removed some of the stigma from being included in the welfare system, they failed to provide money for needy citizens. In 1913 Isaac Max Rubinow, a doctor and reformer, published *Social Insurance*, which offered a means to redistribute money from taxpayers to welfare recipients. Social insurance, as practiced in Germany and England, substituted a sure small loss for a possible large one and protected against social hazards such as industrial accidents, sickness, disability, death, and unemployment. The average workman could not accumulate sufficient resources to provide for these hazards, but their incidence was statistically predictable. Accordingly, Rubinow defined social insurance as a "well-defined effort of the organized state to come to the assistance of the wage-earner and furnish him something he individually is quite unable to attain." Rubinow envisioned an elaborate state apparatus to provide this insurance. Ironically, the wide-spread appeal of social insurance lay precisely in the fact that its implementation required minimal state effort. In particular, social insurance might be linked with the private sector insurance system.[7]

Several professional organizations managed to work from the Webb and Rubinow theories and produce recommendations for the amendment of America's public welfare system. Two groups stood out in this effort: the social workers who belonged to the National Conference on Charities and Corrections, and the social scientists who formed the American Association for Labor Legislation (AALL). The National Conference on Charity and Corrections, founded in 1879, formulated its proposals at the insistence of Jane Addams. When she became president of the organization in 1910 she assigned Paul Kellogg, a prominent social reformer, to head a committee that would, in Kellogg's words, "crystallize in men's minds an industrial program of minimums." From 1910 to 1914 the committee presented just such a program, complete with detailed suggestions for minimum standard laws regarding wages, child labor, education, and social insurance.[8]

For the members of the AALL, workers' compensation and related forms of social insurance became a special interest. By 1911 the AALL had created a model workers' compensation proposal and supported state attempts to pass such laws.[9] In that year, then, plans for reform of the public welfare system had reached the same stage as plans for the reform of the private welfare system. Professional forums existed to spread the reforms in both sectors; in the one case to state governments, in the other to employers.

THE FATE OF THE PUBLIC POLICY PROPOSALS

At base the two sets of reform proposals were not in conflict. Both systems located the private employer at the focal point of social action, and both systems justified the creation of new welfare institutions with the same rationalizations—those of cost efficiency. Individual differences, however, between welfare-minded businessmen and reformers were often marked. Jane Addams' desires to restore preindustrial community lasted longer than those of E. A. Filene or Henry Dennison. Despite these differences, both groups agreed that the establishment of minimum welfare standards in the public sector necessarily followed in the wake of pioneering experiments by employers. Constraints imposed by the small size of the public sector made employer-initiated programs the linchpin in the evolution of socially desirable welfare standards.[10]

Employers who accepted the rationalizations of cost efficiency tended to support both private and public welfare measures. For this reason the NCF, the organization that led the private welfare movement among employers in the Progressive Era, also participated in the public welfare movement by becoming one of the leading advocates of workers' compensation. Government-enforced minimums had the additional advantage of providing relief from problems posed by "free riders," firms that were unwilling to undertake the expenses involved in introducing welfare arrangements and thereby gaining competitive advantages in product markets. At the same time they indirectly benefited from the improved business environment that welfare experiments created.[11]

Even the logic of cost efficiency, however, did not appeal to employers who believed that this rationale failed to apply to them. Employers fearful of interstate competition tended to oppose both private and public welfare proposals as threats to their very existence.[12]

The creation of a public welfare system was, therefore, not a uniform or simple phenomenon. As were businessmen, upper-class progressives who advocated the creation of this system often were more effectively organized on the municipal and state levels than they were on the national level. The progressives presented different proposals in different states. The combinations and permutations of the struggle created a diverse array of legislative and administrative clashes regarding minimum standard welfare legislation. Like many infinite series, however, the sum of these struggles was finite. By 1920, minimum wage laws existed in fifteen states; workers' compensation statutes, in forty-five.[13]

MINIMUM WAGES

The adoption of the minimum wage for women in Massachusetts and Oregon illustrated how competitive pressures undercut business support for minimum standard measures in some states and produced highly fragmented state control over industrial conditions in others.

In Massachusetts a minimum wage law for women arose in model fashion. After Florence Kelley of the National Consumer's League (NCL) spoke on the subject of minimum wage legislation at a public meeting in December of 1910, representatives of organized labor, the NCL, and the Massachusetts branch of the AALL formed a committee to agitate for legislative passage of the measure. The activities of this committee led to the appointment of a state investigatory commission under the direction of patrician-reformer Mrs. Glendower Evans of the Women's Trade Union League. Mrs. Evans' report, written largely by Mary W. Dewson, later the head of the women's committee of the Democratic Party during the New Deal, painted a dreary picture of an industrialized state where "the employers may dictate their own terms" concerning labor contracts. It lamented the fact that only the impersonal laws of supply and demand determined wage levels. Within such an environment there was "not even the check of humane sympathy that might exist in the personal relations of employer and employee."[14]

Despite the persuasive report and the prolabor sympathy generated by a nationally publicized International Workers of the World (IWW)-led strike at Lawrence, Massachusetts, in 1911, minimum wage advocates succeeded in obtaining only a compromise measure. Richard Olney, a business representative on the commission and the former Attorney General of the United States under Grover Cleveland, suggested the idea of retaining the legislation by making compliance nonmandatory. After the minimum-wage advocates accepted this compromise the bill encountered little debate. It cleared both houses of the

legislature with only two votes recorded against it, and became law on
June 4, 1912.[15]

The bill created the Massachusetts Minimum Wage Commission,
which had power to investigate individual industries and publish
minimum wage recommendations for those industries. The law's
effectiveness depended upon the efforts of the Minimum Wage Commission, in particular on who served as a commission member. At first
minimum wage advocates controlled the commission. H. LaRue Brown,
an attorney and a leading supporter of the measure, served as its first
chairman. When he retired, however, opponents of the minimum wage
took over. By World War I a textile manufacturer who had previously
condemned the law headed the commission.[16]

In the brief time minimum-wage advocates held sway they
managed to recommend minimum wages for five industries. Small size,
the existence of both mechanized and unmechanized plants, and a high
percentage of female employees characterized these industries. Significantly, the board chose the brush industry for its first wage decree. This
tiny industry employed less than 9,000 people of both sexes nationally,
over 10 percent of whom worked in Massachusetts. Even in this small
industry the board decided to set its wage recommendation below the
figure suggested by its committee investigating conditions in the
industry. It rationalized this decision on the grounds that a higher
decree, although the decree was not mandatory and applied only to
women, would drive the brush industry out of the state. The commission ruled that the minimum wage was a "principle wise and businesslike" but not a principle capable of withstanding interstate competition.
The president of the largest brush company in the state concurred in
this judgment and told an investigating committee in 1921 that, even
with its safeguards, the bill had forced him to give up the production of
low-grade brushes. (Obviously, his company was a step removed from
the large, technology-intensive companies that belonged to the NCF's
Welfare Department.)[17]

The brush decree was promulgated in 1915. By that time a broad
range of Massachusetts businesses opposed the minimum wage law.
The National Association of Manufacturers (NAM) attacked the minimum wage as a "failing experiment." Other industrialists, such as the
owners of laundries and the makers of paper boxes, took the Minimum
Wage Commission to court, contesting the right of the state to inspect
their payrolls. By 1916 small business organizations such as the Massachusetts Industrial Protective Association had introduced a bill in the
state legislature calling for repeal of the measure. At hearings held in
1922 this organization claimed that 95 percent of the manufacturers
from all branches of industry favored repeal of the law.[18]

If the Massachusetts experience suggested that business as a group opposed minimum standard legislation, Oregon's experience with a minimum standard law for women showed exactly the opposite. On September 1, 1916, the Oregon Industrial Welfare Commission issued the first mandatory wage decree for women in America. The decree made a careful distinction between employers in Portland, the only large urban center in a state with less than 750,000 inhabitants, and those outside Portland. The state asked Portland employers to pay a higher minimum wage than employers in the rest of the state. Significantly, the decree set such other conditions for the employment of women in Oregon as the maximum number of hours they could work at night, the minimum rest periods they required, and the size of plant rest rooms. In this sense the Oregon Industrial Welfare Commission attempted to govern a woman's entire industrial life.[19]

If an explosion was expected from the business community, none came. After the decree the Commercial Club and the Portland Chamber of Commerce remained strongly in favor of the law. When Oregon box manufacturers decided to contest the law's constitutionality the Oregon Supreme Court upheld the law and most businessmen concurred in the decision. After the U.S. Supreme Court declared all minimum wage laws for women unconstitutional in 1923, the Oregon Manufacturers and Merchants Association resolved "to be governed in the future as we have in the past by the rulings of the Industrial Welfare Commission." Florence Kelley, the national leader of the minimum wage movement, corresponded with the Oregon Manufacturers Association and received assurances that "many employers of women . . . would [continue] to regard the minimum wage of this state as the law of the land."[20]

Why should Oregon and Massachusetts employers have reacted so differently to a similar law? Simply stated, Oregon employers faced far fewer competitive threats than Massachusetts employers. Oregon employers hoped to capture the long-run improvements in worker and managerial efficiency that a minimum wage could produce. Isolation from national product markets freed them from the fear that out-of-state competitors would undercut their prices and take away their market shares before these improvements could be realized. Massachusetts employers, on the other hand, were more closely linked to national markets for staple industrial goods such as cotton textiles, and employed many women in the mills and factories that produced such items. A minimum wage law in Oregon's relatively self-contained market meant comparatively little in terms of business survival. A similar minimum wage decree in Massachusetts put many employees in basic industries in a far less secure position. These companies faced competition from southern producers with lower labor costs. Such contrasting conditions and experiences relating to the implementation of an important minimum standard statute clearly illustrates what Robert D. Cuff terms the "decentralized and regional" nature of the American business community in the Progressive Era.

THE SOCIAL INSURANCE ALTERNATIVE: WORKERS' COMPENSATION

Social insurance approaches often succeeded where minimum standard statutes failed or achieved only partial acceptance. The same businessmen who failed to see why minimum wages were in their self-interest actively supported social insurance laws such as workers' compensation. They owed their support to the fact that workers' compensation, unlike minimum wages, promised immediate benefit. Workers' compensation laws lowered operating costs in the short rather than the long run. Workers' compensation, therefore, posed fewer threats to a firm's survival in a competitive market.

In the years before World War I, workers' compensation became the classic example of the success of a cost-efficiency approach to public welfare. Workers' compensation laws became the foundation of the state welfare system created during the Progressive Era. As such they clearly exemplified the extent to which public programs were modeled according to economic and administrative criteria provided by the private sector.

The history of workers' compensation and the development of its administrative apparatus are complicated matters, but they are important for understanding the nature of public sector social welfare efforts. Part of the complication lies in the legal origins of workers compensation, for workers' compensation was, at base, the solution to a legal puzzle. By the early twentieth century, laws governing work accidents required major changes to reflect changes in American industry.

When the first colonists arrived in America they brought with them legal traditions. One of these traditions obligated a master to care for his servant if the servant became disabled in his service. Noblesse oblige was a required duty. By the nineteenth century, however, the relationships between a master and a servant mandated in a preindustrial age were increasingly out of place.[21]

In 1842 a case arose in the Massachusetts Supreme Court that expressed the changes that had occurred in the law since colonial days. Nicholas Farwell, a railroad engineer for the Boston and Worcester Railroad, drove over a stretch of track whose switch had been improperly left open by a switchman. His engine derailed and as a result he lost the use of his right hand. Chief Justice Lemuel Shaw ruled that the railroad was not responsible for Farwell's injuries. The decision formalized the "fellow-servant" rule: An employee injured by another employee's negligence could not sue the employer for damages. By accepting employment on the railroad Farwell assumed the risks of working on the railroad; one risk was the possibility that a switch along the way might be left open.[22] In time, the doctrine that an employee assumed the risks of a work place by accepting employment and the notion that employee negligence accounted for injuries created a formidable array of defenses for employers when injured employees sued them.

Almost immediately these defenses began to crumble under their own weight. By the end of the nineteenth century an employer brought to court in an injury case faced serious difficulties. As early as 1855, Georgia, a state crisscrossed by railroads on their way to someplace else, enacted a law modifying the defenses a railroad might use if an injured employee sued for damages. Other rural states passed similar statutes. Urban states also passed laws modifying employer's defense in work accidents. People everywhere regarded work accident cases as a means of striking back against a powerful and arrogant elite.[23] Just as twentieth-century juries awarded large sums to people injured by physicians widely regarded as rich and insensitive, so late nineteenth-century juries punished industrial employers for injuring employees on the job.

As a direct result of this change in people's attitudes, the volume of litigation and size of jury awards increased. If a skillful lawyer representing an injured employee got past the judge and maneuvered his case in front of a jury he then had a reasonable surety he would win the case. In one sample of appellate court cases tried between 1875 and 1905, juries decided in favor of the employer in only 98 of 1043 cases. During this same period the number of workers' compensation cases rose from 92 to 736 per year.[24]

Employers reacted to this epidemic of litigation by insuring themselves against the risk of paying large awards to injured employees. As the chance of paying such awards increased the price of insurance premiums, which was the cost of averting the risk, rose. In the state of Washington, where in 1910 50 percent of court time was spent on accident litigation, the cost of industrial liability insurance tripled between 1905 and 1910. The dollar value of industrial liability insurance for the nation rose from $200,000 in 1887 to more than $35 million in 1912. Employers, therefore, wanted an industrial disability system that cost them less.[25]

Employers were discontented with damage claims paid to injured workers determined or lucky enough to get their cases before a jury. A majority of injured workers, however, never made it that far. In the state of Washington injured workers collected money from their employers only ten per cent of the time. Across the nation the Aetna Insurance Company managed to avoid paying any damages in 80 percent of the cases it handled. As these examples suggest, employees, as well as employers, suffered from an ineffective work injury law.[26]

This situation was one in which the position of both parties could be improved without making either party worse off. In such situations minimum standard and social insurance measures held their greatest appeal. In this particular situation members of the AALL and other reform groups offered employers and employees workers' compensation. The two parties adopted this suggestion eagerly.

For the old, court-oriented system, workers' compensation laws substituted the new principle of "employer's liability without fault." The laws required an employer to assume the responsibility for any work-related injury that occurred in his plant. Without need of further investigation the employer paid a fixed amount of money, which varied with the severity of the injury, to the worker involved in the accident.

According to the AALL and other workers' compensation advocates, workers' compensation offered advantages over the old system to both the employer and employee. The new law enabled more workers to receive quicker benefits than under the old laws. The old laws gave an injured employee a choice among alternatives. He could accept the benevolence of his employer or initiate a lawsuit. If he accepted the second alternative he needed to hire a lawyer, secure expert testimony, and even then he faced the strong possibility of losing the case.[27] Even if the worker won the case he still had to pay the legal fees and live without wages during lengthy court proceedings. According to Crystal Eastman, co-author of a pathbreaking survey of industrial conditions in Pittsburgh during the Progressive Era, almost half of any award went for the "fighting necessary to get it."[28] By contrast, under workers' compensation injured workers would receive benefits as a matter of right, without need of extensive litigation.

In addition, the new laws offered quick compensation payment. The Illinois courts, for example, required the wounded workman or his family to wait long years, without means of support, for a decision. If the worker won an initial decision he then faced the possibility his employer would appeal. The result was delayed compensation which, at the very least, might produce "an ever-present fear of undeserved want" and destroy a worker's "hopefulness and enterprise." More likely it would lead to prolonged incapacity, needless death, and the destruction of the worker's family. Workers' compensation eliminated the court proceeding, promised a quick recovery of damages, and lessened the social evils produced by delayed payment. Cost-efficiency arguments were obvious and often made.[29]

Such reasoning persuaded labor leaders. Samuel Gompers supported workers' compensation in 1911. Businessmen were swayed by the more basic argument that workers' compensation laws lowered insurance premiums. In a remarkable show of unity, state legislators responded to their constituents and, between 1911 and 1920, passed workers' compensation laws in 45 states. Eventually every state in the union passed such a law, making it the most universal form of social insurance in America in the years between 1911 and 1940.[30]

WORKERS' COMPENSATION IN PRACTICE

Despite this repetition of the same basic process in each state, the compensation laws still reflected the decentralized nature of the American political economy. The national appeal of the AALL for a standard state compensation law revealed the differences among the state laws. The AALL wanted coverage under the law to be universal, yet many states excluded casual, farm, or domestic workers. The association favored strict insurance regulations to put the force of law behind an employer's obligation to compensate his injured employees. The state laws offered a wide variety of insurance arrangements, including, in many states, the right of the employer to insure himself. The association favored a week's waiting period before an injured employee received compensation; the state laws contained a wide variety of waiting times.[31]

The state laws fell farthest behind the association's expectation and contained the widest variations in the amount of money workers received. In 1914 the Association recommended that benefits adequate to meet an accident's cost should include medical, surgical, hospital expenses, and two-thirds of an employee's wages, not to exceed $20 or fall below $5 per week. Most states failed to meet this standard; instead, they followed New Jersey's lead and adopted a schedule that equated the loss of a particular part of the body with a certain number of weeks of compensation payments. The levels chosen probably reflected the experience of private insurance companies that had learned how to distribute accidents by the part of the body damaged. This distribution enabled them to compute insurance rates. The result of this approach by workers' compensation officials was a scheme that disregarded a worker's disability in favor of providing what I. S. Rubinow called "a price list of certain irreplaceable parts of the human body." And the price list differed widely from place to place.[32]

In theory, passage of workers' compensation, even with these wide differences and imperfections, marked a significant imposition of public control over private processes. In practice, as we have seen, this public control had already existed in the form of the court system and, in fact, workers' compensation added few public services to the state welfare system. Like the other Progressive Era minimum standard and social insurance laws passed by the states, workers' compensation laws relied on the actions of private employers to provide for their employees. The public bureaucracies created by these laws might be called skeletal bureaucracies of control—organizations that attempted to police the actions of external private parties, not perform those actions themselves. Yet, even the creation of such indirect bureaucratic entities produced two significant results. One was the permanent institutionalization of workers' compensation laws and the other was the inclusion of state workers' compensation laws as a concern of the federal government.

At first some of the states failed to provide for any formal institutions to administer workers' compensation laws and, as a result, the laws remained the province of the courts. In such states the operation of the laws was presumed to be automatic. An injured employee received compensation from his employer without the intervention of the state. In Minnesota, for example, employers met their workers' compensation obligations by subscribing to employers' mutual insurance. As standard practice the insurance companies sent checks to an employer and he presented his employee with a company check. No governmental party intervened in the process. During the first three years of the New Jersey law state authorities became involved in less than 7 percent of all compensation settlements.[33]

But the compensation advocates of the AALL objected to merely legislating compensation laws and leaving them to the courts; instead, they worked hard to create industrial commissions to administer the law. Largely the creation of Wisconsin professor and AALL/NCF member John R. Commons, these commissions, a fourth branch of government removed from the partisan executive, judicial, and legislative branches, drafted the minimum standards for each particular industry and listened to the disputes that the standards created. Although the compensation advocates rationalized this new branch of the public sector as a joint labor-management exercise with few elements of overt public control, the industrial commissions testified to their belief in the management of industrial processes by a well-educated elite. The right person, the professional expert, in the right setting—the industrial commission—should administer compensation laws and settle disputed cases.[34]

Working from within these commissions the experts attempted to reduce labor conflict. By making employer and employees adversaries in a legal proceeding, the old industrial disability system intensified conflict. One of the common metaphors in workers' compensation propaganda compared the old system to war. Engaging in lawsuits that were "retribution for personal wrong," workers were "drilled to a combative attitude." Employers responded to increasingly harsh liability laws by banding together to resist them. No law, argued one state commission, ought to be framed "which history proves must have the inevitable tendency to deepen, widen, and inflame social distrust and opposition of interests."[35]

It followed that if states passed workers' compensation laws but failed to provide for an administrative body other than the courts they would not get the full benefits of the law. Specifying the payment of compensation for all accidents and allowing workers to appeal to the courts perpetuated the disadvantages of the old system. Employers and employees remained combatants. Creating an industrial commission ushered in an era of industrial peace. Employers and employees from each industry jointly drafted laws and solved conflict through informal agreement.

Industrial commissions offered the essential advantage of replacing the capriciousness of the legal system with the professional discipline of expert administration. To demonstrate the advantages of rule by experts the AALL conducted a full-scale investigation of the New Jersey workers' compensation law, the first American law to take effect. The New Jersey legislature had provided no administrative agency. If not satisfied with the disposition of a particular case, workers and employers retained the right of appeal to the Court of Common Pleas. S. Bruce Black, later to become president of a private insurance company, investigated how the New Jersey law worked for the years 1914 and 1915.[36]

His report, which harshly condemned the New Jersey law, demonstrated what expert administration would accomplish. Court administration lacked provision for systematic reports on industrial accidents. An industrial commission would require such reports and by reducing uncertainty about accident rates would lower insurance premiums and promote safety programs. Court administration, like the old industrial disability system, took time to process cases; Black's investigation estimated the average case lasted 34 weeks from accident to award. An industrial commission, specialized in the compensation law, would facilitate prompt settlement. Court administration involved a great deal of unnecessary expense. One New Jersey worker hit by a train had to pay $25 to secure a physician's testimony and to pay the wages of two fellow workers for the days they testified. Meanwhile the man's wife and five children supported themselves on charity. An industrial commission could eliminate all of these expenses and keep the worker's family off charity. Court administration resulted in not enough cases receiving benefits. Without an agency to publicize the law the ordinary laboring man, the Commissioner of Labor reported in 1913, was "woefully ignorant of the law." An industrial commission would correct this ignorance and make sure workers got what was coming to them.

Worst of all, court administration led to incorrect settlement of compensation cases. The courts' very nature made them unfit to hear and settle workmen's compensation cases. Judges had no knowledge of industrial conditions and had neither the time nor the opportunity to become specialists in the law. As a result they made inconsistent and inaccurate decisions. "In all of these respects," the association report concluded, "a commission especially entrusted with the task of settling compensation claims would obviously be superior." Schooled in industrial conditions, functionally specialized welfare experts would apply the compensation law with precision, order, and efficiency.[37]

The AALL's campaign to create state industrial commissions worked almost as well as the original campaign to create workers' compensation laws. New Jersey took administration of the compensation statutes away from the court system in 1919. By 1920, 34 of 45 states with workers' compensation laws administered those laws through industrial commissions.[38]

As soon as the employees of the industrial commissions were installed they took steps to formalize their jobs and to create the type of national forums through which groups defined themselves as professionals. Acting through the Bureau of Labor Statistics the federal government supplied the impetus for the movement to bring state compensation officials together. Only three years after the first state industrial commission was created (in Wisconsin), Royal Meeker, the U.S. Commissioner of Labor Statistics, convened a conference for the purpose of standardizing accident forms and statistics. By October, 1914, all of the compensation interests were participating in this effort, including the large railroad and steel companies, the National Safety Council, insurance companies such as Metropolitan Life, and the AALL.[39]

Meanwhile, the International Association of Industrial Accident Boards and Commissions (IAIABC) was formed in Lansing, Michigan in April 1914. This group, which became the official organization of workers' compensation officials, viewed its purpose as bringing the compensation boards and commissions "into closer relation with one another." Such proximity would breed "uniformity" in workers' compensation laws.[40] The market for the relief of industrial accidents was slowly and gradually being made national in scope.

The efforts of the U.S. Commissioner of Labor Statistics and of the IAIABC came together when the commissioner became the secretary of the IAIABC. At the same time the Bureau of Labor Statistics agreed to publish the IAIABC's proceedings. Speaking at the IAIABC's third annual meeting, Commissioner Meeker claimed that his bureau, the "natural and obvious medium to unify and coordinate the activities of all state agencies," would "eliminate useless and irritating duplication of effort."[41]

Here, then, was an attempt to coordinate the industrial disability sector of America's welfare system. States could apply a common methodology to local conditions and work to improve that methodology through national forums sustained in part by the administrative resources of the federal government. Federal bureaucrats could mediate the voluntary application of uniform minimum standards among the states. State bureaucrats, in turn, could mediate the application of uniform minimum standards among employers. Both levels of public authority could attempt to persuade laggards to operate up to the most enlightened existing norms established by the activities and experiences of enlightened employers in the private sector. Creation of this Progressive Era welfare structure marked the first hesitant entrance of the federal government into the twentieth-century welfare system.[42]

Two important effects accompanied the formation of government welfare bureaucracies on the state and, to a much lesser extent, the federal levels. The process eliminated a degree of flexibility from the American welfare system and created the potential for antagonism between public and private bureaucrats. The original public welfare agencies, such as the courts, were multipurpose institutions able to perform a wide range of tasks. Industrial commissions were specialized institutions to deal only with labor laws. The interests of the courts were tied to no particular law; the interests of industrial commissions were intertwined with workers' compensation, the most important law these commissions administered. Because the identity of the industrial commissions came from workers' compensation laws, the employees of these agencies had a vested interest in preserving such laws. The continued existence of industrial commissions, therefore, insured the continued existence of workers' compensation laws and perpetuated a state-by-state approach to disability.

In addition, the industrial commissioners duplicated the role of the increasing numbers of welfare bureaucrats operating within private industry. Both professionals served many of the same functions—in particular, settling disputes between workers and management. Although the limited power of the state or federal governments prevented overt conflict between the two groups throughout the early decades of the twentieth century the potential for such conflict existed.

In the years between 1900 and 1920 the federal government made its entrance into the modern social welfare system. Overseeing the actions of private companies and the states served as the dynamic and the rationale for the federal government's activities. Receiving public welfare changed from a **sign** of failure to a matter of right in the case of industrial accidents and, to a lesser degree, in the case of working conditions for women and children. Although businessmen remained the more important welfare innovators, the minimum standard and social insurance legislation of the Progressive Era provided an impetus for continued state involvement in welfare matters. When federal bureaucrats mounted their first real challenge to businessmen in the 1930s, these Progressive Era precedents held great significance. First, however, came a very different era.

NOTES

1. Eric Goldman, *Rendezvous with Destiny: A History of Modern American Reform* (New York: Random House, 1953).

2. This classic example is taken from Richard Hofstadter, *The Age of Reform* (New York: Vintage Books, 1955), pp. 231–32.

3. David Rothman, *The Discovery of the Asylum* (Boston: Little Brown, 1971); Gerald Grob, *Mental Institutions in America: Social Policy to 1875* (New York: Free Press, 1973).

4. Arthur H. Holcombe, "The Legal Minimum Wage in the United States," *American Economic Review* 2 (1912): 31.

5. Sidney and Beatrice Webb, *Industrial Democracy* (London: Longmans, 1887), p. 729.

6. Sidney Webb, "The Economic Theory of a Legal Minimum Wage," *Journal of Political Economy* 20 (1912): 977, 982.

7. J. Lee Kreader, "Isaac Max Rubinow: Pioneering Specialist in Social Insurance," *Social Service Review* 50 (September 1956): 408–09.

8. Paul Kellogg speaking before National Conference of Charities and Corrections, *Proceedings* (1910), p. 374.

9. Robert F. Wesser, "Conflict and Compromise: The Workmen's Compensation Movement in New York, 1890's–1913," *Labor History* 11 (Summer 1971): 346–47; "Review of Labor Legislation," *American Labor Legislation Review*, December, 1915; *Proceedings of the First Annual Meeting: American Association for Labor Legislation* (Madison, 1907), p. 3.

10. See note 25, Chapter 1, for "enlightened" business interest in minimum standard legislation.

11. We take the concept of the free rider from Douglas North and Robert Paul Thomas, *Institutional Change and American Economic Growth* (New York: Cambridge University Press, 1971).

12. L. A. Boettinger, *Employee Welfare Work* (New York: Ronald Press, 1923); William Graebner, "Federalism in the Progressive Era: A Structural Interpretation of Reform," *Journal of American History*, September, 1977.

13. The best overview of both types of laws remains John R. Commons et al., *History of Labor*, vol. 3 (New York, 1935). See also Robert H. Bremner, *From the Depths: The Discovery of Poverty in the United States* (New York: New York University Press, 1956), pp. 249–57 and Hace Sorel Tishler, *Self-Reliance and Social Security* (Port Washington, N.Y.: Kennikat Press, 1971), pp. 108–41.

14. Clara M. Beyer, *History of Labor Legislation for Women in Three States* (Washington D.C.: G.P.O. 1929), p. 56; Goldmark, *Impatient Crusader*; James T. Patterson, "Mary Dewson and the American Minimum Wage Movement," *Labor History* 5 (1964): 134; *Report of the Commission on Minimum Wage Boards* (Boston: State Printing Office, 1910).

15. H. LaRue Brown, "Massachusetts and the Minimum Wage," *Annals* 48 (1913): 15.

16. Anthony F. Lucas, "The Legal Minimum Wage in Massachusetts," *Annals* supplement, 130 (1927): 72.

17. Massachusetts Minimum Wage Commission, *Statement and Decree Concerning the Wages of Women in the Brush Industry in Massachusetts* (Boston: State Printing Office, 1914), p. 2.

18. Beyer, *History of Labor Legislation for Women*, p. 59; National Industrial Conference Board, *Minimum Wage in Massachusetts* (New York: National Industrial Conference Board, 1927), p. 11.

19. Victor P. Morris, *Oregon's Experience with Minimum Wage Legislation* (New York: Columbia University Press, 1930), p. 124; Edwin V. O'Hara, *A Living Wage by Legislation: The Oregon Experience* (Salem, Oregon: State Printing Office, 1916).

20. Secretary of Oregon Manufactureers and Merchants Association to Florence Kelley, n.d., National Consumers League Papers, Library of Congress, Washington, D.C.

21. See John Demos, *A Little Commonwealth: Family Life in Plymouth Colony* (New York: Oxford University Press, 1970) for a description of the obligation of master to servant in early America.

22. Leonard W. Levy, *The Law of the Commonwealth and Chief Justice Shaw* (Cambridge: Harvard University Press, 1957), pp. 166–83.

23. See Lawrence Friedman and Jack Ladinsky, "Social Change and the Law of Industrial Accidents," *Columbia Law Review* (1967), and U.S., Department of Labor, *Growth of Labor Law in the United States* (Washington D.C.: G.P.O., 1962), p. 159.

24. These statistics come from Richard A. Posner's pathbreaking article, "A Theory of Negligence," *Journal of Legal Studies* (January, 1972): 44–95.

25. Joseph F. Tripp, "An Instance of Labor and Business Cooperation: Workmen's Compensation in Washington State," *Labor History* 17 (Fall 1976): 537; Lubove, *Struggle for Social Security*, p. 51.

26. Tripp, "An Instance of Labor and Business Cooperation," p. 537; Crystal Eastman, "The American Way of Distributing Industrial Accident Losses," *Proceedings of the Second Annual Meeting of the American Association for Labor Legislation* (Madison, 1909), p. 44. See also Crystal Eastman, *Accidents and the Law* (New York: Russell Sage Foundation, 1913), p. 279.

27. Charles Henderson, "Workingman's Insurance in Illinois," *Proceedings of the First Annual Meeting: American Association for Labor Legislation* (Madison: American Association for Labor Legislation, 1907), p. 74.

28. Eastman, "The American Way," p. 51.

29. Henderson, "Workingman's Insurance in Illinois," p. 74; E. H. Downey, *Workmen's Compensation* (New York: Macmillan, 1924), p. 8.

30. Among the many state documents bearing on this process see *Report of the*

Connecticut State Commission on Compensation for Industrial Accidents (Hartford, 1911); *Report of the Employer's Liability Commission of the State of Illinois* (Chicago, 1910); *Report of the Special Commission on Industrial Insurance* (Madison, 1911); all of which are available at the Department of Labor Library, Washington, D.C. The best overview of the process is Herman A. and Anne R. Somers, *Workmen's Compensation: Prevention, Insurance, Rehabilitation of Occupational Disability* (New York: John Wiley and Sons, 1954).

31. "Review of Labor Legislation."

32. Evelyn Ellen Singleton, "Workmen's Compensation in Maryland" (Ph.D. diss., Johns Hopkins, 1933), p. 50. Arthur Reede, *Adequacy of Workmen's Compensation* (Cambridge, Mass.: Harvard University Press, 1947), p. 119.

33. Robert Asher, "Radicalism and Reform: State Insurance of Workmen's Compensation in Minnesota, 1910-1933," *Labor History* 14 (Winter 1973): 58; "Three Years Under the New Jersey Workmen's Compensation Law: Report of an Investigation under the Direction of the Social Insurance Committee of the American Association for Labor Legislation," *American Labor Legislation Review* 5 (1915): 58.

34. John R. Commons to Henry W. Farnam, March 16, 1911, Commons Papers, Wisconsin State Historical Society, Madison Wis.; "The Administration of Labor Laws," *American Labor Legislation Review* 5 (1915): 679; Singleton, *Workmen's Compensation in Maryland*, p. 62.

35. Henderson, "Workingman's Insurance in Illinois," pp. 75, 81.

36. See Monroe Berkowitz, *Workmen's Compensation: The New Jersey Experience* (New Brunswick: Rutgers University Press, 1957).

37. Ibid., pp. 116-17; "Three Years Under the New Jersey Workmen's Compensation Law," pp. 38-39, 41, 47, 58.

38. Asher, "Radicalism and Reform," p. 33; Wallace D. Yapple, "Administration by Courts or by Commission," *American Labor Legislation Review* 5 (March 1915): 117-19; Carl Hookstadt, "Comparison of Workmen's Compensation Laws of the United States and Canada up to January 1, 1920," in Bureau of Labor Statistics Bulletin no. 275 (Washington D.C., 1920), p. 114.

39. "Standardization of Industrial Accident Statistics," in Bureau of Labor Statistics Bulletin no. 276 (Washington D.C.: G.P.O., 1920), pp. 8-9.

40. Ibid., p. 10.

41. "Proceedings of the Third Annual Meeting of the IAIABC," in Bureau of Labor Statistics Bulletin no. 210 (Washington D.C.: G.P.O., 1917), p. 7.

42. It should perhaps be noted that our approach to workers compensation differs from the conventional one, which tends to center on the question of whether business or labor was most responsible for the laws. As we indicate, both were responsible and the laws' significance lies outside the nuances of this particular historiographic nonargument. See James Weinstein, *The Corporate Ideal in the Liberal State* (Boston: Beacon Press, 1968), and Robert F. Wesser, "Conflict and Compromise: The Workmen's Compensation Movement in New York, 1890-1913," *Labor History* (Summer 1971): 345-72.

3

AN ATMOSPHERE OF ORGANIZATION: THE RISE OF WELFARE CAPITALISM, 1910-1930

If the Progressive Era witnessed the beginning of a modern public welfare system it also provided the foundations for the welfare capitalism of the 1920s. During the years between 1910 and America's entrance into World War I the discovery of new production techniques led to new means for dealing with labor and labor relations. These new methods involved the ability to identify, measure, and therefore quantify, discrete components of the production process. The war speeded the introduction of these techniques, frequently summarized by the term "scientific management," into private industry. Building upon these new techniques, businessmen managed to stay ahead of the public sector and to dominate the new welfare environment that the war helped to create.

PROLOGUE TO WAR

In the decade before World War I heightened efforts to harness science to industry underlined the virtues of order, predictability, and coordination within the bureaucratic order of large American corporations. This trend was particularly evident in new science-based industries such as electrical manufacturing and chemicals. Cooperative networks linked growing numbers of companies with technical experts in private foundations, government departments, and universities. Scientists and engineers exercised increasing power and influence within America's basic industries: steel, petroleum, rubber, and automotive. The same forces that impelled industrialists to pioneer in industrial research forced them, in David Noble's words, to look outside of industry for solutions to the problems they faced within it. . . . [T]he historical, philosophical, and geographical distinctions between the workshop and the laboratory, the industries and the universities, applied and fundamental research, were collapsing in practice, in the daily functioning of the industrial system.[1]

New techniques and new men were needed to implement these changes and to train the tens of thousands of managers necessary to administer the complicated operations of an expanding industrial order. The scientific management movement of the prewar period provided the most visible example of these new techniques.

Since the late 1890s the structure of production processes and the act of human labor itself had been objects of intense study. Investigations by engineers including Frederick Winslow Taylor and H. L. Gantt led to increased efforts at measuring the efficiency of workers in terms of a collection of specialized labor components. Systematized planning procedures replaced random production, scheduling, and training techniques. Once-powerful foremen became subordinates within a functionalized bureaucratic order.

By 1910, scientific management techniques offered an increasingly congenial rationale to employers experimenting with various forms of industrial betterment. These same techniques obtained the support of a wide spectrum of upper-class reformers anxious to discover some calculus of industrial felicity by which workers, their employers, and the general public might all benefit. Shop improvements that boosted production by decreasing waste and inefficiency, in their view, created positive stimuli toward humane industrial evolution. As a result, scientific management techniques were considered profitable investments in human, as well as inanimate, capital; as "social engineering," rather than philanthropy. These techniques, moreover, were not limited to one firm or industry. The degree to which industry implemented F. W. Taylor's notions of efficiency could, therefore, serve as a yardstick to measure industrial progress.[2]

When Frederick W. Taylor died in 1915 a further elaboration of scientific managerial technique was underway. Until 1915, upper-level business administrators had trained workers and assumed increased powers over the operations of foremen. After 1915 the principles of scientific management and business administration were extended to the upper levels of management. Increasingly, executives were made, not born.

Systematized management education, which occupied a larger and larger role on the American corporate scene, provided one new approach to training managers who were responsible for social welfare work. In 1909 the first textbook on scientific management for corporate administrators was published. By 1910, Cornell, Harvard, Penn State, Carnegie Tech, and the Massachusetts Institute of Technology (MIT) offered programs of "works administration." Twelve years later ten colleges and universities offered instruction in the science of management. After another decade that total had tripled. Managers in science-based industries proclaimed the virtues of specialization and professionalism within their companies. These proclamations were also calls for increased use of company welfare plans.[3]

A less scientific element, the fear of labor violence, also accounted for the growth in corporate welfare schemes after 1915. Masses of industrial workers were not quietly accepting major alterations in the pace and organization of their working lives. The years from 1910 to 1915 witnessed a pattern of labor unrest, the severity of which matched that of the 1890s. Bloody strikes in Paterson, New Jersey, and Ludlow, Colorado, accented the depths of worker discontent. "Regardless of cause, geographic location, type of industry, or ethnic group," Graham Adams noted, "turbulence in industrial relations flared all over the United States." Even such conservative employers as John D. Rockefeller, Jr. decided to follow the lead of Edward A. Filene and an earlier generation of beneficent employers and institute welfare programs within their firms. Unlike earlier employers, however, Rockefeller was able to capitalize on the shared experience represented by the NCF's Welfare Department and leading organizations of the Progressive Era social welfare movement such as the AALL.[4]

As we have seen, the federal government confined its role within America's Progressive Era social welfare system to coordinating the decentralized social insurance and minimum standards efforts being variously undertaken by the states. Federal officials also cooperated with private organizations such as the NCF to spread the gospel of social welfare and efficiency among businessmen generally. Woodrow Wilson, the president with whom businessmen would have to deal during the war, exemplified these Progressive Era traditions of minimal government and voluntary social welfare action. Wilson looked to the federal government to provide a solution to the "curse of bigness" and restore to the greatest extent possible the virtues of a decentralized market system. Once purged of anticompetitive excesses free market institutions would allocate society's resources optimally and adequately. Only in unusual cases of market failure should the state intervene in any way, such as in the case of child laborers who lacked the facilities to participate fully in the market, or in the case of women who lacked the strength to be full-fledged competitors. Others in Wilson's world were presumed to be able to handle their own welfare problems.

The war put a severe strain on Wilson's theories. Within the federal government militant antitrust stands gave way to efforts to maintain the confidence of businessmen. At the same time, the war accelerated the organizational trends that had been developing in the private sector for some time. World War I, therefore, solidified private welfare structures without significantly expanding public ones.[5]

WAR AS SOCIAL WELFARE EXERCISE

For nearly three years after Sarajevo, America enjoyed the economic advantages of neutrality. Billions of dollars of Allied orders for weapons, raw materials, and agricultural products revived a sluggish economy and inflated profit margins without necessitating direct military or political involvements.

In April 1917, the United States entered the world conflict. Unprecedented efforts were required to organize industry to produce the myriad devices requisite for complex technological war. Western science and technology had, almost unnoticed, forever changed the nature of war. These changes had an economic dimension as well. Airplanes, tanks, flame throwers, and field telephones could not be bid for with the same simplicity as blankets, shovels, and bayonets. War had become a matter of complex machines, as well as of men. To solve the problems of nationwide planning, coordination, and resource allocation, the federal government became involved in the infinite nuances of wartime production.

Increased federal involvement in the economy might have expanded the federal government's social welfare responsibilities, but, considered as a test of public versus private power, World War I was an almost uncontested victory for the private side. In July 1917, a new War Industries Board (WIB) received primary responsibility for industrial mobilization. The board, "the greatest concentration of public bureaucratic power to that point in American history," posessed wide concerns. Assisted by a network of industrial trade associations the WIB oversaw coordination, allocation, production, and supply decisions arrived at by military and corporate groups, and attempted to fix prices for strategic commodities. In April 1918 President Wilson augmented emergency controls over the industrial economy by creating a National War Labor Board (NWLB) to prevent strikes and to help guarantee uninterrupted production schedules. NWLB mediators affected industrial relations within 1100 plants (711,500 employees) created 125 works councils within individual firms, and even seized a small number of companies. For the first time in United States history the federal government entered the arena of industrial relations in an effort to guarantee collective bargaining rights to American workers.

Despite this expansion of public power, corporate bureaucrats remained in a dominant position vis-à-vis their opposite numbers in the public sector. Instead of relying on the group of professional state administrators to run the wartime mobilization agencies, key administration officials asked businessmen to come to Washington and serve for the duration. Financier Bernard M. Baruch took control of the WIB. He then called upon Edwin F. Gay of the Harvard Business School to run the new agency's Planning and Statistics Section. Gay, in turn, recruited Henry S. Dennison as his assistant. Gerald Swope of the General Electric Company, Walter Gifford of American Telephone and Telegraph, and other corporate welfare innovators also played key roles in the wartime agencies. With the exception of Bernard Baruch few of these company officials transferred their loyalties to the federal government. When the war ended in November 1918 they speedily left Washington and returned to company headquarters. The federal agencies they had manned, including the NWLB, were abruptly dismantled.

The ending of wartime economic planning agencies was not to the liking of all business and government interests. Throughout the early months of 1919, Department of Commerce officials sought peacetime substitutes for the war arrangements, chiefly revisions of the antitrust laws to allow price setting by national industry trade associations. Steel industry executives provided strong support for such efforts. But both federal and corporate councils proved too fragmented to enable substantial collaboration to take place.

The dismantling of federal war production agencies faithfully reflected Wilson's preferences for minimal government and for voluntarism in industrial affairs. "The United States government," Robert Cuff concludes, "made no more preparations to leave the war than it had to enter it." Instead, it sought to assume its traditional role as an umpire regarding bargaining between labor, capital, and the public.

Businessmen, too, shed few tears over the demise of the WIB and allied agencies. Throughout the wartime emergency these agencies lacked clear statutory authority to enforce their decisions. As a result, the mobilization program that they administered was "fundamentally dependent upon voluntary administration and the private cooperation of corporate interest groups." Officials of national industrial trade associations, not Bernard Baruch, were the true czars of the planning process. Once the war ended, however, the rationale for continued institutional synthesis between organized business and the federal government evaporated. Businessmen sought the advantages of self-regulation without the complicating factor of institutionalized governmental participation in the process.[6]

Although businessmen opposed an expanded independent regulatory role for the federal government, that did not mean that the Washington establishment should disappear entirely from the industrial scene. The wartime emergency had demonstrated the federal government's usefulness as a facilitator of compromise among occupational and industrial groups. In periods of crisis, government officials might expedite the voluntary arbitration of outstanding disputes if and when the agreement of the major antagonists was obtained. Government, in short, should provide forums in which private parties could formulate enlightened welfare procedures, but it should go no farther.

Prevention of federal interference was hardly difficult. If war had unsettled customary political and economic procedures, a broad agreement continued to exist among government, corporate, and middle-class leaders that primary responsibility for the operation of the industrial system rested in businessmen's hands.

President Wilson's reaction to the strike wave of 1919–20 illustrated the continuities between prewar and postwar federal procedure. During the war, federal officials had ordered firms in key defense industries to create employee representation agencies. This order marked an attempt to replicate a key component of enlightened business's welfare procedure within firms producing war materials. After the war, however, the federal government failed to restrain employers from abolishing or watering down existing representation plans.

Labor reacted predictably, particularly in the steel industry. The number of strikes and lockouts surged upward, and Wilson convened two unprecedented national industrial conferences to discuss the problem of industrial unrest. Leaders of organized labor and organized business attended the conferences. Government as a distinct interest was not represented in the negotiations. It remained an umpire in which private organizations set the rules, performed experiments, and created concrete programs. Federal officials limited themselves to expediting compromise between corporate and labor leaders in a manner reminiscent of the NCF.[7]

The government's efforts to end labor unrest failed. Conservative employers, led by Elbert H. Gary of United States Steel, refused to countenance any form of employee representation within industry. Employers launched attacks against industrial union drives within the mass production trades. As a result total trade union membership plummeted from 5.1 to 3.6 million between 1920 and 1923. Syndicalist

and Socialist unions, notably the IWW, fared even worse. Restoration of
the status quo ante bellum appeared to sum up business desires.

In this case appearances were deceiving. For all of the NAM's
alarmist rhetoric Elbert Gary's views were not universally shared.
During the deliberations of Wilson's national industrial conferences a
small number of articulate capitalists argued for a rapprochement with
labor as one component of a corporate welfare system. Among these
men were representatives of giant corporations such as Gerald Swope
and Owen D. Young, both of the General Electric Company. These men
inherited earlier welfare capitalist traditions and would be chiefly
responsible for their elaboration during the postwar decade.[8]

WELFARE CAPITALISM IN THE 1920s: GERARD SWOPE AND OWEN D. YOUNG OF GENERAL ELECTRIC

The installation of Swope and Young as the chief executive officers
of the General Electric Company (GE) in December 1921 illustrated the
arrival of a new era in American industrial life. During this era complex
managerial bureaucracies, not captains of industry, commanded large
corporations. The age of the owner-capitalist was past and the future
belonged to the professional who felt comfortable with functionally
specialized administration and the routinization of management procedure.

To a great extent new professionals worked in oligopolistic product
markets. In the 1920s these managers looked forward to what they
called ethical competition. Ethical competition, of course, meant non-
price competition, a situation that earlier capitalists would have regarded as no competition at all. Oligopoly, therefore, produced a new
sort of corporate logic. Stabilized profit margins permitted the long-
term investment planning that was increasingly necessary to develop
new techniques and products. Simultaneously, oligopoly provided
businessmen with greater opportunities to finance welfare programs by
passing costs on to consumers and by spending the increased profits.
The postwar leadership of GE exemplified how one company took
advantage of these opportunities.

Owen D. Young and Gerard Swope, GE's new men of the corporate world, were professionally trained bureaucrats who had risen
through the elaborate corporate ranks. Born in 1874, Young grew up
poor on a farm in upstate New York. He managed to attend a local
college on a series of scholarships and loans and then received a law
degree from Boston University in 1896. Having reached the city Young
kept his eye on the main chance and entered the burgeoning field of

public utilities law. He was soon marked as a man to watch. Finally, in 1912 Young was recruited to head GE's legal department and made a corporate vice-president in charge of overall public policy.

Although Gerard Swope was only two years older than Young, he came from a different world. His father was a relatively affluent St. Louis watch case manufacturer, a German Jew finding success in America. Gerard soon developed a penchant for basement tinkering, and, since money was no object, he eventually attended MIT. He earned his engineering degree in 1895. At MIT Swope received an education with a remarkable group of fellow engineering students, many of whom would rise to prominence in corporate circles. This group included Alfred P. Sloan, Jr., a man whose fortunes became intertwined with a young corporation with the uninspiring title of General Motors, Paul W. Litchfield of Goodyear, and Irénée DuPont of the DuPont Company. Swope and his peers found an engineering education an important asset in the managerial world.

After 20 years at Western Electric, the manufacturing division of the American Telephone and Telegraph Company, Swope was hired away by GE and made president of the corporation's international sales subsidiary. Shortly afterward, Swope's combination of Prussian efficiency and manufacturing and merchandising know-how propelled him toward the presidency of the parent corporation. At the same time, Owen D. Young, whose talents were primarily legal, financial, and diplomatic, was installed as chairman of the board.[9]

The administrative style that GE's new leaders initiated set a standard followed by many other large American corporations in the postwar decade. Owen D. Young, known colloquially as "Mr. Outside," went public and became, in effect, GE's ambassador-at-large to the business and political world. Throughout Young's career he espoused doctrines of corporate trusteeship for the welfare of an industrial society. The doctrines differentiated enlightened postwar entrepreneurship from the buccaneering proclivities evident in earlier stages of corporate development. According to Young, the specialized bureaucracies that now ran American corporations were composed of managerial professionals, rather than robber barons. An occasional ignorant leader still existed. The growing separation of ownership from administrative responsibility and control, however, had created a willingness among upper-level managers to act as stewards for the welfare of stockholders, employees, and the consumer public. The reign of rules that resulted from the new corporate procedures allowed a benign industrial oligarchy to improve the welfare of the masses.[10]

The views of Gerard Swope, the "Mr. Inside" of GE's leadership team, on the virtues of corporate self-regulation contrasted sharply with Young's. Young's conceptual style was predominantly legalistic. He placed exhaustive definition of desired goals above procedural tinkering. Swope, however, possessed an engineer's mind. Like Henry S. Dennison, Swope saw the welfare capitalism of the postwar era as an exercise in social engineering, rather than trusteeship or philanthropy. Enlightened entrepreneurship consisted of an awareness that scientific management principles earlier enunciated by Frederick W. Taylor could be applied to the entire spectrum of human and production relations in corporate society. GE spent millions of dollars for basic scientific research, and millions more to ensure that its production machinery was maintained in the highest possible state of efficiency. By the same token, it must invest large sums to maintain its human machinery in as frictionless a state as possible. Such intelligently selfish improvements in the welfare of the corporation's human capital would boost overall productivity, profitability, and power for all groups concerned in the capitalist process. As Swope, a one-time resident at Jane Addams' Hull House, concluded in an essay written for *Survey* magazine in 1924,

> If the engineer [managerial capitalist] can make contributions that will not only reduce human effort in production so that goods may be made at less cost and so be available to an ever increasing number of people, but can also cooperate with others, whether in the ranks of labor or in the social service professions, who are applying the scientific method to the wider problems of society, he will come into his own.[11]

Working collectively, Young and Swope created their own version of a welfare state within GE during the early 1920s. They made major efforts to standardize welfare procedures throughout all of the company's plants.

General Electric's approach to company unionism highlighted the trend. Until the end of World War I, company administrators had issued occasional mollifying statements regarding collective bargaining in elite business associations like the NCF. But diplomatic utterances did not extend into the realm of tolerance for experiments. As early as 1918, however, Young sought labor relations counsel from William Lyon MacKenzie King, an adviser to Rockefeller. The next year, Young and A. C. Bedford, another Rockefeller aide, provided the impetus for the formation of a Special Conference Committee to enable industrial relations executives to standardize their procedures. Officials from industry giants including Bethlehem Steel, DuPont, General Electric, General Motors, Goodyear, International Harvester, Standard Oil of New Jersey, U.S. Rubber, Westinghouse, U.S. Steel, and American

Telephone and Telegraph availed themselves of this national forum for policy development. Finally, between 1922 and 1924, Young and Swope initiated employee representation plans at all GE plants. Low-level managers often worked to negate these challenges to their power and authority. Gradually, however, regulations requiring regular elections, secret balloting, and the arbitration of grievances were formalized.[12]

General Electric also routinized a broad range of corporate welfare procedures. Life insurance, retirement pensions, and disability programs were made less discretionary than before. Workers were allowed to buy company stock at preferred rates. Company-guaranteed mortgages enabled higher-paid company personnel to obtain homes. The firm agreed to match the funds that workers contributed to an employee relief and loan society. Efforts were made to create an unemployment insurance program acceptable to both managers and employees. The company reorganized production schedules to decrease the necessity of seasonal layoffs. Paid vacations were awarded to workers with over ten years of continuous service. General Electric's leadership engaged in what one academic economist termed "one of the most ambitious social experiments of the age." Here was a multifaceted effort to formulate a new responsibility for the preservation of mass welfare standards. This responsibility was based within the private corporation, rather than within the isolated island-community, the trade union, or the federal government.

These liberal procedures derived important ideological legitimacy from the new discipline of psychology. In addition, these principles interfaced neatly with the social engineering viewpoints of H. S. Dennison and Gerard Swope. Following America's entrance into World War I, mobilization programs had benefited from a variety of new social science techniques, particularly standardized intelligence (IQ) tests first developed in France in 1905. Such measurements of specific mental skills allowed the American armed forces to measure the quality of labor and the intellectual efficiency among recruits. Human intelligence was broken down into component parts that could be incorporated into production equations.

Businessmen were not uninterested in the possibilities presented by these techniques. Scientific management allowed managers to gauge efficiency of action. Psychological techniques offered the additional possibility of measuring (and perhaps controlling) the mental and emotional processes that underlay the act of labor itself. Workers were more than a set of divisible labor components. They were, in addition, a mass psychology to be measured, gauged, modified, and understood. Psychology, in such a view, need not concern itself with analyzing the nature of human consciousness; rather, it could confine itself to studying concrete human behavior as it interacted with social and work surroundings.

The decade immediately after the Armistice witnessed ambitious elaborations of welfare capitalist procedure based upon the "management of men on a human basis." Elton Mayo's experiments begun in 1924 at the Hawthorne Works of the Western Electric Company further underlined the virtues of behavior modification through managerial consultation and teamwork with employees. Accenting the entrepreneurial understanding of the internal group dynamics of workers, Mayo's theories provided a strong rationale for the creation of company unions. More than philanthropy, such representation agencies provided an institutional means for involving workers in, and harmonizing workers with, their industrial environments. After visiting a GE plant in 1926, Robert W. Bruere observed that the company's welfare system, complete with company unions, was more a device for promoting technical efficiency than a means of forwarding a democratization of industrial procedure.[13]

General Electric's policies, however, reaped impressive social and economic dividends. Pioneer welfare capitalists Edward A. Filene and H. S. Dennison joined muckrakers Ida M. Tarbell and Lincoln Steffens in identifying Owen D. Young as an enlightened capitalist of the first order. Business periodicals agreed with this opinion. Young maintained extremely good relations with Republican party leaders and became a trusted adviser on international banking questions. In 1924 and 1929 Young acted as an unofficial United States representative at important European war reparations conferences. The Democrats, too, wanted to obtain the benefits of Young's stature and influence. By 1926, for example, Eleanor Roosevelt publicly announced a preference for Young over Tammany liberal Robert F. Wagner in the New York Democratic Party senatorial primary. At the same time, New York's Governor Alfred Smith listened to the advice of Young's associate Gerard Swope on important political matters. By 1928 the New York *Times* was booming Young as a dark-horse presidential nominee. All the while, GE plants, assets, profits, and dividends mounted. Occasional antitrust suits were brushed aside or avoided by corporate divestiture of affected properties. The corporation expanded its production range into the markets for consumer durables such as electric radios, refrigerators, and washing machines.[14]

General Electric's policies and procedures served as a model for what was increasingly termed the "welfare capitalism" of the postwar United States. Statistics highlighted the trend toward systematization of welfare procedures throughout large segments of the American corporate order. Between 1919 and 1922 no less than 317 company unions were created—26 times the total established by employers during the preceding 20 years. Prominent among the firms involved were corporations such as Goodyear Tire and Rubber, Inland Steel, International Harvester, and the Pennsylvania Railroad. "By 1926," one authority noted, "the number of employees working under [company union] plans was above 1,400,000, compared with a little over 400,000 in 1919. And of these, nearly a million worked for companies with more than 10,000 employees" in the steel, electrical, utilities, coal, textile, food processing, railroad, and meat-packing industries.[15]

Simultaneously a new breed of industrial relations executives emerged within companies operating in oligopolistic markets. High-level staff specialists at Standard Oil of New Jersey, U.S. Rubber, General Electric, and U.S. Steel accelerated the growth of welfare programs. Personnel departments with overall responsibility for administering welfare and employment procedures had been rare in American industry until World War I. By 1929 more than half the firms employing over 5,000 people surveyed by a national employers' association possessed such bureaucratic agencies. Six years later the percentage rose to 80 percent.[16]

Nor was this all. Between 1915 and 1917, larger United States corporations created over 340 programs that enabled their employees to purchase company stock at preferred rates. Other traditional welfare activities became generally accepted. By the end of the postwar decade over 90 percent of companies surveyed in one national study operated safety programs; 70 percent operated group insurance plans; and 60 percent had mutual aid associations. In the 15 years after 1910 more than 181 companies established retirement pension programs to minister to the needs of workers with continuous employment records within individual firms. Benefits depended upon good employee behavior. If the worker struck, joined an AFL union, or appeared to hold radical political beliefs he could lose his benefits, low as they often were. Despite these elements of old-fashioned social control, however, a precedent was being established that systematic retirement benefits of some sort were due to faithful employees. This development occurred at a time when state retirement plans were few and fragmentary, and federal programs were nonexistent.[17]

Corporate welfare innovations were impressive in scope. At the same time, however, (it should be emphasized) welfare capitalism remained a minority phenomenon largely confined to prosperous firms operating in national markets. As late as 1929 only one corporation out of every five surveyed provided formalized pension, stock purchase, or savings and loan programs for its workers. For the majority of America's industrial labor force, it was business as usual throughout the 1920s.

Welfare capitalism, however, enjoyed growing intellectual, social, and political support among nonbusiness groups. Hesitant and partial as businessmen's innovations might be, theirs remained the most active role in the provision of welfare services. The very weakness of public and trade union response to the human problems of a complex industrial age accented entrepreneurial achievement and legitimized corporate purpose. Governmental preferences for voluntarism and established craft union strategies of organizing only skilled laborers allowed managerial bureaucrats to maintain a clear responsibility for the preservation of the "public interest" in the commercial and industrial affairs of the nation. The future appeared to belong to enlightened advocates like Owen D. Young and social engineers like Gerard Swope.

In the 20 years between 1910 and 1930, welfare capitalism indisputably arrived on the American social and political scene. The welfare efforts of an earlier generation of business pioneers were being integrated into a system within a nationalized corporate system. Welfare arrangements that had earlier been characterized by piecemeal formulation and informal administration were now centralized, routinized, and functionally coordinated by specialized managerial bureaucracies administering the various affairs of large corporations.

A new capitalism had emerged—one that regulated its affairs to abolish the excesses and insecurities of the old order. An American experience of war made the corporation the major model for administering welfare services. America's approach to welfare throughout the 1920s demonstrated the results of these perceived realities.

Compared to private sector developments, therefore, federal welfare programs faced an uncertain and confusing future. After all, they possessed fewer ties to the market place. Nonetheless, in the 1920s Washington bureaucrats sought to expand their welfare responsibilities. In the process they created programs organized and rationalized in the same terms as the private programs. In other words, no distinction between a public and private approach to social welfare had yet been made. Throughout the 1920s, then, large corporations continued to dominate the social welfare field.

NOTES

1. David Noble, *America By Design: Science, Technology, and the Rise of Corporate Capitalism* (New York, 1977), pp. 111-12. See also Alfred D. Chandler, Jr., *The Visible Hand: The Managerial Revolution in American Business*, (Cambridge, 1977) p. 415.

2. Standard works for the influence of the scientific management impulse include Samuel Haber, *Efficiency and Uplift* (Chicago: University of Chicago Press, 1964); Milton J. Nadworny, *Scientific Management and the Unions* (Cambridge: Harvard University Press, 1956). For useful contemporary estimates, see Louis D. Brandeis, *Business, A Profession* (Boston: Small, Maynard and Company, 1914) and John R. Commons, *Industrial Government* (New York: Macmillan, 1921).

3. Noble, *America By Design*, p. 276. Alfred D. Chandler, Jr.'s *Strategy and Structure: Chapters in the History of American Industrial Enterprise* (Cambridge, 1962), chapter 7, provides the best single source for the influence of "functional" management models across the spectrum of America's various industrial sectors.

4. Graham Adams, *The Age of Industrial Violence, 1910–1915* (New York: Columbia University Press, 1966), p. 228. For the Rockefeller initiatives see Irving Bernstein, *The Lean Years: A History of the American Worker, 1920–1933* (Baltimore: Penguin, 1966), pp. 114–89; F. A. McGregor, *The Fall and Rise of Mackenzie King* (Toronto: University of Toronto Press, 1962); John D. Rockefeller, Jr., *The Personal Relation in Industry* (New York: Boni and Liveright, 1923); Peter Collier and David Horowitz, *The Rockefellers: An American Dynasty* (New York: Holt, Rinehart & Winston, 1976), chapter 8.

5. For two important statements of Wilsonian belief see Woodrow Wilson's speech "Government in Relation to Business" (May 23, 1912), in *The Public Papers of Woodrow Wilson*, vol. 2, edited by Ray Stannard Baker (New York: Harper, 1925), p. 430, and William C. Redfield, *The New Industrial Day: A Book for Men Who Employ Men* (New York: The Century Company, 1912).

6. Robert C. Cuff, *The War Industries Board: Business-Government Relations During World War One* (Baltimore: Johns Hopkins Press, 1973), pp. 243, 264; Robert F. Himmelberg, "Business, Antitrust Policy, and the Industrial Board of the Department of Commerce, 1919," *Business History Review* 42 (Spring 1968): 1–23; Melvin I. Urofsky, *Big Steel and the Wilson Administration* (Columbus, Ohio: Ohio State University Press, 1969), pp. 248–91; Leverett S. Lyon, *Government and Economic Life*, vol. 2 (Washington D.C.: Brookings Institute, 1940), pp. 1062–85.

7. W. Jett Lauck and C. Watts, *The Industrial Code* (New York: Funk and Wagnalls, 1920) covers the postwar National Industrial Conferences. See also Haggai Hurvitz, "The Meaning of Industrial Conflict in Some Ideologies of the Early 1920's: The AFL, Organized Employers, and Herbert Hoover," (Ph.D. diss., Columbia University, 1971).

8. An important statement of General Electric's labor policies is the confidential report, "General Electric Industrial Relations" prepared for the corporation's Board of Directors sometime in 1919 now in the Owen D. Young Collection (privately held), Van Hornesville, N.Y. (hereafter cited as Young Collection). McQuaid, "Henry S. Dennison," pp. 85–96, deals with Dennison's activities during the immediate postwar period of labor unrest. In addition see David Brody, "The Rise and Decline of Welfare Capitalism," in *Change and Continuity in Twentieth Century America: The 1920's*, edited by J. Braeman, R. H. Bremner, and D. Brody (Columbus, Ohio: Ohio State University Press, 1968), pp. 147–48; Sumner H. Slichter, "The Current Labor Policies of American Industries," *The Quarterly Journal of Economics* 43 (May 1929): 393–435; Abraham Epstein, "Industrial Welfare Movement Sapping American Trades Unions," *Current History*, July, 1926, pp. 516–22; Robert W. Dunn, *The Americanization of Labor* (New York: International Publishers, 1927).

9. Young and Swope's careers at General Electric are covered more fully in Kim McQuaid, "Young, Swope, and General Electric's 'New Capitalism'... 1920–1933," *American Journal of Economics and Sociology* 36 (July 1977): 323–34; and "Competition, Cartellization, and the Corporate Ethic: General Electric's Leadership During the New Deal Era, 1933–1940," *American Journal of Economics and Sociology* 36 (October 1977): 417–28; Ida M. Tarbell, *Owen D. Young: A New Type of Industrial Leader* (New York, 1932); and David Loth, *Swope of G.E.* (New York: Simon and Schuster, 1958). The Oral History Memoir of

Gerard Swope at the Columbia Oral History Collection (Columbia University, New York, N.Y.) is also useful, but it only covers the period up until 1923.

10. Owen D. Young, "What is Right in Business," *Review of Reviews* 79 (March 1929): 75–78; Owen D. Young, "Dedication Address . . . [at the] Harvard Graduate School of Business Administration, June 4, 1927," *Harvard Business Review* 5 (July 1927): 389–94.

11. Gerard Swope, "The Engineer's Place in Society," *Survey* 51 (March 1, 1924): 635.

12. Committee on Education and Labor, *Hearings . . . [regarding] Interference with the Right of Labor to Organize and Bargain Collectively, Part 45, Supplementary Exhibits: "The Special Conference Committee"* (Washington, D.C.: G.P.O., 1939). These hearings are perhaps succinctly known to historians as the "LaFollette 'labor spy' Hearings." See also Irving Bernstein, *The Lean Years*, p. 168.

13. Gerard Swope, "Management Cooperation with Workers for Economic Welfare," *Annals of the American Academy of Political and Social Science* (Columbia University) 154 (March 1931): 131–35; J. T. Broderick, *40 Years with General Electric* (Albany, New York, 1929), pp. 134–44; Charles A. Coffin, "Employer-Employee Counsel in Industry," *Electrical World*, May 24, 1924, pp. 1082–83; Charles M. Ripley, *Life in a Large Manufacturing Plant* (Schenectady, New York: General Electric Company, 1919); Robert W. Bruere, "West Lynn," *Survey* 56 (April 1, 1926): 27; Slichter, "Current Labor Policies," p. 432. Loren Baritz, *The Servants of Power: A History of the Use of Social Science in American Industry* (Middletown, Connecticut: Wesleyan University Press, 1960); R. Alan Lawson, *The Failure of Independent Liberalism, 1930–1941*; and issues of *Law and Labor* magazine, a personnel relations/welfare capitalist mouthpiece that appeared throughout the 1920s, are all exceedingly useful sources for the background and environment of larger corporations' welfarisms.

14. F. W. Stearns to Owen D. Young, March 25, 1919; Young to Stearns, October 18, 1920; Young to Calvin Coolidge, March 5, 1925, Box 7, Young Collection; Joan Hoff Wilson, *American Business and Foreign Policy, 1920–1933* (Lexington, Kentucky: University of Kentucky Press, 1971), pp. 123–56; B. S. Beach to Young, March 25, 1921; Herbert Hoover to Young, March 23, 1920; Young to Hoover, January 5, 1926; Young to C. F. Smith, May 8, 1920, Box 9, Young Collection; E. A. Filene to Young, July 3, 1922, Box 300, Young Collection; Young to Hoover, August 10, 1928, Box 9, Young Collection; New York *Times*, August 9, 1929, p. 2.

15. John R. Commons, D. Lescohier, and E. Brandeis, *History of Labor . . .*, vol. 3, pp. 347–50; Robert Dunn, *The Americanization of Labor*, p. 129; Stuart D. Brandes, *American Welfare Capitalism*, p. 119; Ray Stannard Baker, *The New Industrial Unrest: Reasons and Remedies* (Garden City, New York: Doubleday, 1920); Kim McQuaid, "Corporate Liberalism in the American Business Community, 1920–1940," *Business History Review* 52 (Fall 1978).

16. Baritz, *The Servants of Power*, pp. 119–20; Brody, "Rise and Decline of Welfare Capitalism," p. 161; Clarence J. Hicks, *My Life in Industrial Relations* (New York: Harper and Brothers, 1941), pp. 41–52; Hurvitz diss., p. 245; Robert Ozanna, *A Century of Labor-Management Relations*, p. 156; LaFollette Committee Hearings (1939), p. 16777; Henry Eilburt, "The Development of Personnel Management in the United States," *Business History Review* 33 (Fall 1959): 350.

17. Brandes, *American Welfare Capitalism*, pp. 83, 104–07; Philip H. DuBois, *A History of Psychological Testing* (Boston: Allyn and Bacon, 1970), pp. 29, 60–66; Herman Krooss, *Executive Opinion*; Reinhard Bendix, *Work and Authority in Industry*, p. 287; David Brody, "Rise and Decline of Welfare Capitalism," pp. 160–62.

4

FEDERAL SOCIAL WELFARE
IN THE 1920s

At the end of World War I, federal administrators faced an uncertain future. Although emergency mobilization had demonstrated the possibilities of unprecedented nonmarket management of the nation's industrial economy, the Wilson administration proved unwilling to transfer wartime planning procedures into peacetime settings; instead, Washington bureaucrats resumed their established roles as expediters and coordinators of state minimum standard and social insurance legislation and as facilitators of enlightened welfare procedures by private groups, particularly businessmen.[1]

In the decade following the Versailles peace conference federal administrators cautiously expanded their welfare responsibilities. Under the terms of legislation passed during and immediately after the war modest amounts of federal funds were supplied to the states to maintain the health of children, to rehabilitate disabled workers, and to create vocational education programs. Previously, war veterans and Indians had been the only recipients of federal funds on a regular, contractual basis. The 1920s witnessed a growth in federal willingness to supply public monies through the states to less traditional welfare clients.

The resulting federal welfare programs were administered by tiny bureaucracies of fiscal control.* Handsful of federal officials dispensed funds to illustrate the effectiveness of a small number of welfare activities. These welfare activities, in turn, were legitimated as profitable investments that increased social efficiency and decreased waste.

---

*By a bureaucracy of fiscal control we mean a small organization that dispenses funds to other organizations.

The social engineering undertaken by Washington in the 1920s created new opportunities for federal activity in the welfare field. The new programs did not, however, displace businessmen as the chief welfare providers in America's industrial society; in fact, they furthered cooperation between business and the state.

Herbert Hoover's career exemplified the cooperative theme of federal welfare efforts in the 1920s. As wartime relief administrator, postwar Secretary of Commerce, and, finally, president, Hoover encouraged contacts between businessmen and government officials, aimed at a humane and efficient management of the economy. Through such contacts, Hoover reasoned, the United States could enjoy the benefits of an expanded and improved industrial order without suffering the adverse effects of excessive regulation by the federal government.[2]

Hoover's concept of government was a complex, sometimes metaphysical, phenomenon. Paradoxically, as Ellis W. Hawley has noted, Hoover saw himself as both a planner and an antistatist. His idea of the federal government's proper role resembled an airport hotel and convention center. Private citizens from across the country met at the hotel, discussed their problems, and flew home with the solutions in their briefcases. The government ran the hotel, encouraged people to attend meetings, but was strictly not responsible for interests left unattended. In this manner public power helped businessmen and others to arrive at (and depart with) private understandings.

Hawley writes that Hoover believed the government should "serve as a midwife to a new, non-statist commonwealth" composed of private interest groups. After assisting in the creation of such a federation the federal government would serve as a caretaker of an expanding welfare capitalist order.[3]

As for the private parties involved in the process, they would create new organizations such as industrial trade associations, to spread their enlightened ideas. According to Joan Hoff Wilson, he encouraged such trade associations "to regulate themselves by developing and adhering to socially responsible ethical and business codes which the government would periodically review and promulgate as fair standards of practice." These standards, created by organized business, would serve as the key element in defining an American social welfare system.[4]

INFORMAL FEDERAL WELFARE SERVICES

Two events, one at each end of the decade, illustrated the ways in which the federal government responded to social welfare problems in the 1920s. The first occurred in September 1921 when President Warren G. Harding convened an unprecedented national conference on unemployment, chaired by Secretary of Commerce Herbert Hoover.

Characteristically Hoover approached the conference with a firm idea of how it would help solve the problems of postwar unemployment. Unemployment, the former engineer believed, was a direct function of waste in industry. Improperly used resources led to low productivity which, in turn, was an important source of unemployment. Eliminating waste required cooperation among producers, and the conference publicized the need for such private sector cooperation.

The conference also attempted to outline proposals for public action. An economic advisory committee of the Department of Commerce performed most of the preparatory work for the conference and anticipated many of its final recommendations. Regarding public policy toward the relief of unemployment, the committee decided that local and state governments should be urged to assume additional administrative responsibilities. Local and state governments possessed the best organized public social welfare bureaucracies and, therefore, they held special responsibility for unemployment relief. In this instance, states and localities that had not already done so should create employment offices to provide centralized data on employment opportunities and gather statistics on unemployment. Intensive efforts should also be made to design public works projects to be initiated when unemployment in an area rose markedly. In this manner decentralized elements of the public sector, like the decentralized components of the corporate sector, would learn the virtues of rationalization, coordination, and efficiency.

Meanwhile the federal role would remain that of a clearing house. Washington would publicize ways in which cities, states, and private groups prevented and relieved unemployment. Groups across the country would then select those strategies most relevant to their particular social and economic circumstances. No necessity for a direct federal involvement with unemployment relief programs existed; instead, a process of what might be called "decentralized eclecticism" would evolve to meet welfare needs.[5]

When the unemployment conference was finally convened in Washington it speedily endorsed the advisory committee's ideas. The Department of Commerce made well-publicized efforts to implement this vision of voluntary cooperation. Scattered improvements in the provision of unemployment relief were made by both business and government groups. Fiscal conservatives quashed efforts to provide federal assistance for a new system of employment offices. Despite the spottiness of the conference's effect, Hoover and his supporters believed that the experience of the unemployment conference would gradually become a model for the future. Acting on this assumption the federal government, usually led by a branch of Hoover's Department of Commerce, held many similar conferences throughout the 1920s. All were aimed at providing forums in which cooperative solutions to social welfare problems could be worked out by the private parties most directly affected.[6]

Widespread flooding along the Mississippi in 1927 occasioned a different sort of informal federal welfare initiative. When the river flooded its banks Secretary Hoover responded as he had to the problems of European nations during World War I. He became the chairman of a special Mississippi flood committee appointed by President Coolidge, and solicited money from both private and public sources for the relief of flood victims. More than half of the $27 million that Hoover raised came from a nationwide radio appeal sponsored by the American Red Cross. Having secured the money, Hoover proceeded to give it away to the 1.5 million people that the flood had left homeless. The money also repaired dikes and rescued stranded individuals. In partnership with private charitable institutions the federal government was providing direct relief to its citizens.

After this direct relief phase concluded, a second and longer lasting phase of indirect relief for flood victims began. In this phase, private lending institutions made money available for the rehabilitation of property destroyed by the flood. Hoover helped to organize the credit facilities involved in this effort. He was instrumental in integrating local banks into regional financial institutions such as the Arkansas Farm Credit Company. Through the U.S. Chamber of Commerce he helped to establish another organization that provided an additional $10 million in low-interest loans. Acting cooperatively, private institutions were revitalizing a region with the help of federal expertise. In the eyes of contemporary observers the handling of the Mississippi flood provided a textbook case of the principles of progressive American social welfare.[7]

Separated by five years these isolated incidents—an unemployment conference and a flood—demonstrated the abilities of the decentralized welfare system engineered during the 1920s. Within this system specific problems such as unemployment or poverty were treated as symptoms of general malfunctions in the economy. Improving the economy through the spreading of scientific administrative and managerial techniques would eliminate the problems. Correcting the major systemic problems of America's economy, of course, did nothing to correct welfare problems caused by external factors such as natural disasters or other acts of God. An efficient economy, however, could solve these externally imposed problems with a minimum of friction. When mobilized by the federal government, as in the case of the Mississippi flood, private facilities and expertise could be diverted to problem areas until the flood waters (actual and metaphorical) receded. If such problems created discontinuities in the economy, America's private sector was organized and powerful enough to restore long-run equilibrium. As Hoover acknowledged his duty to become president in 1928, therefore, his faith in the vision of a cooperative system operating with efficiency allowed him to prophesy an imminent end to traditional welfare problems.[8]

FORMAL FEDERAL WELFARE SERVICES

Unlike many of his fellow citizens, Herbert Hoover lived in a logically complete world. Yet, even he believed that the federal government owed special obligations to well-defined disadvantaged groups: children and disabled workers, in particular. Acting upon these beliefs Hoover assisted in unsuccessful efforts to pass a constitutional amendment banning child labor in the 1920s and gave support to the implementation of federal vocational rehabilitation, vocational education, and infant and maternal health programs. These programs represented more than mere institutional manifestations of Herbert Hoover's personal emotions; they also interfaced neatly with the political and ideological environment of the postwar era.[9]

Vocational education was the first of the new federal programs. Created by the passage of the Smith-Hughes Act of 1917, federal support for vocational education reflected a longstanding concern to provide training that meshed with industry's importance in America's occupational structure. Vocational education, indeed, was often conceived of by its supporters as a public sector counterpoint to the managerial training provided by corporations and universities in the private sector.

As was the case with many reforms successfully advocated during the Progressive Era, the vocational education movement depended upon a coalition of business and labor interests for its political support. Both the NAM and the AFL cooperated with the prewar Commission on National Aid to Vocational Education, whose very existence owed much to their efforts. The commission's report published in 1914 stressed that vocational education "conserved" labor and contributed to overall economic "efficiency." As such it was a legitimate recipient of federal funds.[10]

The major sticking point in carrying out the commission's recommendation to provide federal aid for vocational education came over the propriety of using federal money to finance what many still regarded as a local welfare function. Despite the long tradition of granting federal lands for public schools and agricultural colleges, some congressmen saw federal grants-in-aid as a real threat to local self-sufficiency. They feared (rightly, as it turned out) that creation of an ongoing program of federal grants would be the first step in effecting a permanent shift from local to federal control within the structure of the American social welfare system.

American entrance into World War I, however, facilitated the passage of vocational education legislation. Emergency mobilization and a cessation of immigration from Europe heightened the need for trained industrial manpower and made the need for enhanced vocational education programs seem more urgent and more likely to contribute to economic efficiency than ever before. With the strong backing of organized America—businessmen, laborers, and professionals—Congress legislated federally subsidized vocational education. War had legitimated an important welfare innovation.

The other two components of the formal federal welfare system of the 1920s—vocational rehabilitation and infant and maternal hygiene—also owed existence to the enhanced opportunities for administrative innovation that World War I provided. Civilian vocational rehabilitation marked an extension of state workers' compensation programs into new areas at federal expense. The argument for rehabilitation programs as a necessary adjunct to workers' compensation began with the notion that modern medical technology and vocational training techniques made it possible to do more than compensate the victims of industrial accidents. Much of an injured person's productive capacity could be restored through the use of rehabilitation procedures. Because the injured worker and society at large would reap the benefits of rehabilitation, its costs could be charged to society or the injured, instead of to the employers who paid the costs of workers' compensation. The injured, however, were likely to be in relatively poor economic condition at the time that their rehabilitation was initiated, so vocational rehabilitation programs required new sources of public funds.

The founding of the International Association of Industrial Accident Boards and Commissions (IAIABC) in 1913 provided state workers' compensation officials with a forum to spread their rehabilitation ideas and to lobby for public funds for rehabilitation. By the end of the decade a number of states had responded to these efforts. In 1918, for example, Massachusetts authorized its State Industrial Accident Board to provide vocational training and job placement services for the industrially disabled. Not satisfied with such scattered efforts, the IAIABC began lobbying for a national industrial rehabilitation law.[11]

War facilitated such endeavors. In 1918 Congress passed a rehabilitation law for veterans. Veterans, who had long enjoyed federal workers' compensation payments in the form of disability pensions, would now receive vocational training from a new Federal Board for Vocational Education and medical services from agencies designated by the U.S. Surgeon General's office.

On July 1, 1918, the two full-time employees of the new Federal Board for Vocational Education awaited the first injured veterans. The veterans promptly tore the doors down. By December, 1919, no less than 21,000 of them were involved in federally funded vocational training. By August 1921 this number had risen to 113,000. A total of 296,940 veterans had been declared eligible for such training.[12]

The veterans' experience provided the lobbyists of the IAIABC with just the opportunity they were seeking. If federal rehabilitation services were to be provided to veterans they should also be provided to those who had served their nation on the home front. Observing the veterans' rehabilitation act in operation the association noted that, although the war had "shocked" the nation into initiating rehabilitation for traditional recipients of federal welfare services, an even greater need existed to restore "industry's cripples." This logic proved persuasive enough to enable congressmen to pass legislation that initiated a program of federal grants-in-aid to state bureaus of vocational education for the purpose of establishing vocational rehabilitation programs.[13]

A year after ratifying a civilian vocational rehabilitation law Congress passed an infant and maternal health program in the form of the Sheppard-Towner Act. This program was the last of the three formal federal welfare programs created during the 1920s. Infant and maternal health was less a product of wartime emergency than either vocational education or vocational rehabilitation; it was a political response to a new force in American politics—women. World War I marked the culmination of a long drive by women to earn the vote. Sheppard-Towner's provision of federal grants-in-aid for state projects designed to decrease infant and maternal mortality demonstrated congressional responsiveness to its new constituents.[14]

By contemporary standards the three new welfare programs undertaken by federal administrators were modest in scope. In 1924, for example, four physicians, a nurse, an accountant, a secretary, and a stenographer composed the entire staff of the Washington office of the infant and maternal health program. As late as 1920, 96 percent of aggregate federal welfare expenditures were confined to war veterans. The remaining 4 percent of expenditures represented "less than six percent of the comparable [public welfare] spendings of the country as a whole." In 1928, federal bureaucrats disbursed only $1,585,000 to promote vocational rehabilitation and infant and maternal health combined. A federal government that spent $.09 per capita on welfare expenditures (exclusive of aid to veterans) in 1913, spent only $.25 per capita 15 years later.[15]

Ideological barriers to the expansion of direct federal welfare activities remained strong. All of the formal welfare programs created during the 1920s operated on the principle of federal grants-in-aid to the states. This principle meant that state governments, which had to match federal grants dollar for dollar, spent the increased welfare appropriations. Each of the programs, therefore, involved state provision of services to welfare clients. The clients received advice or training from a professional counsellor or teacher, not money from the federal government. Further, all formal federal welfare programs relied on private labor markets for their ultimate effectiveness. Welfare clients could remain on the rolls of programs such as vocational rehabilitation for only a limited time period. No expectation existed that the federal government would provide continuing protection against life's hazards. In fact, federal programs did not even guarantee that all who could benefit from them would do so. Federal programs served more to demonstrate the social effectiveness of a particular welfare activity, such as rehabilitation or the pasteurization of milk for infants, rather than to provide permanent federal support for these activities.

Even with all of these limitations the new programs escalated the level of the federal government's social welfare responsibility. No longer would the federal government be limited to supervising state minimum standard laws or providing for its own wards such as soldiers, sailors, Indians, and Eskimos. Beginning in the 1920s the federal government had begun to act as a source of funds for states to initiate new welfare activities.

THE FEDERAL PROGRAMS IN ACTION

The new federal programs, then, occupied a unique place within America's social welfare system. The elements of cooperation and efficiency characterized governmental welfare activities and linked formal federal programs with the informal web of activities undertaken by trade associations and other private interest groups.

The operation of the federal vocational education program clearly illustrated how private demands and interests shaped public welfare policy. In 1925 the Federal Board for Vocational Education reported on its cooperative activities with the National Association of Retail Grocers. The association had approached federal administrators with a proposal to increase the average grocer's efficiency through vocational training. Because the Federal Board knew that no such training programs existed, it agreed to cooperate with the National Association to create one.

In the decade's most enlightened style a series of conferences between businessmen and bureaucrats ensued. First, a group of successful retail grocers met to identify the factors that made them more efficient that their competitors, then the Federal Board's commercial education service held a series of meetings with the successful grocers. These meetings resulted in the preparation of 20 lessons that would teach grocers how to perform more profitably. At the association's next annual convention the assembled grocers adopted the federal board's program and agreed to establish an education bureau. After the convention, officials of the federal board, working with the association's education director, organized experimental classes of grocery store employees in public evening schools and tested the 20 lessons on them. When this process was completed the federal board and the assocation cooperated to spread their new gospel of efficiency to state capital and corner grocery store alike.[16]

Administrators of the two other federal welfare programs made similar cooperative efforts. The Infant and Maternal Health Program brought officials of private public health associations such as the Milbank Memorial Fund to local communities to explain the latest in public health techniques. Federal rehabilitation administrators urged their peers in the states to undertake "organized cooperation" to "secure in each community, city, or county, some clearing agency which will take the responsibility of locating, reporting, and investigating cases." State agencies might establish rehabilitation councils and place "the president or secretary of a manufacturers association, a Rotary, or a Kiwanis Club" in charge of them.[17]

Along with the ideal of cooperation each of the federal welfare programs struggled to meet the decade's standards of efficiency in conducting their internal affairs and in defining their external purposes. The well-run public program was perceived to resemble the well-conducted business—it performed its operations at the least possible cost, and it created products that society valued. This desire for program efficiency through businesslike administration was the characteristic that most clearly defined the 1920s style of public welfare.

In the case of the vocational rehabilitation program the drive for efficiency on the part of public administrators was so influential that it transformed the program into something quite different from the public service envisioned by its creators. As the program became more and more committed to efficient administration, measured in cost-benefit terms, it moved farther and farther away from its original mission of cooperating with state workers' compensation officials to rehabilitate industrial accident victims. By the end of the 1920s, indeed, workers' compensation and vocational rehabilitation had evolved into completely separate programs. Their separation illustrated the differences between Progressive Era and New Era social welfare programs.[18]

When the vocational rehabilitation program began in 1920, federal and state administrators stated its objectives in both humanitarian and economic terms. The program's virtue, in fact, lay precisely in the fact that it combined the humanitarian and cost-effective courses of action in the treatment of the disabled. It cost less to cure a disability than to support one, and rehabilitation promoted a "fitness to work" that was one of the preconditions of both economic efficiency and personal satisfaction.

Within a few years, however, the rhetoric used to justify the vocational rehabilitation program changed. The efficiency objective was more explicitly emphasized. Program officials now argued that the "efficiency problem" should determine the course of social policy. This view meant that program activities should be considered in terms of "securing the greatest social return for a dollar expended."[19]

The triumph of a cost-benefit approach marked the departure of workers' compensation from the vocational rehabilitation program. This phenomenon occurred despite the fact that workers' compensation officials in the IAIABC, more than any other group, had pressured Congress to initiate a federal vocational rehabilitation program. Not surprisingly, Congress debated the proposed new program in terms of the effects that it would have on the older program. The completed federal vocational rehabilitation law mandated that each state furnish a plan of cooperation between its rehabilitation and compensation agencies as a precondition for receiving federal aid. The Federal Board for Vocational Education, which administered the vocational rehabilitation program, reiterated that "the work of vocational rehabilitation is supplementary to that of compensating injured workers."[20]

In one of the board's annual reports it even illustrated how the relationship between vocational rehabilitation and workers' compensation should proceed. A piece of wood flew into a 31-year-old carpenter's eye, blinding him in that eye. Because the accident occurred at work, the carpenter received medical treatment for his injured eye through workers' compensation. At the same time the state's rehabilitation agency helped the carpenter retain the vision in his remaining eye and counseled him on ways to adjust to his impairment. The board found the carpenter's case "particularly interesting" because it demonstrated "where the work of the bureau of rehabilitation takes up what is left incomplete by the workmen's compensation bureau."[21]

At least part of the Federal Board for Vocational Rehabilitation's interest in the aforementioned carpenter stemmed from his uniqueness. Few other workmen's compensation clients managed to make such a smooth transition from compensation to rehabilitation. If, for example, the carpenter had been injured in Georgia in 1921 he would have had to come to the attention of one of the state's two vocational rehabilitation caseworkers, only one of whom worked full time. The process of rehabilitation itself was a painstaking matter of direct interviews between the clients and their counselors. "There is no such thing as rehabilitation in general," the federal office noted. "It is always rehabilitation in particular." Because of rehabilitation's custom-made nature, each rehabilitation counselor could handle only 75 to 100 cases at any one time. In Georgia the two counselors managed to see only 207 people in fiscal year 1921. If the carpenter was one of the lucky 207 he was still faced with formidable barriers before actually receiving rehabilitation. The counselors might tell him that he was "not susceptible" to rehabilitation (as they told five other people that year), or that he was not eligible for program services.

In fact, of the 207 people who managed to see the State of Georgia's rehabilitation counselors in fiscal 1921, only 12 received some form of vocational training and only 3 eventually obtained a job as a result of that training. In fiscal 1922 the story was the same. The same two counselors saw 66 new cases. Of these, three were deemed not eligible, 8 were deemed not susceptible and 20 decided to reject the agency's services. Despite the cooperation of private charities, the Red Cross, the state board of health, and the Georgia Industrial Commission, the Georgia rehabilitation program hardly made a dent in dealing with the disability problem in the state—whether such disabilities originated from industrial accidents or from any other source.[22]

The situation was not much different in other states. The state of New York depended upon two full-time directors and ten other employees to run its vocational rehabilitation program. In fiscal 1921 they closed 46 cases. Of these, 4 cases rehabilitated themselves, 17 cases rejected the agency's services, and 5 were declared not eligible for services. In the nation as a whole, state vocational rehabilitation agencies consistently rehabilitated less than one-third of the people who applied for their services.[23]

Federal bureaucrats soon did their bit to put an optimistic face on affairs, By the end of the 1920s the Federal Board for Vocational Education simply stopped issuing statistics on the numbers of clients turned away by state rehabilitation agencies. Their statistics concentrated instead on the number of people such agancies had successfully rehabilitated. During the 1920s this annual calculus of felicity reached a high of 5,852 cases in 1925. By the board's own admission this accomplishment came at a time when between 50,000 and 70,000 potential rehabilitation cases were being created every year.[24]

Because of limited staff, funds, and influence, the Washington office of the federal rehabilitation program could do little to improve the situation. An average of six people worked in this office during the 1920s, five of whom spent most of their time on the road. One federal regional supervisor was in charge of overseeing program operations in Massachusetts, Connecticut, New York, New Jersey, Pennsylvania, and Virginia. The chief responsibilities of the federal office for vocational rehabilitation were to inform Congress of the program's progress in the states and to fight to maintain its small congressional appropriation.[25]

Even these modest tasks proved difficult to accomplish for a program that throughout the decade never managed to spend all of its annual congressional allotments. This failure stemmed from the requirement that states receiving federal grants for vocational rehabilitation match Washington's contribution dollar for dollar. As the federal office explained: "There are some states in which the rehabilitation program has not been sufficiently developed to require the expenditure of all available funds." Congress became so annoyed that in the first half of fiscal 1925 it simply did not appropriate any money for rehabilitation. Federal rehabilitation officials, however, refused to intervene in state programs or politics to get them to put up more money. "Each state," the Washington office announced, "has its own problems and must establish its own policies and procedures in order to deal with its problems effectively." So spoke the authentic voice of New Era voluntarism.[26]

The vocational rehabilitation program, therefore, reached so few people and was conducted on such a small scale that each successful rehabilitation resembled a demonstration or pilot project more than it formed part of an ongoing social process. Rehabilitation was not conceived of as a social service in which the federal government helped finance the nation's disabled citizens; it was a sporadic, widely dispersed activity that rationed its available resources to dramatize its welfare potential. Through the vocational rehabilitation program, state and federal bureaucrats publicized an efficient way of dealing with welfare problems in much the same way as the Department of Commerce publicized a new production technique. In both cases the private sector had the obligation—a moral obligation reinforced by its cost-reducing, efficiency-promoting possibilities—to spread this technique across the entire spectrum of the nation's industrial order.

It was precisely the pilot project, efficiency-oriented nature of vocational rehabilitation programs that obliterated any chances for a cooperative relationship between them and the workmen's compensation programs established during the Progressive Era. In the states of California and Ohio, for example, workers' compensation officials viewed the arrival of vocational rehabilitation optimistically in the belief that rehabilitation would serve an adjunct role in improving compensation procedures. The California workers' compensation bureau dumped 1,580 cases into the new rehabilitation agency's lap. Of these, only 280 reached the stage of vocational training. Meanwhile, Ohio workmen's compensation authorities were having their own troubles. Data that they accumulated on the origins of rehabilitation clients in their state showed that only one-third of the caseload of Ohio's vocational rehabilitation bureau came from the workmen's compensation agency. National statistics told the same story of declining interest in compensation clients on the part of rehabilitation agencies. Less than one-half of the individuals successfully rehabilitated in 1927, 1928, 1929, and 1930 had disabilities that originated in employment accidents.[27]

The growing separation between the caseloads of workmen's compensation and vocational rehabilitation agencies reflected important differences between Progressive Era and New Era practices. Like other Progressive Era welfare programs, workmen's compensation asked private employers to meet a set of industrial standards and to pay for the increased costs, if any, themselves. By contrast, vocational rehabilitation spent money from the general revenue of the public sector to demonstrate rehabilitation's utility. Workmen's compensation functioned automatically as an independent and self-financing no-fault insurance fund. An injured employee received his compensation without any state intervention. Rehabilitation, however, depended for its effectiveness on intensive interaction between a state official and a disabled client. Rehabilitation, in short, was intrinsically a matter of state intervention; workmen's compensation was not. Not limited by the level of government appropriations, workmen's compensation programs could expand to encompass all industrial disability. Tightly bound by state and federal budgets, rehabilitation agencies could only go as far as their program funds allowed them to go. Unlike workmen's compensation, vocational rehabilitation programs had continually to demonstrate that they put the taxpayers' money to good use. Vocational rehabilitation programs were efficient because, in the long run, they returned more to society than they cost. Despite the best inten-

tions of Congress and government officials, therefore, the very structure of vocational rehabilitation and workmen's compensation programs doomed them to become isolated from one another.[28]

Once separated from workmen's compensation, vocational rehabilitation developed its own image—one that underlined the close ideological fit between public and private sector welfare activities throughout
the 1920s. According to the ideology that justified the vocational
rehabilitation program, it generated economic returns by acting like a
profit-making loan company. Vocational rehabilitation agencies loaned
a disabled client vocational training. The client then repaid the loan in
the form of taxes, which reflected his new productivity. A similar
analogy was applied to vocational education by the public bureaucrats
involved in financing it. The Infant and Maternal Health Program was
rationalized in only slightly different terms. In preventing babies from
dying, and preserving the health of their mothers, public officials were
strengthening the nation's reserves of human capital and, by only a
slight extension in reasoning, increasing the gross national product as
well. Although each of the three federal welfare programs created
during the New Era cost the government money in the short run, they
saved the public sector money in the long run. As such these federal
welfare programs exemplified smart business practice.[29]

The cost-benefit approach undertaken by public authorities demonstrated the strength of the link between the welfare operations of
private businesses and those run by the federal and state governments.
To show how large the government's profits were under the New Era
welfare programs, officials in Washington and various state capitals
adopted private sector accounting techniques. The efforts of W. F.
Faulkes, a director of the state of Wisconsin's vocational rehabilitation
program, proved particularly memorable. Faulkes refined his calculations down to the penny. The program he administered cost
$11,659.36, increased total earning power by $1,722,419.76, and produced a net gain of $1,610,760.40 for the state.

For the entire nation the gains were equally impressive. The
average weekly wage of all persons rehabilitated in fiscal 1924 was
$26.07. These rehabilitants would live, on the average, for at least
20 years. In those 20 years, therefore, they would collectively earn
$147,004,000. To generate the impressive sum of $147 million in
additional national income the federal and state governments had spent
only $1,124,500. The vocational rehabilitation program for fiscal 1924,
therefore, had reaped returns of over 10,000 percent on investment.
Not bad even by New Era standards.[30]

These fulsome statistics possessed a darker side. The clear desire of
many vocational rehabilitation program administrators to turn a profit

for society held important implications for the sorts of persons that they accepted as rehabilitation clients. It influenced the age, sex, race, level of education, and physical characteristics of the caseload, and it meant that the public sector would provide special help for precisely that group of people with the best chance of receiving help from the private sector.

Like any loan company, in short, government had to take the best risks. People who gave "irrefutable evidence of the economic benefits of rehabilitation" were "young persons with academic training of at least eight years." These same young people had the most productive years remaining to pay off the loan, and young people with education already had a lot invested in their future. It also helped, of course, if the young person being considered for rehabilitation were white and male, because that person would encounter the least prejudice in the job market. Blacks and females, among others, faced a restricted labor market and would have a comparatively hard time paying off loans.[31]

Finally, it helped if the person's disability was comparatively mild. Severely disabled persons were bad rehabilitation risks, because they cost more to train and were more restricted in their physical abilities even after such training. In 1927, for example, one state rehabilitation supervisor instructed his employees not to spend money on "shut-in cases" or people confined to wheelchairs but to concentrate on "better material." One observer in Illinois noted in 1929 that the vocational rehabilitation program there "appears especially desirous of working with young persons and does not wish to take chances on cases in which success is improbable." Such was the New Era welfare system.[32]

LASTING RESULTS

Depression wiped out much of the ideological basis for the social welfare system of the New Era. The informal part of the system would be hampered in its effectiveness by growing popular suspicions that business groups no longer possessed either the wisdom or the funds to solve social problems. The formal part of the system would suffer from the fact that the level of return on the government's investments no longer justified spending money on vocational rehabilitation or maternal health. The once-splendid cost-benefit demonstrations undertaken by federal and state bureaucrats would now, in depressed economic circumstances, show that the cost of educating, rehabilitating, or medically treating welfare clients far outweighed the benefits that these clients could return to society by their participation in the industrial marketplace. On these grounds alone the public social welfare system of the 1920s could be dismissed as merely a temporary phenomenon of interest only to antiquarians.

In retrospect, however, the 1920s marked an important transition between a traditional and a modern welfare system—a transition that had permanent effects upon American social welfare practice. In the 1920s the federal government's bureaucratic structure was changing even though it was still locked in the occupational mold left over from the Progressive Era. Officially, welfare bureaucracies created in the Washington establishment still needed to include representatives from the departments of Commerce, Labor, and Agriculture in their formal organization charts. The Federal Board of Vocational Education, for example, contained the secretaries of Labor, Agriculture, and Commerce, as well as lay business, agricultural, and labor representatives appointed by the president. States also accepted the parties-at-interest principle in administering their vocational education and rehabilitation programs.[33]

But in the New Era, unlike in the Progressive Era, representatives of the occupational parties-at-interest were no longer sufficient to run a federal welfare program. In the 1920s federal welfare responsibilities widened to embrace the awarding of funds to the states and the overseeing of their proper dispersal. This new function or strategy required the presence of technically trained specialists with loyalty to the service they performed, rather than to the groups they served. Eventually it would lead to a new structure for the social welfare system. In the 1920s the desire for a new structure took the form of demands for the creation of a department of education and social welfare.

The educational caliber of the Federal Board of Vocational Education's technical staff demonstrated the functional specialization of federal welfare bureaucrats. These 25 people, rather than the cabinet-level secretaries or the lay dignitaries appointed by presidents, performed most of the board's actual work. All but four of these 25 held college degrees. Ten had earned master's degrees from such places as Chicago, Yale and Harvard.[34] These credentials hinted at the important fact that, like welfare capitalist managers in the private sector, government welfare administrators were themselves becoming professionalized.

The 1920s, then, marked a period of harmony between the public and private sectors. Both the formal and the informal components of the welfare system engineered during this decade depended upon a unity of goals between public and private welfare practitioners based upon the concepts of cooperation and efficiency as determined by the dollars-and-cents dictates of a market economy. These shared goals and understandings, in turn, gave the formal welfare programs their distinctive identities and proved a factor in the slow evolution of the federal bureaucracy from an occupational to a functional or service orientation.

The trouble with the system, of course, was that public and private welfare programs moved in unison. A shock to one system produced sympathetic contractions in the other. In 1929, however, as Herbert Hoover became president of the United States, many regarded the close relations—organizational and otherwise—between the public and private sectors as one of the New Era's greatest welfare accomplishments.

NOTES

1. Robert F. Himmelberg, "Business, Antitrust Policy, and the Industrial Board of the Department of Commerce, 1919," *Business History Review* 42 (Spring 1968): 1–23; Melvin I. Urofsky, *Big Steel and the Wilson Administration* (Columbus, Ohio, Ohio State University Press, 1969), pp. 248–91; William C. Redfield, *The New Industrial Day: A Book for Men Who Employ Men* (New York: Century Company, 1912). (Redfield was Wilson's Secretary of Commerce.)

2. Among the many biographic studies of Hoover see especially Craig Lloyd, *Aggressive Introvert: A Study of Herbert Hoover and Public Relations Management* (Columbus, Ohio: Ohio State University Press, 1972), pp. 37–59 and Harris Gaylord Warren, *Herbert Hoover and the Great Depression* (New York: Oxford University Press, 1959), pp. 19–39.

3. Ellis W. Hawley, "Herbert Hoover, the Commerce Secretariat, and the Vision of an 'Associative State', 1921–1928," *Journal of American History* 61 (June 1974): 117. Hawley has recently broadened his argument in his as-yet-unpublished essay "Techno-Corporatist Formulas in the Liberal State, 1920–1960: A Neglected Aspect of America's Search for Order."

4. Joan Hoff Wilson, *Herbert Hoover, Forgotten Progressive* (Boston: Little Brown, 1975), p. 69. Barry D. Karl's "Presidential Planning and Social Science Research: Mr. Hoover's Experts," *Perspectives in American History* 3 (Cambridge: Harvard University Press, 347–409 surveys the academic middlemen in the business-government relation.

5. Carolyn Grin, "The Unemployment Conference of 1921: An Experiment in National Cooperative Planning," *Mid-America* 55 (April 1973): 83–107 is the best single survey of the conference. Haggai Hurvitz, "The Meaning of Industrial Conflict in Some Ideologies of the Early 1920's: The AFL, Organized Employers, and Herbert Hoover," (Ph.D. diss., Columbia University, 1971) and John D. Hicks, *Rehearsal for Disaster: The Boom and Collapse of 1919–1920* (Gainesville, Florida: University of Florida Press 1961). Pages 1–32 provide useful background data on the environment in which the unemployment conference was held.

6. Barry D. Karl, "Presidential Planning and Social Science Research," p. 364; Herbert Hoover et al., *Recent Social Trends in the United States: Report of the President's Research Committee on Social Trends*, two vols. (New York: McGraw-Hill, 1933) provides a complete discussion of the proposals made by the many conferences federal administrators sponsored.

7. Herbert Hoover, *The Memoirs of Herbert Hoover* (New York: Macmillan, 1951–1952), vol. 2, pp. 125–26; L. C. Spears, "The Sort of Man Herbert Hoover Is," New York *Times Magazine* 29 (January 15, 1928), p. 3; Bruce Alan Lohof, *Herbert Hoover and the Mississippi Flood of 1928* (Syracuse, New York: Syracuse University Press, 1968).

8. Joan Hoff Wilson, *Herbert Hoover*, pp. 114–16.

9. For a ringing statement of Hoover's ideals see "The Children's Charter" in William Starr Myers and Walter H. Newton, *The Hoover Administration: A Documented Narrative* (New York: Charles Scribner and Sons, 1936), pp. 456–61.

10. Charles A. Prosser and John C. Wright, *The Development of Vocational Education* (Chicago: American Technical Society, 1950), p. 81; Berenice M. Fisher, *Industrial Education: American Ideals and Institutions* (Madison: University of Wisconsin Press, 1967), pp. 134–35; Public Law 347 (The Smith Hughes Act) 64th Cong.

11. Mary E. Macdonald, *Federal Grants for Vocational Rehabilitation* (Chicago: University of Chicago Press, 1944) and E. Esco Obermann, *A History of Vocational Rehabilitation in America* (Minneapolis: Dennison Publishers, 1965) provide useful surveys of the early growth of the vocational rehabilitation movement.

12. *Fifth Annual Report of the Federal Board for Vocational Education* (Washington, D.C.: G.P.O., 1921), p. 29.

13. *Congressional Record*, vol. 59, p. 8 (Washington, D.C., 1920), p. 7598.

14. J. Stanley Lemons, "The Sheppard-Towner Act: Progressivism in the 1920's," *Journal of American History* 55 (March 1959): 776–86; Dorothy E. Bradbury, *Four Decades of Action for Children: A Short History of the Children's Bureau*, U.S. Children's Bureau Publication no. 358 (Washington, D.C.: G.P.O., 1956).

15. Howard W. Odum, "Public Welfare Activities," in Herbert Hoover et al., *Recent Social Trends*, vol. 2, pp. 1255–63; *Twelfth Annual Report of the Secretary of Labor* (Washington, D.C.: G.P.O., 1928), p. 119.

16. *Ninth Annual Report to Congress of the Federal Board for Vocational Education* (Washington, D.C.: G.P.O., 1925), p. 36.

17. *Seventh Annual Report to Congress of the Federal Board for Vocational Education* (Washington, D.C.: G.P.O., 1923), p. 120.

18. Macdonald, *Federal Grants for Vocational Rehabilitation*, p. 304.

19. *Eleventh Annual Report to Congress of the Federal Board for Vocational Education* (Washington, D.C.: G.P.O., 1927), p. 21.

20. *Fifth Annual Report*, p. 316; *Sixth Annual Report*, p. 349, 352; *Ninth Annual Report*, p. 49.

21. *Sixth Annual Report*, p. 355.

22. Ibid., p. 396; *Tenth Annual Report to Congress of the Federal Board for Vocational Education* (Washington, D.C.: G.P.O., 1926), p. 120; *Fifth Annual Report*, p. 28.

23. *Sixth Annual Report*, p. 331; *Thirteenth Annual Report of the Federal Board for Vocational Education* (Washington D.C.: G.P.O., 1929), p. 97.

24. *Tenth Annual Report*, p. 120. For a remarkable example of how rehabilitation data was used see *A Study of Occupations at which 6,097 Physically Disabled Persons Are Employed after Being Vocationally Rehabilitated*, Federal Board for Vocational Education Bulletin no. 96 (Washington, D.C.: G.P.O., 1925).

25. *Sixth Annual Report*, p. 2.

26. *Ninth Annual Report*, p. 47; *Eighth Annual Report to Congress of the Federal Board for Vocational Education* (Washington, D.C.: G.P.O., 1924), p. 23.

27. *Ninth Annual Report*, p. 49; *Sixth Annual Report*, p. 378, 366; *Fourteenth Annual Report of the Federal Board for Vocational Education* (Washington, D.C.: G.P.O., 1930).

28. This point is developed further in Edward Berkowitz, "Vocational Rehabilitation and Workers Compensation," unpublished report to the Interdepartmental Workers Compensation Task Force of the U.S. Department of Health, Education, and Welfare (Washington, D.C., 1975).

29. Edward Berkowitz, "Rehabilitation: The Federal Government's Response to Disability," (Ph.D. diss., Northwestern University, 1976), pp. 84–86; William H. Chafe, *The American Woman: Her Changing Social, Economic, and Political Roles, 1920–1970* (New York: Oxford University Press, 1972), p. 27.

30. *Proceedings of the Fourth National Conference on Vocational Rehabilitation*, Federal Board for Vocational Education Bulletin no. 121 (Washington, D.C.: G.P.O., 1927), p. 81; *Proceedings of the National Conference on Vocational Rehabilitation of the Civilian Disabled*, Federal Board for Vocational Education Bulletin no. 93 (Washington, D.C.: G.P.O., 1924), p. 15.

31. *Vocational Rehabilitation in the United States*, Federal Board for Vocational Education, Bulletin no. 120 (Washington, D.C.: G.P.O., 1927), p. 34.

32. *Proceedings of the Fourth National Conference on Vocational Rehabilitation*, Federal Board for Vocational Education Bulletin no. 121 (Washington, D.C.: G.P.O., 1927); Earl P. Beckner, *A History of Labor Legislation in Illinois* (Chicago: University of Chicago Press, 1929), p. 463.

33. *Eighth Annual Report to Congress of the Federal Board for Vocational Education* (Washington, D.C.: G.P.O., 1924), p. 2.

34. *Ninth Annual Report to Congress of the Federal Board for Vocational Education* (Washington, D.C.: G.P.O., 1925), p. 39.

5

SEEKING A NEW EQUILIBRIUM: RESPONSES TO THE DEPRESSION, 1930–1935

Depression posed fundamental challenges to established welfare procedure, but the early 1930s provided no points of immediate discontinuity in the American social welfare tradition, and Franklin Roosevelt did not arrive in Washington armed with an irrepressible urge to experiment. Instead, influential welfare capitalists cooperated with federal bureaucrats to organize and administer emergency programs aimed at preserving the welfare standards of the 1920s. These activities, exemplified by the creation of the National Recovery Administration (NRA), were undertaken on the principle that Washington should promote self-regulation by organized occupational interest groups. In this way, hoped articulate businessmen such as Gerard Swope and Henry S. Dennison, the nation's largest firms could continue to provide the organizational and conceptual initiatives for enlightened welfare practice. Although government might sponsor private sector activities as it had done during World War I, it would not become an independent actor in the social welfare field, nor would it begin to provide welfare services directly to the people.

Many factors combined to wreck welfare capitalist efforts to mitigate the evils of the depression. External pressures from new political constituencies complicated social welfare politics. The elderly and the advocates of industrial unions, among others, pushed the government to recognize the rights of new welfare clients and even to begin to supply welfare services directly from Washington to the people. Welfare capitalists faced internal pressures as well—pressures that made it impossible for them to maintain united positions on key industrial policy questions. In the area of collective bargaining, for example, liberal employers were willing to compromise with the leadership of the American Federation of Labor and to make a bargain. By the terms of the bargain the unions could conduct organizing drives in return for agreeing to limit strikes. Liberal employers were also willing to allow federal enforcement of employment and other standards in areas of American industry that had not been affected by welfare capitalism in the 1920s. Conservative businessmen, even conservative welfare capitalists, refused to go along with these concessions. They continued to equate trade unions and the federal government with sin. These external and internal pressures, then, made the welfare capitalists less effective in leading the nation in social welfare matters than they had been in the 1920s.

As unity among the welfare capitalists fractured, fears grew that the corporation would no longer be the organizational model for social welfare activity. These fears sharpened the reactions of many businessmen to New Deal reform and induced a surly negativism toward federal policy. A minority of businessmen, however, continued to maintain an influential presence in Washington and hoped their presence would influence New Deal social welfare law and practice. Solutions to social welfare problems, these businessmen continued to believe, should still reflect the experience and discipline of the marketplace and the lessons of their own welfare capitalist experience.

The efforts that this welfare capitalist minority made to influence the New Deal were complex. To understand these efforts we must first analyze the mélange of public policy that was the early New Deal. Once having analyzed these events we can proceed to examine a characteristic late New Deal program—Social Security—to see how this program married welfare capitalist precedent to federal administrative initiative.

THE POLITICAL ECONOMY OF INERTIA, 1930–1932

By the end of the 1920s conventional wisdom held that federal welfare and other governmental efforts should operate within a conceptual universe set by corporate welfare precedent. To businessman and bureaucrat alike, social welfare programs gained legitimacy to the extent that they contributed to industrial efficiency, measured in terms of private sector profit and loss. In this regard, social welfare was conceived of as a corollary of the market, rather than something extra that public authority had to provide for the industrial system. Operating within a free market, individual companies sought to improve productivity and profits through coordinated welfare procedures such as those welfare initiatives that contributed most to overall economic well-being. Companies that experimented successfully enjoyed concrete financial benefits; companies that did not, felt the spur of declining profits. The enlightened selfishness of the market could, therefore, achieve progress in welfare that public interference could not achieve.

According to this theory there was an inevitability to the dissemination of welfare capitalism. Liberal employers such as Filene, Dennison, Swope, and Young believed that once businessmen understood the profitability of welfare salvation they would make haste to invest in it. Far from dismissing such views, government and professional experts tended to believe in them as strongly, or more strongly, than businessmen themselves. President Herbert Hoover echoed contemporary opinion when he argued that government should attempt to expedite private efforts through established techniques of information and publicity but under no circumstances enter the welfare scene as an independent actor.

The anxiety-ridden period of economic contraction in the years following the stock market crash of October 1929 created quite a different emotional and ideological climate but did not produce any immediate challenge to corporate welfare primacy. The federal government continued to rely upon private methods such as charity campaigns, and private expertise such as personnel experts to cope with the growing social consequences of unemployment.

Unlike previous presidents, however, Herbert Hoover recognized an increased federal obligation to do something about the business downturn. At first he limited his actions to statements designed to reinstill confidence among private entrepreneurs, investors, and consumers. When the situation continued to deteriorate, Hoover decided to expedite relief efforts. He used the White House as he had once used the Department of Commerce. The president's office became a clearing house for private efforts to solve welfare problems. Through the President's Emergency Committee for Employment, headed by Walter C. Teagle of Standard Oil of New Jersey, and the President's Organization on Unemployment Relief, headed by Walter S. Gifford of American Telephone and Telegraph, businessmen and community leaders compared their approaches to relief and attempted to standardize their efforts. Straining the limits of the federal government even further, Hoover finally established the Reconstruction Finance Corporation to lend funds to banks, railroads, and other institutions and supported similar federal loans to the states for their relief efforts.*[1]

Hoover's cautious experiments took the federal government to its conceptual and administrative limits. At the start of the Great Depres-

---

*Herbert Hoover only very reluctantly endorsed federal funds for unemployment relief.

sion, as in the decades preceding, the Washington establishment served as little more than an umpire among well-organized, competing interest groups. Although the president or some other federal official could coax the groups to act in a socially responsible manner or facilitate transactions among them, the federal government was not conceived of or constituted as an important force in its own right. In Hoover's view the best contribution that government could make toward the preservation of mass social welfare lay in the encouragement of "voluntary cooperation in the community." Throughout Hoover's tenure in office he opposed efforts to expand federal welfare powers to direct federal relief grants to the states, federally funded public works programs, or the establishment of federal-state employment exchanges.[2]

The similarity of public and private welfare programs added to Hoover's difficulty, and the fact that public and private programs were so similar compounded Hoover's and America's social welfare dilemmas during the depression. Both company welfare plans and community charity plans depended upon accumulating funds to be set aside for emergencies. The depression forced a crisis in both types of funds—contributions to the funds decreased, and payments from the funds increased. When this unstable situation persisted both types of funds dwindled to nothing. Other contemporary welfare schemes faced similar difficulties. Programs like vocational rehabilitation that trained people to receive jobs in private employment were only as strong as the private labor market. When wages fell below the subsistence level, as they often did in the early 1930s, the usefulness of such programs as welfare devices ended. Programs that loaned institutions money were only as strong as those institutions' ability to invest the money in productive ways. When the interest rate fell close to zero the usefulness of this approach was extremely limited.[3]

Despite these limitations in social welfare approaches that so closely linked the public and private sectors, Franklin Delano Roosevelt continued to use many of them during his first two years as president. His program came in two parts, the first of which dealt with emergency relief problems. Within weeks of his inauguration Roosevelt asked Congress to authorize federal grants to the states for unemployment victims, and the emergency relief phase began. By May 20, 1933, Congress had approved the request, and Harry Hopkins was appointed director of the Federal Emergency Relief Agency (FERA). This agency was intended as an emergency measure that would end with the depression. Shortly thereafter, temporary federal public works jobs began to be provided to the citizenry by agencies including the Civilian Conservation Corps (CCC) and the Public Works Administration (PWA).[4]

For extension beyond such immediate measures Roosevelt and his aides also pieced together legislation to reorganize the economy and effect a permanent recovery. The antecedents of this most important early New Deal effort demonstrate the extent to which businessmen and bureaucrats continued to see their welfare efforts as essentially complementary phenomena in the midst of an unprecedented crisis in the nation's peacetime industrial economy.[5]

NATIONALIZING A WELFARE CAPITALIST ORDER: THE SWOPE PLAN AND THE NRA

By the time that the Roosevelt administration arrived in Washington influential business men were well aware of the fact that traditional welfare procedures could not cope with the social and economic disorganization caused by the depression. Welfare capitalist spokesmen Owen D. Young, Edward A. Filene, Henry S. Dennison, and Gerard Swope called for increased federal assistance for private sector efforts to maintain welfare and employment standards.

To get such assistance these welfare capitalists were willing to move beyond the voluntaristic ideas expressed by Herbert Hoover. Dennison, for example, complained to his old friend Ida M. Tarbell that his "old notions" of improving welfare standards "through preachment as to good management" had "gone to the winds." In a book published in 1932 Dennison argued that "businessmen through voluntary effort rarely succeed in covering ten per cent of the necessary field of action, and seldom get as high as three per cent." To achieve more than the "bare beginnings" of an improved welfare capitalist system, he concluded, businessmen "must be willing to imagine a referee with a power and influence greater than that which any group from the business world would be willing voluntarily to grant him and maintain in him." The federal government, in short, must be brought into a closer supervisory connection with big business in matters of work and welfare. Business must reorganize itself under federal auspices just as it had done during World War I.[6]

Such ideas were controversial. The cooperation between government and industry during World War I had occurred in a period of industrial and economic expansion: Income and employment expectations were generally optimistic and the dangers facing the nation's political and industrial leadership came from foreign, not domestic, sources. Depression, however, produced the opposite effects. Contracting markets and revenues meant businessmen faced the possibility that the "doctor's bill" for federal assistance might require them to engage in the difficult matter of apportioning losses, as opposed to the cheerier task of distributing gains. For all that, liberal welfare capitalists such as Gerard Swope agreed with Dennison that business proposals for national recovery must include the federal government.

Swope's opinions were not a matter of theory, but of stark industrial fact. By 1931 the General Electric Company's welfare programs were in a shambles. Company officials were reduced to sending free baskets of groceries to the homes of thousands of laid-off employees. Swope realized that further corporate inactivity would only cause businessmen's stature to plummet further in popular estimation. In September 1931, GE's president unveiled an ambitious proposal for corporate leadership in economic reconstruction.

In essential respects the Swope plan marked the culmination of welfare capitalist trends operating since the Progressive Era. The industrial economy would be cartelized under the auspices of the federal government. First, government would allow industry to stabilize itself through price fixing and production limitations, then industry would provide greater employment opportunities to the American labor force. In these respects Swope sought to resurrect Wilson's War Industries Board.

Leaving the past behind, Swope invited the federal government into his system as an enforcer of enlightened standards. He proposed a corporate welfare state with a national system of unemployment, retirement, life insurance, and disability programs and standards. A "federal supervisory body" would approve these programs and set overall accounting and reporting requirements. But administration of all programs would remain in the hands of industrial trade associations. To insure that refractory business interests would not hamper his efforts Swope added another plank to his recovery program. All companies with "fifty or more employees, and doing an inter-state business" would be required to adopt all minimum standard and social insurance welfare provisions drawn up for their industry within three years. If all else failed, the national government would enforce welfare capitalist standards.

Swope proposed that businessmen set welfare standards for their industries under loose federal oversight. Then powerful businessmen would run a national, but nongovernmental, welfare system; the federal government would enter the system only as a policeman for welfare capitalist interests. Creation of this system would help to eliminate the problem of "free riders." It would allow businessmen in firms with high welfare standards to operate without fear of losing their market shares to employers with low welfare standards.[7]

The Swope plan sparked interest in business, academic, and intellectual circles.* President Hoover opposed the plan, but he was clearly a lame-duck president. Swope ignored Hoover's characterization of his program as "fascist and monopolistic" in tendency, and concentrated on bargaining with influential Democrats. When Roosevelt won the 1932 election Swope found himself among a large company of business interests jockeying for White House attention. Important spokesmen for small business, notably the NAM and the U.S. Chamber of Commerce, were not enthusiastic about welfare capitalist proposals that threatened their members with higher operating costs. The programs of these groups advocated price fixing and relaxation of the antitrust laws, and failed to provide for national welfare standards. Roosevelt decided not to act on matters of industrial reorganization until businessmen were more united in their opinions and were ready to agree on a specific plan.[8]

Roosevelt, however, reckoned without the impatient Democrats in Congress whose demands for instant action forced his hand. In April and May 1933 the White House pieced together the National Industrial Recovery Act that was stormily debated in Congress and signed into law on June 16, 1933. General Hugh S. Johnson, an aide to former War Industries Board head Bernard Baruch, became director of the National Recovery Administration (NRA) created by the act.[9]

The Roosevelt administration's NRA differed from Gerard Swope's welfare capitalist proposals in important respects. The antitrust laws were relaxed to allow industries to formulate "codes of fair practice" through their various trade associations. The president also received the right (which he never exercised) to force codes on industries unable or unwilling to create their own. Swope's proposal that national industrial trade associations supersede states and localities at the center of the public sector welfare system was not included in the act. Instead, in Progressive Era style, three advisory boards representing management, labor, and the consumer public were created to represent the welfare of parties-at-interest during the period of NRA code formulation and implementation. Section 7-A of the act, in addition, tendered vague guarantees that workers possessed rights to organize and bargain collectively under representation of their own choosing. Finally, NRA was an emergency agency whose mandate would run for only two years before congressional renewal was required.[10]

---

*It is important to note that the recovery programs of the United States Chamber of Commerce and the National Association of Manufacturers did not propose an enhanced federal role regarding welfare measures in any but the vaguest terms. The NAM and the U.S. Chamber of Commerce simply proposed voluntary cartelization—and wanted none of Swope's welfare capitalist enforcement provisions.

For all of the complexity, however, the Roosevelt administration's recovery legislation recapitulated business and government's twentieth-century welfare experience. It permitted private parties organized into large interest group blocs to meet under government auspices and solve their problems, provided only that their solutions met certain minimum standards.[11]

CREATING A WELFARE CAPITALIST DIRECTORATE: THE BUSINESS ADVISORY COUNCIL

If the government exercised all of its rights under the NRA, in particular if federal officials imposed codes spelling out pricing, employment, marketing, and labor standards for particular industries upon business leaders in those industries, then the role of the federal government within the American social welfare system would be greatly expanded. Articulate welfare capitalists such as Swope, Dennison, and Walter C. Teagle worked to insure that the federal government did not go beyond its established role as a facilitator of compromise and an enforcer of privately determined standards and become involved in actively managing the economy.

In this effort to limit governmental influence the Business Advisory Council (BAC) of the Department of Commerce proved helpful. This organization became an institutional bridge between the welfare capitalism of the 1920s and the early New Deal. This fact owed much to the efforts of Secretary of Commerce Daniel C. Roper and NRA director Hugh Johnson. In April 1933 Roper began to create the BAC to provide the administration with a necessary reservoir of corporate managerial talent. Three men, Gerard Swope of GE, Walter Teagle of Standard Oil of New Jersey, and Henry I. Harriman of the U.S. Chamber of Commerce occupied a central place in early procedures and selected most of the council's first members. The advisory agency that resulted from their efforts was an unprecedented attempt to enroll corporate expertise within the peacetime federal government on a permanent basis.[12]

The 41 (later 60) members recruited to the BAC possessed impressive credentials. In addition to Harriman, Teagle, and Swope (who became the first chairman of the BAC), the roll included Henry S. Dennison, Pierre S. DuPont (chairman, DuPont de Nemours), Alfred P. Sloan, Jr. (chairman, General Motors), Robert E. Wood (chairman, Sears, Roebuck), Fred I. Kent (treasurer, National Industrial Conference Board), A. Lincoln Filene (chairman, Filene Department Stores), and Winthrop W. Aldrich (chairman, Chase National Bank). If an honor guard of welfare capitalist leadership existed anywhere during the formative stages of the New Deal, the BAC was the place where it was headquartered.[13]

On June 26, 1933 the BAC held its first meeting. Hugh S. Johnson, the keynote speaker, came right to the point. He wanted high-level corporate advisers to man the Industrial Advisory Board (IAB) created within the NRA structure to represent management interests during and after the period of code making. Although labor and consumers also possessed advisory boards, Johnson wished particularly to obtain support from an elite group of corporate leaders: men with whom federal officials could create a consensus on questions of industrial welfare.

BAC chairman Swope proved receptive to Johnson's desire, and the frantic pace of early NRA procedures put a premium on the BAC's advice.* Working through the IAB, BAC members concentrated their efforts in two areas. First, they advised top NRA administrators concerning overall agency policy; second, they assisted trade associations in drafting and presenting code proposals at the hearings that were the key to NRA's ratification process.[14]

In both realms BAC members exercised impressive influence. Hugh S. Johnson and his chief assistants were more than willing to allow larger corporations the primary responsibility for industrial reorganization.[15] At early code hearings administration spokesmen repeatedly stated that NRA was not trying to "dictate" to business; rather, it intended to allow "in large measure, almost complete self-government, excepting where the action of one [trade group] will interfere with the other."[16]

WELFARE CAPITALISM AND ORGANIZED LABOR: THE CREATION OF THE NATIONAL LABOR BOARD

Despite the smooth organization and demonstrated ability of the BAC and the IAB, welfare capitalists faced opposition to their policies from the trade union leaders who made up the Labor Advisory Board of the NRA. These labor leaders also wanted to play a role in the creation of a rationalized economy and to benefit from newly created social welfare standards. In particular, they wanted to exploit Section 7-A of the National Industrial Recovery Act, which gave them unspecified

---

*Gerard Swope had worked as Hugh S. Johnson's assistant during the period of the War Industries Board.

rights to organize workers in industries that adopted codes. Intense worker unrest in the textile, rubber, and steel industries throughout 1933 and 1934 revealed the possibilities for trade union growth.[17]

BAC members responded to the problem of labor organization on August 3, 1933 when the IAB hosted a meeting with NRA's Labor Advisory Board. During this meeting the participants created a plan for a National Labor Board that would arbitrate strikes and lock-outs, report violations of labor standards such as failure to pay minimum wages, and obtain voluntary consent to Section 7-A from employers and employees. Senator Robert F. Wagner of New York was proposed as chairman; William Green, John L. Lewis, and Leo Wolman would represent the AFL; Gerard Swope, Walter Teagle, and Louis Kirstein of Federated Department Stores represented the welfare capitalists of the IAB/BAC. Within 48 hours Roosevelt ratified the proposal in toto.[18]

The National Labor Board (NLB) was an institutional manifestation of a traditional social welfare compromise. Acting under the loose organizational sponsorship of a federal umpire, trade union and big business representatives had met together to solve their common problems. Federal officials then ratified the proposals emanating from these private interest groups, rather than seeking to formulate independent strategies of their own. In an unprecedented peacetime emergency the Roosevelt administration sought to reinstitute the labor relations institutions of World War I. In Wilson's time a National War Labor Board composed of five AFL leaders, five businessmen, and two public chairmen had been created. The NLB replicated the strategy and structure of its wartime predecessor and aimed to duplicate its experience as well.

Welfare capitalists such as Gerard Swope understood the lessons of the Wilsonian past. During World War I, AFL leaders had surrendered the right to strike in return for obtaining increased business and government tolerance for the right to organize. Samuel Gompers' AFL had learned the virtues of no-strike pledges, voluntary arbitration of industrial disputes, and toleration for company unionism during emergency situations, and Swope hoped that William Green's AFL would do the same. Of course, this compromise depended not only on labor's agreement with Swope that, indeed, the AFL would benefit, but also on the disciplining of conservative businessmen such as Alfred Sloan who opposed unionization, emergency situation or not.[19]

At first, this compromise and the overall structure of NRA itself appeared to work. The alphabetical agencies were in the proper order; BAC members on the IAB expanded corporate influence within the NRA. The federal government lacked its own industrial planning agencies, and policy makers were in no rush to create them. In October

1933, for example, Hugh S. Johnson informed Walter C. Teagle that leaving final responsibility for the administration of national industrial codes in the hands of public officials would create "too bureaucratic" a setup. Instead, "self-government of industry" should be achieved by rotating panels of "outstanding men from industry and business generally" to oversee the operation of the codes. IAB members enthusiastically agreed, and code authorities often became equivalent to dominant trade associations within individual industries. The American Iron and Steel Institute oversaw the NRA's Iron and Steel Code. The National Electrical Manufacturers Association Administered the code for the electrical manufacturing industry.[20] Even the small number of government members on code authorities were appointed from among the ranks of businessmen with "intimate knowledge" of the industries they regulated. It was not unusual for these men to be members of the BAC.[21]

Despite the initial success of welfare capitalists in bending early New Deal industrial recovery measures to their purposes, frictions appeared among business leaders by the spring of 1934, and the organizational cohesion of the BAC, the NRA, and the NLB began to decline. Blows fell hardest on the NLB. In January the NAM strongly criticized the board. Two important firms, Wierton Steel and Budd Manufacturing, refused to allow the NLB to hold collective bargaining elections for their employees, and a host of smaller employers made haste to jump on the antiunion bandwagon.

These attacks by conservative businessmen made it difficult for the compromise-minded welfare capitalists on the BAC to persuade their more skeptical peers of the necessity of wooing the AFL leadership. A majority of the BAC opposed the creation of arbitration boards within industries "relatively unorganized from either the industrial or labor standpoint," and could not agree among themselves on the proper interpretation of Section 7-A. If a majority of the employees in a given plant voted for a union affiliated with the AFL, would that union then bargain for all workers or only that proportion of the employees who selected it? Would employee minorities possess rights under 7-A to be represented by company unions that many large corporations had established as alternatives to independent trade unions? Or were single worker collective bargaining agents essential to achieving the purposes of the statute?

Liberal welfare capitalists had answers to these questions. They were willing to countenance AFL-led organizing drives in return for AFL acquiescence in a mixed system of company and independent unionism based upon the principle of proportional representation. To further such compromise, Swope and Dennison were also willing to use the NLB to enforce "majority rule" interpretations of Section 7-A on employers who failed to recognize unions. Such logic failed to persuade employers who refused to consider company unions and trade unions as complementary—or those who opposed any efforts, by whomever instituted, to force antiunion entrepreneurs into line with the procedures of enlightened corporations such as GE. Men such as these branded Swope and his allies on the NLB as radicals. Such criticism caused AFL leaders to doubt the ability of the BAC to control the antiunion activities of corporate conservatives. Calling upon federal bureaucrats to aid them, the AFL demanded majority rule under 7-A.[22]

On March 1, 1934, the NLB came out publicly for majority rule. For the first time a board decision was not unanimous. Recently-appointed employer delegate Pierre S. DuPont dissented, reaffirming the virtues of proportional representation. Within days, Roosevelt effectively repudiated the decision of a majority of the NLB's employer and labor members by allowing Hugh Johnson to work out an emergency agreement with the automobile industry "that not only allowed for proportional representation but also created an Automobile Labor Board independent of the NLB." To further confound affairs the president later announced that the decision he had just made had been "unfortunate." All this did nothing to resolve the growing confusion regarding what, if any, collective bargaining policy his administration possessed.[23]

By the end of March the NLB had effectively ceased to exist. Roosevelt's indecisiveness delivered the coup de grace to BAC-initiated attempts to evolve a national compromise based upon proportional representation and a recognition of the AFL's right to enjoy a modest existence within the mass production trades. With the creation of the first National Labor Relations Board in the summer of 1934, primary influence in the creation of a national labor policy shifted to congressional liberals and the advocates of industrial unionism and away from welfare capitalists, leaders of AFL craft unions, and the executive branch of the federal government.[24]

As the NLB fell apart the NRA itself was coming under attack. Early in 1934, independent Republicans and conservative Democrats in Congress grew restive with the price fixing aspects of the NRA codes. Code authorities, they argued, were setting prices to discriminate against small business. In March, Hugh Johnson responded by appointing a National Recovery Review Board to gauge the extent of unfair practices.

The board soon complicated NRA's existence. Bypassing agency channels it issued a series of scathing, often slapdash, attacks upon NRA. Though ideologically muddled, the review board's criticisms increased opposition to NRA procedures within Congress, the Brookings Institution, and the NRA's own Consumer Advisory Board. In June 1934 some of the lawyers and academic economists on the NRA staff attempted to abolish the price control aspects of the national industrial codes in all but shortrun emergency situations. Counterattacks by the Industrial and Labor Advisory Boards, NRA deputy administrators, and code authorities speedily ended these efforts to restore the hoped-for virtues of free market forces. Public bickering improved neither NRA's internal cohesion nor its morale.[25]

The NRA was becoming a political liability. Facing congressional elections in the autumn of 1934, FDR began to speak of stricter antitrust enforcement. In May he exempted small service, luxury, and retail trades from the NRA codes. Finally, in August he eased Hugh S. Johnson out of the government. To replace him Roosevelt established a five-man National Industrial Recovery Board headed by BAC member S. Clay Williams[26]

By late summer, however, the idea that organized business should continue its collaboration with federal officials was becoming progressively less attractive to important elements of the BAC. IAB policy statements became increasingly captious. NRA officials should cease "tinkering" with codes. Attempts to deny government contracts to companies that refused to allow NLB-style representation elections were unwarranted efforts to "license" industry. Unannounced surveys of businessmen's compliance with the wage and hour provisions of NRA codes were an illegitimate extension of federal power. Disgruntled BAC members including John Jacob Raskob of General Motors apocalyptically announced that businessmen must stop federal officials from destroying capitalism.[27]

While BAC members squabbled the agency created for them started to unravel. Mass resignations of NRA administrators took place, and severe difficulties were encountered by BAC personnel in finding corporate managers to replace them. Council members including Arthur D. Whiteside (Dun and Bradstreet) and S. Clay Williams (Reynolds Tobacco) used their positions of power within the NRA bureaucracy to block efforts by labor and consumer interests to weaken businessmen's influence. Small businessmen steadily increased the scope of their attacks.[28]

Finally, in August 1934 the BAC was shaken by the resignation of the representatives of General Motors and DuPont. Alfred P. Sloan, John Jacob Raskob, and Pierre S. DuPont struck at the heart of the business-government alliance, which made NRA possible, by leaving the council to establish an American Liberty League devoted to defeating Roosevelt, trade unions, liberal Democrats in Congress, "communism", and assorted social welfare causes. Simultaneously the U.S.

Chamber of Commerce and the NAM accelerated their attacks on the New Deal. NRA survived until its eventual invalidation by the Supreme Court in the Schecter Case on May 27, 1935, but it was left to a ragged collection of small retail and service firms to defend the agency in its final months.[29]

As NRA disintegrated, the welfare capitalists of the BAC tried to formulate some common plan of action to replace it. In conferences held between January and April 1935 the BAC worked out terms upon which a majority of its members were willing to see the NRA continued for another two-year trial period. Council statements illustrated the growing disjunction between welfare capitalist leadership and New Deal policies. Industry, not government, should have the dominant responsibility for formulating and enforcing codes. Industry should have the right to withdraw its compliance with any code provision "it might have voluntarily accepted." Government had no constitutional right to administer laws to favor trade unions at the expense of company unions. Organized business represented the true "public interest" in economic affairs. The president should give up the right (which he had never exercised) to impose codes on especially uncooperative industries.

Government, at base, should gather data from industry, state its recommendations to national trade associations, and bargain for the fulfillment of these recommendations. It should not possess powers of compulsion, particularly in the field of labor relations. In short, Washington should not move beyond the self-regulatory precedents acceptable to mainstream welfare capitalist opinion.[30]

Such corporate proposals died unborn. Relations between the BAC and the Roosevelt administration worsened. By July 1935, disaffected welfare capitalists were resigning from the BAC in such numbers that the organization's leaders feared for its survival. Opinions were expressed that a "breathing spell" from further federal welfare and industrial experiment was required.[31]

THE WELFARE CAPITALISTS REGROUP

Worsening relations between the welfare capitalists of the BAC and the executive branch formed only part of the story. By the middle of 1935, important elements of the business community had broken off cooperative relations with the New Deal administration. Included among these businessmen were a majority of the operators in important industries such as steel, automobiles, rubber, and chemicals. Conservative spokesmen such as Henry Ford and Alfred P. Sloan, Jr. never forgave "that man" Roosevelt for not forthrightly opposing organized labor's claim to national legitimacy.

Businessmen confused cause and effect. Roosevelt and his advisers could no more have ignored an aggressive and expanding union movement than they could have created one. Conspiracy theories that compared the New Deal with creeping socialism allowed businessmen to externalize problems from the structure of the industrial system and to fasten them upon a small group of "un-American" or "communist" government bureaucrats who were, presumably, hell-bent on creating an absolutist state.

Such theories also allowed antagonistic businessmen to ignore the fact that, up to 1935, little about the American social welfare system had changed. The federal government provided some direct relief to American citizens, all of which was placed under the rubric of short-term emergency. In this regard the states received grants to aid the unemployed, and banks, corporations, and local governments accepted Reconstruction Finance Corporation loans to remain solvent. Of the early New Deal programs only a very few, most notably the Tennessee Valley Authority, posed any threat to established welfare and employment folkways. Welfare capitalists such as Gerard Swope, H. S. Dennison, E. A. Filene, and W. Averell Harriman appreciated these facts, even if other businessmen did not.[32]

And yet something had changed. Welfare capitalists now lived with the knowledge that their company programs required a substantial federal underpinning to be effective. The NRA experiment had revealed the limits of voluntary business organization to solve the nation's problems. Businessmen lacked the unity necessary to defend themselves successfully against challenges to their authority, particularly challenges from organized labor. In addition, this business disunity was an implicit invitation for the federal government to solve the nation's welfare problems on its own, without the benefit of business advice. Still, by 1935 government had not accepted the invitation, and continued business control of America's social welfare system was as likely a possibility as any.

NOTES

1. Albert U. Romasco, *The Poverty of Abundance* (New York: Oxford University Press, 1965); Herbert G. Warren, *Herbert Hoover and the Great Depression* (New York, 1959); Caroll H. Wooddy, *The Growth of the Federal Government, 1915–1932* (New York: McGraw-Hill, 1934).

2. J. J. Huthmacher, *Senator Robert F. Wagner and the Rise of Urban Liberalism* (New York: Atheneum, 1968), pp. 98, 101–02, 76–89.

3. For the effect of the depression on the vocational rehabilitation program see Edwin E. Witte, *The Development of the Social Security Act* (Madison: University of Wisconsin Press, 1962), pp. 189–90.

4. William E. Leuchtenburg, *Franklin D. Roosevelt and the New Deal, 1932–1940* (New York: Harper & Row, 1963), pp. 121–25.

5. Ellis W. Hawley, "Herbert Hoover, the Commerce Secretariat, and the Vision of an 'Associative State', 1921–1928," *Journal of American History* 61 (June 1974): 116; Robert F. Himmelberg, *The Origins of the National Recovery Administration: Business, Government, and the Trade Association Issue, 1921–1933* (New York: Fordham University Press, 1976), pp. 5–69; Barry D. Karl, "Presidential Planning and Social Science Research: Mr. Hoover's Experts," *Perspectives in American History* 3 (1969): 347.

6. Owen D. Young to Bruce Barton, November 25, 1932, Box 19, Young Collection, Van Hornesville, N.Y. (privately held); O. P. White, "Doubts of Owen D. Young," *Collier's*, July 9, 1932, p. 42; H. S. Dennison to Ida M. Tarbell, March 14, 1935, Dennison Collection, Baker Library, Harvard School of Business Administration, Cambridge, Mass.; H. S. Dennison, *Ethics and Modern Business* (Boston: Houghton Mifflin, 1932), pp. 58–59.

7. For complete texts of the Swope plan and other recovery programs see Charles A. Beard, ed., *America Faces the Future* (New York: Vanguard, 1932), pp. 160–95. For Hoover's reaction to the Swope plan, see *The Memoirs of Herbert Hoover: The Great Depression, 1929–1941* (New York: Macmillan, 1952), pp. 334–35, 420.

8. James MacGregor Burns, *Roosevelt: The Lion and the Fox* (New York: Harcourt, Brace, 1956), p. 177. The spectrum of welfare capitalist opinion regarding government-industry "planning" on the eve of the New Deal can be seen in U.S. Congress, Senate, Committee on Manufacturers, "Hearings on a Bill to Establish a National Economic Council," S. 6215 (Washington, D.C.: G.P.O., 1932).

9. R. F. Himmelberg, *Origins of the N.R.A.*, p. 204.

10. Sources for the principles and the creation of the NRA include Leverett S. Lyon et al., *The National Recovery Administration* (Washington, D.C.: Brookings Institution, 1935); Charles F. Roos, *NRA Economic Planning* (Bloomington, Indiana: Principia Press, 1937); Ellis W. Hawley, *The New Deal and the Problem of Monopoly: A Study in Economic Ambivalence* (Princeton: Princeton Univ. Press, 1966); Bernard Bellush, *The Failure of the NRA* (New York: W. W. Norton, 1975). Frances Perkins' *The Roosevelt I Knew* (New York: Viking Press, 1947) discusses Roosevelt's ambiguities on "planning" questions.

11. This aspect of the NRA legislation is more fully covered in Kim McQuaid, "The Frustration of Corporate Revival during the Early New Deal: Or, The Revisionists Revised" *The Historian* (August, 1979).

12. Daniel C. Roper, *Fifty Years of Public Life* (Durham, N.C.: Duke University Press, 1941), pp. 284–85. Extremely valuable primary materials regarding the creation and early history of the Business Advisory Council are contained in Boxes 783–87 of the General Records of the Department of Commerce (hereafter cited as GRDC) and in Boxes 8336, 8415, 8416, and 8764 of the Records of the National Recovery Administration—both in the National Archives, Washington, D.C.

13. For the BAC see Kim McQuaid, "The Business Advisory Council of the Department of Commerce, 1933–1961: A Study in Corporate-Government Relations," in *Research in Economic History*, vol. 1, edited by Paul Uselding (Greenwich, Conn. JAI Press, 1976), pp. 171–97. For an accessible listing of BAC membership between 1933 and 1938 see Roper, *Fifty Years*, pp. 404–07.

14. Hugh S. Johnson, *The Blue Eagle from Egg to Earth* (Garden City, New York: Doubleday, 1935), pp. 91, 97. See also "History of the Industrial Advisory Board," vol. 1, p. 1, Record Group 9, Series 37, National Recovery Administration, Miscellaneous Report and Documents Series, Box 8336, National Archives (hereafter cited as "History of the IAB"); Roos, *NRA Economic Planning*, p. 68; Lyon et al., *The National Recovery Administration*, pp.

100-02, 148, 156; "History of Code Making" (March 2, 1935), pp. 1-4, Record Group 9, National Recovery Administration, Miscellaneous Report and Documents Series, Box 8784, National Archives (hereafter cited as "History of Code Making").

15. William Leuchtenburg, "The New Deal and the Analogue of War," in *Change and Continuity in 20th Century America*, edited by John Braeman et al. (Columbus, Ohio: Ohio State University Press, 1964), pp. 123, 128-29; Donald Richberg, *The Rainbow* (Garden City, New York: Doubleday, 1936), pp. 115-16; Johnson, *Blue Eagle*, pp. 216, 348, 393; "Hearings on the Proposed Code for the Lumber & Timber Products Industry," p. 212, Box 7161, National Recovery Administration Records.

16. "History of the IAB," vol. 1, pp. 6-7, 111-12; "Industrial Advisory Board, Minutes of the Regular Meetings, 1933-1934" file (Meetings of August 22, 1933 and October 31, 1933), Box 8415, National Recovery Administration Records, National Archives (hereafter cited as IAB Regular Meetings File); "Industrial Advisory Board, Minutes of the Dinner Meetings, June, 1934-June, 1935" file (meeting of November 16, 1933), Box 8416, National Recovery Administration Records, National Archives (hereafter cited as "IAB Dinner Meetings File").

17. Lewis Lorwin and Charles Wubnig, *Labor Relations Boards* (Washington, D.C.: Brookings Institution, 1935), pp. 87-91.

18. "Minutes of the Joint Meeting of the Industrial Advisory Board and the Labor Advisory Board held at the Shoreham, August 3, 1933," pp. 1-6, IAB Regular Meetings File; "Combined Meeting of the Industrial Advisory Board and the Labor Advisory Board, August 4, 1933 in the Department of Commerce Building," pp. 1-4, IAB Regular Meetings File; F. W. McCulloch and T. Bornstein, *The National Labor Relations Board* (New York: Praeger, 1974), p. 11.

19. Irving Bernstein, *The New Deal Collective Bargaining Policy* (Berkeley: University of California Press, 1950), pp. 58-59; Lorwin and Wubnig, *Labor Relations Boards*, pp. 92-94, 106. For background regarding labor unrest see Irving Bernstein, *The Turbulent Years: A History of the American Worker, 1933-1940* (Boston: Houghton Mifflin, 1970); Melvyn Dubofsky and Warren Van Tine, *John L. Lewis* (Chicago: Quadrangle Press, 1977).

20. Bellush, *Failure of the NRA*, pp. 46, 96; IAB Regular Meetings File (meeting of October 20, 1933); Lyon et al., *National Recovery Administration*, pp. 275-77, 103, 135-36.

21. "History of the IAB," vol. 1, pp. 185-91; "History of Code Making," p. 4.

22. Gerard Swope, "Planning and Economic Organization," *Proceedings of the Academy of Political Science, Columbia University* (January 1934), pp. 84-89.

23. Huthmacher, *Senator Robert R. Wagner*, p. 163; Lorwin and Wubnig, *Labor Relations Boards*, pp. 110-19.

24. Bernstein, *New Deal Collective Bargaining Policy*, pp. 64-130; Arthur M. Schlesinger, Jr., *The Coming of the New Deal* (Boston: Houghton Mifflin, 1958), p. 397; and H. A. Millis and E. C. Brown, *From the Wagner Act to Taft-Hartley* (Chicago: University of Chicago Press, 1950) cover the development of national labor policies after the demise of the National Labor Board.

25. Johnson, *Blue Eagle*, p. 272; Hawley, *New Deal and the Problem of Monopoly*, pp. 97, 102; Schlesinger, *Coming of the New Deal*, pp. 132-35.

26. Leuchtenburg, *F.D.R. and the New Deal*, pp. 67-68; T. E. Vadney, *The Wayward Liberal: A Political Biography of Donald Richberg* (Lexington, Kentucky: University of Kentucky Press, 1970), pp. 120-31; Franklin D. Roosevelt, "Address . . . at the General Conference of Code Authorities . . . March 5, 1934," Box 8385, National Recovery Administration Records, National Archives, Washington, D.C.

27. "History of the IAB," vol. 1, pp. 149-50 and vol. 4, pp. 26-27, 60-62; IAB Regular Meetings File (meetings of November 8, 1933 and January 4, 1934); IAB Monthly Meetings File (meetings of October 25, 1934 and November 9, 1933).

28. Bellush, *Failure of the NRA*, pp. 140-55; IAB Regular Meetings File (meeting of August 23, 1934); "History of the IAB," vol. 1, pp. 11, 14; "Industrial Advisory Board, Minutes of the IAB as Reorganized, July, 1934-May, 1935" files, Box 8416, National Recovery Administration Records, National Archives, Washington, D.C.

29. Herman Krooss, *Executive Opinion*, pp. 162, 176, 183-90; U.S. Congress, House, "Hearings on the Extension of the National Industrial Recovery Act" (Washington, D.C., 1935).

30. "History of the IAB," vol. 1, pp. 115, 226-34; IAB Monthly Meetings File (meetings of January 17, 1935 and February 28, 1935); Business Advisory Council reports on labor policy dated January 15, 1935, March 3, 1935, and May 2, 1935, in Franklin D. Roosevelt Collection, Official File no. 3-Q, Roosevelt Library, Hyde Park, N.Y.

31. Daniel C. Roper to H. P. Kendall, April 17, 1935 and E. W. Jensen to BAC members, April 19, 1935, Box 784, GRDC; New York *Times*, September 14, 1934, p. 1; March 28, 1935, p. 1; May 19, 1935, p. 2; May 18, 1935, p. 16; May 24, 1935, p. 2; William O. Douglas, *Go East Young Man: The Early Years: The Autobiography of William O. Douglas* (New York: Random House, 1974), pp. 263-373; "Business Advisory Council: Views on the Wagner National Labor Relations Bill (S. 1958)," (dated 1935), Box 47, Donald Richberg Papers, Library of Congress, Washington, D.C.; H. P. Kendall to Franklin D. Roosevelt, October 21, 1935; Ernest G. Draper to Daniel C. Roper, October 28, 1935; Draper to BAC members, July 5, 1935; Kendall to Marvin McIntyre, October 12, 1935—all in Official File no. 3-Q, Roosevelt Library; New York *Times*, August 8, 1935, p. 11; December 5, 1935, p. 14.

32. Krooss, *Executive Opinion*, covers this mainstream business reaction thoroughly. See also F. X. Sutton et al., *The American Business Creed* (Cambridge: Harvard University Press, 1950).

6

SOCIAL SECURITY AND THE CREATION OF A PUBLIC SECTOR, 1935-1939

The failure of the NRA raised disturbing questions of just who would maintain the American social welfare system and just how they would go about doing it. The depression testified to a continuing failure to maintain American living standards using conventional means. In the years between 1934 and 1939, therefore, the Roosevelt administration stumbled toward a new approach to welfare problems, one that ultimately involved the direct provision of welfare services by the federal government. This approach produced an unemployment compensation program and a federal program to pay pensions to retired industrial and commercial workers who reached age 65. It also yielded an ambitious reform agenda for what would ultimately become disability and health insurance. In the half decade between 1934 and 1939, therefore, the public sector mounted unprecedented challenges to the private sector.

The federal government's challenge involved two major pieces of social security legislation. Passed in 1935, the Social Security Act represented the New Deal's effort to create a permanent and comprehensive federal social welfare law. Four years later, Congress amended this law to alter its terms even before many of its provisions had gone into effect. These two laws brought the federal government into the American social welfare system as a permanent partner of private employers and state governments. They also occasioned a remarkable growth in the number of federal personnel concerned with social welfare, definite changes in the federal government's bureaucratic structure, and a marked growth of confidence among federal and state program administrators. By the end of the decade, federal personnel were ready to initiate projects abandoned or never undertaken at all by the private sector. Most of these projects did not receive congressional sanction until the 1950s and 1960s, under far different terms and conditions from those envisioned by New Deal planners. Still, the years between 1934 and 1939, which laid the groundwork for the subsequent expansion of the federal government, deserve close scrutiny.

THE FAILURE OF CONVENTIONAL WELFARE APPROACHES

The National Industrial Recovery Act was more than the New Deal's hope for industrial recovery. It was also its primary solution to the social welfare problems of the single most important component of the labor force: industrial workers. What the Agricultural Adjustment Act provided for farmers, the National Industrial Recovery Act was to have provided for industry. In this sense, the legislation marked the last attempt by federal administrators to build a social welfare system in which occupational groups defined and maintained their own living standards. The failure of the NRA to coordinate industrial policy and orchestrate widespread recovery meant that self-regulation by organized groups was not enough.[1] The Roosevelt administration had to look elsewhere for concepts upon which to base its social welfare efforts.

Existing public welfare programs offered few convincing models for an effective ideological or organizational base upon which New Deal bureaucrats might build. Workers' compensation remained the most ubiquitous example of Progressive Era labor legislation. Its spotty achievement record underscored the futility of that era's minimum-standard, state-by-state approach to public welfare. Even the most vigorous proponents of workers' compensation complained of its inability to provide quick and complete relief for those involved in industrial accidents. The program had never realized its initial objectives of eliminating litigation and speeding up the compensation process. Instead, the program had become mired in legal controversies that brought delay and frustration. In these regards, the state programs perpetuated the problems of an earlier court-oriented era.[2]

Furthermore, state administration brought a bewildering variety of rules and regulations. According to the man who ran Wisconsin's relatively advanced program, workers' compensation awards were "inconsistent" and exhibited "wide variations" in compensation for the same disability. The number of weeks of compensation for a particular injury differed by as much as 300 percent from state to state. The laws had a random quality about them, which meant that "lesser injuries were over-compensated and major injuries were under-compensated."[3] Even setting such problems aside, workers' compensation meant absolutely nothing to the millions of workers who were unemployed. Work accidents, after all, were a far less pressing problem than the lack of work.

In a similar manner, federal grant-in-aid programs to the states, such as vocational rehabilitation and other legacies from the 1920s, offered little hope to New Deal planners. They were largely irrelevant to the concerns of depression-era America, since the depression had cut their cost-efficient bases out from under them. Rehabilitation was no longer a good investment. Because of the depression, many handicapped workers who had been rehabilitated lost their jobs; other rehabilitated workers were unable to find jobs at all. By 1931 federal officials were faced with a backlog of over 2,000 people who had successfully completed the rehabilitation process but who still lacked jobs.[4] As a result, society reaped no returns on the tax money spent to restore the physically handicapped. In the middle of the depression, no one seriously thought that the federal government should make major investments in training programs. What was needed was not skills, but jobs; immediate relief mattered far more than long-term investment.

Noting this fact, rehabilitation officials began a discreet retreat from the efficiency rhetoric they had once used to justify their program. Observing the difficulties that physically handicapped workers were having finding jobs, federal officials declared that "economy is only an incidental consideration in rehabilitation of the disabled, which is of course to be justified principally on humanitarian grounds."[5] It was almost as if a time and motion analyst had smashed his stop-watch and gone to study modern dance in Greenwich Village.

Surviving as a humanitarian program proved difficult in the early 1930s, and vocational rehabilitation faced the threat of extinction. This program, like other grant-in-aid programs, needed a handout from Washington. The Roosevelt administration saved the vocational rehabilitation program, but only by diverting relief funds to the rehabilitation programs.[6]

The fate of vocational rehabilitation made it clear that the preservation of existing social welfare programs meant supplying them with increased federal funds. For traditional welfare programs, which operated exclusively on the state and local levels and lacked recourse to federal grants-in-aid, the need for federal funds appeared to be even more urgent. As the new administration studied social welfare questions, it came to believe that the federal government needed to bail out such programs. In an unguarded moment, one young bureaucrat wrote that, "we can never again leave this [welfare] load to the localities." The depression had created shortages of public revenues at a time of increasing demand for the "very services which up to now we have taken to be a local responsibility." This deficit necessitated providing the localities with unprecedented federal assistance.[7]

A few purists such as Supreme Court Justice Louis D. Brandeis remained. Brandeis thought that the federal government should not spend even nominal sums to help state health departments, for fear of sapping local initiative.[8] By 1934, however, such traditionalism was increasingly disregarded by federal administrators. A growing belief existed among federal officials interested in social welfare that federal funds must be supplied to the states and localities on some sort of permanent and expanded basis. Yet shifting the fiscal burden of paying for traditional social welfare programs hardly amounted to a new approach or a new program. Roosevelt administration officials hammered out the details for such a new approach as they debated social security.

THE EVOLUTION OF THE
SOCIAL INSURANCE DEBATE: UNEMPLOYMENT

The administration debated the logistics of federal intervention into the social welfare system intensively between 1933 and 1935. Meanwhile, as might be expected, its first response centered on relief, giving money to governors and mayors. The federal government made little use of its own administrative capabilities; few expected it to do so. Although veterans marched on Washington demanding bonuses to tide them over in time of depression, everyone else marched to city hall or the state capital. Roosevelt brought Harry Hopkins with him to Washington from New York, and Hopkins did what he could to meet the need for relief. Hopkins undertook his activities on temporary basis, as the word "emergency" in the name of Hopkins's Federal Emergency Relief Agency implied.[9]

Giving money to the states and localities, although acceptable, failed to remedy the situation. As the depression continued, the situation required a more coherent response, a plan under which the federal government would take over from the states. NRA's decline made the need for an activist approach all the more pressing; so did the barrage by interest groups who petitioned Congress for permanent, rather than emergency, legislation.

The federal government faced a fundamental difficulty in its efforts to relieve the problems that existed and make sure they never happened again: such a task had never been attempted. Many factors entered into the political calculations. Existing programs, for example, had to be fit into whatever new law was adopted, and questions of financing and administering social welfare laws could not be avoided by the administration or by Congress.

Like the pioneering generation of welfare capitalists, federal planners worked with what they had. Social insurance and minimum standards constituted the major weapons in their conceptual arsenal. Since neither weapon had been designed for a period of mass unemployment, each would require substantial modification.

Consider workers' compensation as an example of a social insurance law. It had been adopted in a burst of optimism and prosperity. Money to fund the program presented relatively few problems. Employers paid for it, in part because they believed that it saved them money. Unlike work accidents, however, the problems of unemployment were immediate, pressing, and costly. Funding a social insurance program for unemployment, therefore, posed difficult, perhaps insurmountable, problems. A fund from which benefits could be paid—a reservoir of money to meet present and future contingencies—needed to be created. Establishing such a reservoir would take time and require financial sacrifice (and forced savings) on the part of workers and industries. But time represented a precious commodity in this era of mass depression, and forced savings took money out of businessmen's and workers' hands, at a time when the economy desperately needed it.

Minimum standards, such as minimum wages, presented many of the same difficulties. They were designed for a time when many were employed and where a strong demand for labor existed and not for an era when unemployment already represented a large and growing problem. Minimum wages and maximum hours might help to spread work around, but they responded to little else about the situation.

Adding to the genuine intellectual quandaries, personal rivalries entered the picture. The "experts" in the field were split into at least two distinct factions: the "Wisconsin group," and the "outsiders group."

The Wisconsin group owed its existence to the energies of John R. Commons, who taught economics at the state university in Madison and became intimately involved in the creation of social welfare policies in that state and in the nation as a whole. A mentally fragile and often distracted man whose own writings lacked coherence, Commons nonetheless inspired generations of graduate students and faculty members at Wisconsin. He involved these groups both in large scholarly enterprises such as a monumental history of labor legislation in America and in weekly discussion groups that were held in his home. His students led the national fight for the passage of labor laws such as workers' compensation and industrial safety laws.[10]

The Wisconsin crowd concentrated on improving workers' compensation and, increasingly after 1929, extending social insurance to cover unemployment. The American Association for Labor Legislation served as the major vehicle that furthered the Wisconsin approach. Led by John Andrews and his wife, Irene Osgood, this association operated out of New York, but it remained in close contact with Commons. Both of the Andrewses, in fact, had been his students. In 1930 this association produced a model proposal for unemployment insurance, the details of which revealed many of the same influences that led Gerard Swope to propose his Swope plan for national recovery the next year.[11]

In particular, the model unemployment bill called for the classification of industry into groups, each of which would have a fund that would pay unemployment benefits. The money in these funds was segregated by industry so that a recession in one industry would not necessarily lead to the withdrawal of funds from another industry. When the state established governing boards for these funds, businessmen were to have a majority of seats on these boards. The law also permitted individual employers to set aside money to meet the requirements of the law by themselves. Another important feature of the model law allowed employers with steady employment records to receive a discount on their contributions to the fund.[12]

The model law mirrored many of the distinctive features of state workers' compensation laws. It required little bureaucratic participation on the part of the states. It more closely resembled self-regulation than government provision of social welfare service. It also tried to use the law as a means of creating market incentives for socially beneficial behavior. It blended welfare capitalism and the welfare state. A safe employer paid lower workers' compensation premiums; a prudent employer who did not lay off workers would pay less for unemployment compensation.

When the state of Wisconsin passed its own unemployment reserve law in 1932, it took a more limited form than the model law of the American Association for Labor Legislation. The Wisconsin act stipulated that each employer of ten or more workers contribute part of his payroll into a reserve fund that the state kept in the employer's name until the contributions amounted to $75 for each employee. If the employer was forced to lay off workers, these employees received benefits from the fund. As long as the fund remained paid up, the employer had no obligation to continue making payments.[13]

According to Paul Raushenbush, a former assistant professor of economics at Madison and a consultant to the Wisconsin Industrial Commission, the act represented a synthesis of corporate and minimum-standards approaches to social welfare. Like Commons, Raushenbush believed that the employer and the work place should be the focal points of social action. To deal with the perplexing problem of unemployment, "efforts should be made primarily by business management with some government help and guidance."[14] Raushenbush would have been offended if his actions were compared with those of Herbert Hoover, yet here was Herbert Hoover with a liberal bouquet in his hands.

The Wisconsin act supplied that public guidance for private action in a pragmatic way that interfered with the workings of the market as little as possible. Raushenbush believed the Wisconsin plan, by adjusting the social cost of doing business, would actually prevent, as well as alleviate, the distress of unemployment. He even thought that earlier adoption of the law might have made "the worst depression in history . . . substantially less severe."[15]

The Wisconsin school separated immediate relief measures from social welfare laws such as unemployment insurance, which permanently changed the terms of employment in labor markets. Although Wisconsin thinkers believed that Washington was a very weak reed upon which to rely—states were the real "laboratories of reform"—the Roosevelt administration invited Wisconsin group members to Washington in large numbers.

The Wisconsin approach failed to attract all of the experts. In the 1920s, the Wisconsin group found itself in an active competition with a group of outsiders, who were not impressed by Commons and his ideas. Since few social welfare laws were being passed, getting it right became as important as getting it done—and led to the sorts of ideological fights common to groups that are out of power. This competition became intensely personal and intensified as time progressed. The ethnic tone of the competition indicated its nasty personal qualities. Commons prided himself on an American approach to social problems; the outsiders were guided by two Russian, Jewish immigrants who were much more influenced by European notions of strong central government than were Commons and his followers.[16]

I. M. Rubinow and Abraham Epstein led the outsiders. Rubinow had been active in the early fights for social insurance, particularly the unsuccessful Progressive Era effort to pass health insurance in the states. Abraham Epstein was his most influential follower. Like Commons, Epstein had his share of personal quirks. He was short, and his eyes tended to wander. His speaking voice was squeaky, and he spoke with a thick accent. He tended to become emotional and to be sensitive to slights, particularly from members of the Wisconsin group.

In the Progressive Era, relative harmony prevailed between the two groups, and in the twenties a division of labor developed. Andrews and the American Association for Labor Legislation concentrated on the improvement of existing workers' compensation laws, while Epstein and his American Association for Old Age Security concentrated on passing state laws in aid of the elderly.

By the end of the twenties, however, a competition developed between Andrews and Epstein over the matter of unemployment. Andrews favored the Wisconsin approach, and Epstein supported what came to be known as the Ohio approach. People who had been friendly with both sides were forced to choose. Aware of how difficult it was to obtain funds to support his organization, Andrews entertained the notion of putting Epstein's group out of business. Epstein became increasingly convinced that Andrews's approach was simply irrelevant to the country's needs in a time of depression.

The Ohio approach favored by Epstein and Rubinow took its name from a 1932 report to the Ohio commission on unemployment. This approach began with the belief that preventing unemployment should not be the primary goal; instead, social programs should deal with the problems already at hand. In the case of unemployment, the problem was how best to get money into people's hands quickly. Separate plant or industry funds made efficient distribution of funds more difficult. Instead, a large pool of funds should be created, with employees and even the government allowed to contribute. The more people and companies contributing to the fund, argued Rubinow, the more likely that the fund would be able to meet its obligations.[17]

The argument between the supporters of the Ohio and Wisconsin plans amounted to a disagreement over the purpose of social insurance. Both agreed that social insurance was the answer. The Wisconsin group believed that such insurance worked best when it adhered closely to the principles of private insurance, in particular to the establishment of a definite relationship between a company's premium and its risks. Epstein and Rubinow ridiculed this emphasis on public insurance imitating private insurance. The insurance principle mattered to public efforts because it provided a means of spreading a particular risk across a large number of people—the substitution of a certain small loss for a possible large one. That did not mean, however, that social insurance was simply mandated private insurance. Instead, it represented a source of funds that could be used to meet social emergencies. Social insurance, Epstein and Rubinow believed, was valuable precisely because it handled situations beyond the reach of private insurance. Social insurance was important, the Commons group asserted, because it brought the efficiency of private insurance to a wider range of problems.

In terms of access to power, the Wisconsin group enjoyed an important advantage over the outsider group. The Wisconsin group knew Frances Perkins, and that made all the difference. Paul Raushenbush had already come to Washington and explained to federal officials how the federal government might enable the Wisconsin law to be adopted by other states. Labor Secretary Frances Perkins proved responsive to Raushenbush's ideas.[18]

Perkins's previous career had forced her to become aware of the Wisconsin approach. Before coming to Washington as the first woman cabinet member in American history, she had spent her entire career working in and around the New York state government. After graduating from Mount Holyoke and working at Hull House, she became the secretary of the New York State Consumers' League in 1910. A decade later she capped her career as a lobbyist for minimum standard laws by joining an agency that administered them, the New York State Industrial Commission. Governor Franklin Roosevelt put her in charge of the commission, a job in Albany that resembled that of the Secretary of Labor in Washington. When he became President, he chose her as Secretary of Labor. In her work as an administrator of the New York workers' compensation law, Perkins had already met many of the leaders of the Wisconsin group. They were her professional peers, fellow administrators of state laws that were considered among the most progressive in the nation.[19]

Perhaps that is why Perkins responded favorably to Raushenbush's proposals. Reflecting typical concerns about the constitutionality of any federal law, Raushenbush proposed that the federal government should legislate a tax on all employers, 90 percent of which could be offset if the employer paid into a state unemployment fund. Frances Perkins was impressed enough with Raushenbush's scheme that she asked him to draft an unemployment insurance bill, with the aid of Thomas Eliot, the department's chief lawyer. By February 1934, Senator Robert Wagner (D-New York) and Representative David Lewis (D-Maryland) had introduced the Raushenbush bill. It became the Wagner-Lewis bill.[20]

OLD AGE ENTERS THE PICTURE

These discussions took place in a rarefied atmosphere removed from the political give and take of Congress. Ironically, as experts engaged in a debate over highly technical matters, another group with no interest in the nuances of social insurance attracted national attention with a simple demand for money.

The group was the nation's elderly, and they practiced social welfare politics of the most traditional sort. The depression forced many older citizens into involuntary retirement and drastically reduced their incomes. In the nineteenth century, the elderly did not exist as a political group, but weakened family ties and improved health conditions isolated the group and increased its numerical strength. Aided by private groups such as the Fraternal Order of the Eagles, advocates for the elderly succeeded in establishing permissive state laws that provided aid to the elderly during the 1920s. These laws and more traditional poor relief laws produced nowhere near the level of funds to meet the elderly's demand for relief.[21]

The elderly had gained respectability because, like soldiers who fought in wars, they were veterans of a long struggle to survive. Most had worked and now wanted to retire. In these respects the elderly managed to separate themselves from other applicants for relief: they could not be accused of being shiftless or irresponsible; their only sin—again like the veterans of foreign wars—was the sin of survival. Emulating the veterans, the elderly called upon the government to grant them a pension.[22]

Led by Francis Townsend, a retired doctor living in California, the Townsend Movement enrolled tens of thousands of elderly members and quickly became a force in the New Deal's political affairs. Townsend vociferously demanded that anyone over the age of 60 be paid a flat pension of $200 a month from the federal treasury on the single condition that the recipients spend the entire amount of money within a month.[23]

Although the Townsend program was bizarre economics, it made very good politics. A $200 federal check at the beginning of each month was a much simpler welfare proposal to grasp than the experts' complicated actuarial calculations. The Townsend proposal cut through the technical cant about pooled funds, accrued liabilities, and the site of administration.

It simply took money from the government and put it into the hands of the elderly, just as Congress had always done for veterans. One young bureaucrat captured the source of the Townsend Plan's appeal when he described it as "more radical than that of the socialists and more conservative than the program of the United States Chamber of Commerce." As the nation's leaders met to design a social welfare program, many interested citizens saw the matter primarily as designing an old-age retirement program that would pay money quickly, and only secondarily as an unemployment insurance program. The bureaucrat described the practical effect of the Townsend Movement as encouraging the "movement for larger old age pension grants."[24]

Meanwhile, Epstein's group remained interested in an old-age pension bill that had been introduced as early as 1931. This bill, refined between 1931 and 1934 and known as the Dill-Connery Bill, authorized federal money to pay one third of the cost of old-age assistance in the states. In 1934, therefore, both the Wagner-Lewis unemployment bill and the Dill-Connery old age bill remained lively topics of discussion in Congress. Indeed, the House passed the old age bill in 1934.[25] Popular pressure, as mediated by experts who influenced the legislative process, threatened to create an *ad hoc* approach toward social welfare problems, an approach heavily influenced by the depression conditions.

THE COMMITTEE ON ECONOMIC SECURITY— UNEMPLOYMENT

Late in 1934 Roosevelt decided to have the administration prepare its own comprehensive bill, covering both old age and unemployment, and to present the bill to the Congress that would convene in 1935. In essence, Roosevelt's actions took control of the bills away from Congress and brought it to the executive branch. Just as the administration had prepared its own recovery program in 1933, it would now present a permanent social welfare program in 1935.

Roosevelt himself had only the vaguest notions of the sort of program he wanted, and the experts, increasingly preoccupied with the technical nuances of unemployment insurance, provided him with little guidance. The President had a vision in his head of cradle-to-grave insurance that would, at one and the same time, be self-supporting, be securely financed, and leave maximum discretion to individuals and to the states. To get beyond this sketchy and contradictory blueprint, Roosevelt turned to the institutional resources at his command, such as the bureaus that comprised the Department of Labor, and to the individuals whose advice he valued.[26]

Businessmen still rated the President's consideration. Despite the growing schism between the business community and the administration, Gerard Swope, among others, continued to maintain cordial relations with the administration. In March of 1934, he discussed GE's pension plans with FDR over lunch. When Roosevelt announced his plans to write a social insurance law in June 1934, he mentioned industrial plans, as well as state and foreign laws, as models for the sort of law he would propose.[27]

The first step in the policy process depended on the work of the Committee on Economic Security (CES), composed of cabinet members specially appointed by FDR to study the problem and issue specific recommendations. Perkins, Hopkins, Treasury Secretary Henry Morgenthau, and Agriculture Secretary Henry Wallace, the principal participants, performed little of the actual work. That task fell to the committee's staff, and to a technical committee from within the federal bureaucracy. Later, the CES and the President established an advisory council composed of business, labor, and academic leaders.

Perkins took the lead in setting up the apparatus, relying heavily on Arthur Altmeyer, who served as Assistant Secretary of Labor. Altmeyer, a former secretary of the Wisconsin Industrial Commission, recruited Edwin Witte, another Wisconsin official associated both with the state government and with the university's economics department. Witte quickly took leave from his post of acting director of the Wisconsin unemployment compensation program and arrived in Washington on July 24, 1934, ready to serve as staff director of the Committee on Economic Security.[28] Through these channels, the Wisconsin group came to dominate the committee staff. Epstein's organization had no similarly cohesive group that could be pressed into service.

Like all presidential commissions, the Committee on Economic Security needed to touch base with the relevant interest groups. The experts, such as Epstein, proved more than happy to oblige. Federal bureaucrats from agencies such as the Children's Bureau also eagerly accepted the offer to participate, since they wanted to gain formal recognition and financial support for their programs through the new legislation.

Unlike the other groups, business and organized labor, who were the most immediately involved, were distracted by other matters. The divisive warfare over a labor law to replace Section 7-A of the NIRA proved a particular distraction. Just as business was divided in its attitude toward federal labor legislation, labor was even more bitterly divided over the question of industrial unionism; it would soon splinter the AFL into two rival groups. As a result, labor failed to take an active role in the deliberations that led to the Social Security Act. Better organized and disciplined, business played more of a role, but not a central role.

Aware of these difficulties, Roosevelt nonetheless encouraged Witte and his staff to consult with business and labor leaders. The President had no wish to alienate any potential source of political support early in the game.

He steered Witte toward the businessmen who still talked with him and who could be used as a source of ideas on meshing federal efforts with existing industrial pension programs. Inevitably, Roosevelt made political choices. He urged Witte to see Gerard Swope, president of General Electric, a Roosevelt intimate from FDR's home state, and the Business Advisory Council's first chairman. Also at the President's request, Witte saw John J. Raskob of General Motors, an important financial donor to the Democratic party. Later Witte learned that Roosevelt had also talked with Owen Young, GE's Chairman of the Board. Witte made the requested calls on these figures, and he also went to see Walter C. Teagle of Standard Oil. Teagle's importance lay in his work on behalf of the Business Advisory Council's Unemployment Insurance Committee. Both Witte and Altmeyer realized that these individuals would also serve on the advisory council that would be established as part of the Committee on Economic Security's work.[29]

As the process of consultation unfolded, the experts reenacted their debate over unemployment compensation, with the stakes considerably heightened. All the experts agreed that unemployment represented the most important subject to be considered, not only because it was the most controversial among themselves but also because it constituted the most serious problem that the country faced. Unemployment consequently generated the most discussion of any topic related to social security.

It also occasioned the most comment from the business community and other interest groups. The fate of the old and the young who had either left the labor market or never entered it was of only peripheral concern to business. The unemployed, by way of contrast, became that way because of business conditions and business decisions. Unemployment could be regarded as one of the social costs of doing business, and whatever remedy the experts devised could end up costing businessmen a great deal.

The Wisconsin proposal gained legitimacy within the committee because of the existence of the Wagner-Lewis proposal, the presence of the Wisconsin representatives on the committee staff, and the President's vague predilections in favor of a state, rather than federal, plan. Despite this favored position, the Wisconsin approach won only a grudging victory in the committee, in part because of the reservations expressed by the government experts and outside advisors. These outsiders, for various individual reasons, tended at first to favor a federal plan.

Early in the deliberations, for example, federal employees on the technical committee advising the CES decided that a federal plan would be best. As federal employees, they naturally turned toward the federal, rather than the state governments for the solution to social problems. On September 26, 1934, they expressed a preference for a national system, rather than one that involved state administration. The proposal of an unemployment subcommittee of the technical committee mixed conservative and liberal elements. On the one hand, it called for pooled contributions, in the style of Epstein, rather than segregated contributions, in the Wisconsin style. On the other hand, the plan allowed industries to contract out and, in effect, to form their own unemployment compensation plans, just as Gerard Swope had earlier proposed. The plan called for contributions from employers and employees, as the businessmen wanted, but it also added provisions for the payment of extended benefits from the federal government, should workers exhaust the funds in the unemployment accounts.[30]

The federal employees who worked on the technical board advising the Committee on Economic Security soon changed directions. Sensing the prevailing sentiment on the President's part in favor of the Wisconsin approach, they abandoned their call for a federal program. Members of an advisory council composed of interested outsiders, however, persisted in their appeals for a federal program into December 1934.[31]

The advisory council served as a forum to discuss ideas. As planned by Arthur Altmeyer of the Department of Labor, the advisory council reflected the traditional Progressive Era attempt to balance the parties at interest. In one memo, Altmeyer suggested that the council be limited to a maximum of 15 members with four employer and four employee representatives, seven members of the general public, and "at least 3 women." The employers on the list reflected the New Deal experience with "progressive" employers who had been involved first in the War Industries Board and later with the NRA. The list of recommended members included Swope, Young, Baruch, Morris E. Leeds of Leeds and Northrup, and Sam Lewisohn of Miami Copper. Others on the list included P. K. Wrigley, who had recently established an unemployment program for his chewing gum company; Walter C. Teagle of Standard Oil, who chaired the BAC committee on unemployment; Lincoln Filene; Marion B. Folsom of Kodak; and Henry Dennison.[32] For the most part, Roosevelt followed Altmeyer and Perkins's advice. Although he wanted Swope or Young to chair the group, he was persuaded by Perkins to appoint Frank P. Graham, a southerner and a college president, as chairman. He selected Swope, Leeds, Lewisohn, Teagle, and Folsom as the business members. All but Lewisohn were BAC members. Thirteen public and five labor members joined them.[33]

Like the technical committee, the advisory council focused almost all of its attention on unemployment insurance. In a crucial vote on unemployment insurance that occurred in December 1934, the advisory council came down in favor of what the experts called the subsidy plan.

Years of debate over unemployment compensation, plus limited industrial and state experience, had been boiled down into three basic alternatives. There could be exclusive federal control, the subsidy plan, or the Wagner-Lewis proposal (a tax offset plan that would establish state programs). Edwin Witte noted that the fundamental issue concerned the extent of federal control. Under exclusive federal control, the law would be uniform from place to place. By ignoring state lines, the law would protect employees' rights when they moved from state to state. At the same time, the creation of a federal unemployment insurance law would force Congress to make decisions about an important social welfare law on the basis of almost no data. Decisions would be needed on the desirability of employee contributions, the creation of funds by plant or by industry, and the rebates to employers with good employment records. The subsidy plan, the second alternative, represented a halfway point between federal and state control. The federal government would collect money for unemployment compensation and then give it back to the states in the form of grants. Although it gave the federal government more power to set standards than did the Wagner-Lewis plan, it fell short of complete federal control. The Wagner-Lewis plan, the third alternative, left almost complete discretion to the states.[34]

The business representatives on the advisory council sided with a majority of the other members and voted in favor of the subsidy plan. The next day they, like the members of the technical committee before them, retreated from this position and left the matter with the Committee on Economic Security to decide. Again, Roosevelt's preference for state administration made the difference. By the end of December, the CES decided to recommend state unemployment plans through the Wagner-Lewis bill, with few strings attached.[35]

Arthur Altmeyer later claimed that this result stemmed from the polarization of expert opinions on unemployment compensation.[36] Since the experts agreed on so little, the cabinet committee to whom the experts reported simply threw the matter back to the states. Their proposal provided a mechanism that would enable the states to establish any sort of unemployment plan they desired. Wisconsin could preserve its segregated reserves; other states could experiment with a pooled fund. Wisconsin could limit contributions to employers; other states could permit both employer and employee contributions. It was possible, therefore, that unemployment compensation could go the way of workers' compensation, as a state system with little federal control.

THE COMMITTEE ON ECONOMIC SECURITY—
OLD AGE

As the experts conducted their specialized debate on unemployment, other staff members struggled to put together a plan to cover the elderly. They worked in relative freedom, almost ignored. As J. Douglas Brown, a Princeton labor economics professor who remained relatively free of the Wisconsin influence, explained his duties as a member of Edwin Witte's CES staff. "We were left largely alone to work out a national system of old age insurance." Witte himself, his hands full with the battles over unemployment insurance, and his interests totally centered on that matter, showed little enthusiasm for Brown's plans.[37]

Despite the relative freedom enjoyed by Brown and the other staff members assigned to old-age security, it proved difficult to create a feasible old-age insurance plan. The first recorded plan, put together by Barbara Nachtrieb Armstrong, a lawyer from the University of California, contained eight variations. Six of these variations involved state or private administration. In one of them, employers and employees each contributed one percent of the employees' wages into a federal fund. States then established old-age insurance plans, and if these plans met federal specifications, the states received a subsidy from the federal government in order to pay old-age benefits. In another variation, private companies, not state governments, established the old-age plans and received the federal subsidy. A week later, Armstrong came up with a different plan, in which the funds were to be segregated by industry. Brown followed these plans with those of his own, in which states or industries could voluntarily elect to be covered under the law.

As these plans revealed, federal social welfare activity was so circumscribed that even compulsory coverage remained an issue in the fall of 1934. By November, however, Brown, Armstrong, Murray Latimer of the Industrial Relations Counselors, and Otto Richter, an actuary from the American Telephone and Telegraph Company, had decided on a federal plan.[38]

Freed from the orthodoxy that inhibited discussion of unemployment compensation, these advisors simply followed the administrative logic to its limits. Brown later noted that the staff members deliberately exaggerated the problems of establishing separate state old-age insurance systems, writing memos to the other staff members with "awesome descriptions of the complexities."[39] As Brown and the others realized, however, the same logic could be applied to unemployment compensation. The real difference was that existing state laws and state-oriented expert opinion blocked a national approach to unemployment compensation; fewer roadblocks stood in the way of a recommendation for a national system of old-age insurance.

The roadblocks may have been fewer, but they still existed. As Brown realized, the other staff members, with their Wisconsin orientations, lacked his "zeal" for old-age insurance. At the time, the constitutionality of an old-age insurance plan remained in doubt. The court had approved few New Deal initiatives. Brown and, particularly, Armstrong decided to carry the fight beyond the genteel confines of the Committee on Economic Security to the Congress and the press. Armstrong went so far as to plant a story in the papers about the administration's lack of interest in old-age problems. Congressmen, responding to pressure from the elderly generated by Dr. Townsend and others, reacted predictably.[40]

In the fight to keep old-age insurance alive, the staff also found an important ally in the businessmen on the CES advisory council. As had been demonstrated by their attitude toward unemployment compensation, these businessmen had little fear of federally administered programs. They already ran industrial pension plans that covered several states, and they might be able to adjust and perhaps even benefit from a federal old-age insurance law. Whatever their motivations, they supported Brown and Armstrong and, in this manner, brought a sense of legitimacy to old-age insurance. Unemployment compensation already had that legitimacy from the Wagner-Lewis bill; old-age insurance needed to gain a similar sense of approval. As Brown noted, Teagle, Swope, and Folsom's "understanding of the need for contributory old-age annuities on a broad, national basis carried great weight with those in authority."[41] No precise measure can be given to this weight; nonetheless it helped old-age insurance to get through the cabinet-level committee and into the hands of Congress.

Considered in relation to radical plans like the Townsend Plan, business support for national old-age insurance made sense. Despite its unprecedented grant of federal power, it represented the approaches to social welfare that private businessmen, not public bureaucrats, had created. The plan retained the joint contributory format reminiscent of private pension plans. Under old-age insurance, workers and their employers would pay into a federal fund from which workers would draw benefits after retirement. In a field that contained a spectrum of policy options that ranged from giving money to all of the elderly immediately (Townsend) to doing nothing beyond preserving industrial pensions for the four millon workers who had them, the proposal chose a fiscally conservative course. It made it possible for America's industrial and commercial workers to be covered by a plan that resembled an industrial pension. Only those with employment records, not simply anyone over 65, would receive benefits. This format would insure that America's social welfare system would continue to be associated with the private labor market.[42]

The old-age insurance portions of the social security bill were not what most businessmen or even big businessmen wanted at the time. In politically volatile times, however, this measure represented the best alternative available to businessmen who, like Folsom and Swope, still cooperated with the administration. The rest of the businessmen sulked in their tents; they would have disapproved of whatever the Committee on Economic Security produced.

CONGRESS CONSIDERS

The persistent pressure of groups like the aged—and the need to respond to existing legislative proposals for the unemployed—sped up the process by which a federal welfare program was formulated and passed by Congress. In essence, Roosevelt presented Congress with an omnibus measure that combined programs covering children, the unemployed, and the elderly into a single legislative package. Since this package had the administration's approval and the administration had just won an impressive victory in the congressional elections, Congress acceded to FDR's wishes. Few congressmen understood the details of the legislation; one inside observer stated after the bill's passage that the "Congressmen have a very confused idea of what this whole program is about. . . . They mix up old-age insurance with unemployment insurance."[43] Almost no one, as Witte later noted, read the technical reports that the staff had prepared.[44] Instead, the Congress acquiesced in the plans of the executive branch for a national social welfare law, just as Congress had earlier allowed the President to cooperate with businessmen on the NRA in the hope of producing industrial recovery. Congress's passive approach had the benefit of shifting political criticism from one branch to the other and taking some of the heat away from Congress for not following the Townsend Plan more closely.

Congressional consideration of what became the Social Security Act illustrated the divided opinions of businessmen toward social welfare legislation. Some spokesmen, such as Henry I. Harriman of the Chamber of Commerce and Marion Folsom of Eastman Kodak, appeared as government witnesses and took what might be described as a "yes, but" approach. They accepted the general approach but suggested changes. Swope and Teagle also remained in touch with the congressional situation, in general supporting the bill. Meanwhile other business groups, such as the National Association of Manufacturers and some of the state manufacturers' associations, reacted viscerally to the bill, regarding it as another New Deal measure which had to be opposed energetically and completely.[45]

The Business Advisory Council (BAC), for its part, continued to suggest that federal subsidies be used for unemployment, rather than the more complicated and indirect tax-offset plan. Perhaps the BAC members feared that the states would take a more radical approach to unemployment compensation than the federal government. BAC members also persisted in their demands that employee contributions be mandated by law and that "experience rating" be expressly permitted in the law. Congress showed little interest. It left maximum discretion to the states.[46]

Congress showed much greater interest in the old-age sections of the bill. These included three major provisions. One called for the establishment of an old-age insurance program; another proposed that, for those people not eligible for the old-age insurance program, a voluntary program be established that would allow them to buy old-age annuities directly from the federal government; the final proposal reflected an accommodation of the forces seeking immediate relief and proposed that the federal government help to fund state relief programs for the elderly.

The voluntary-annuity proposal, alone among the President's proposals, died a quick death. The President bartered it away in return for support of the compulsory old-age insurance program. As it turned out, little thought had been given to the measure, and it had received only cursory mention in the Committee on Economic Security's report. When a Connecticut congressman suggested that such direct competition with the insurance industry be eliminated, no one objected.[47]

The old-age *relief* sections of the bill became the bill's most popular features. Edwin Witte later suggested that if the other features had not been bundled together with them, the bill might never have passed.[48] The popularity of these measures was not difficult to discern. The bill did not challenge the primacy of state and local administration, and it provided a ready source of federal funds that could be distributed almost immediately. Congressmen gratefully accepted these provisions.

THE DEBATE OVER FINANCING

The old-age *insurance* sections of the bill produced the most interesting political maneuvers and established the terms of the political battles that were fought between 1935 and 1939. Those businessmen who accorded the federal government a place in American life tended to favor the program, with two significant exceptions. The Swopes and Folsoms saw positive benefits in a government plan that was meshed with private pensions, rather than one, such as the Townsend program, that lay totally at the mercy of politicians. Faced with an election, these politicians might well decide to vote a handsome increase in appropriations for the elderly. The elderly, after all, were that rarest of social welfare phenomena: a welfare group that voted. Old-age insurance promised a less political, more orderly approach where costs could be predicted: benefits would be based on contributions, and no funds were to come from general revenues. A direct relationship was to be established between a worker's contributions and eventual benefits. The plan even allowed a two-year grace period before contributions would be collected, and five more years before benefits would be paid.

So far, so good. But the funding provisions of the old-age insurance law were not without their problems. As time passed, the costs of the program would increase, even without an extension of coverage or an increase in the generosity of the benefits. The reason was that the percentage of the retired population eligible to receive social security payments would rise over time. For a person who retired in 1936 or before, social security old-age insurance meant nothing. In 1960, by way of contrast, nearly all of the retired people who had worked in covered occupations would expect a pension. Social security would, therefore, cost far more in 1960 than in 1936.

Although the experts recognized this fact, the problem centered on what to do about it. One response was to collect only enough money each year to pay for current expenses. This approach, called pay-as-you-go, meant that social security taxes would be low at first and then gradually rise. Ultimately, it was assumed, the government would have to step in and put general revenues into the fund. After all, depression-era planners predicted a low birth rate and therefore relatively few young people to relieve the burden on the old when the workers of the 1930s retired. Another approach was to collect enough so that general revenues never became necessary. This approach, called fully funded, depended on collecting enough money in the early, cheap part of the program to build up reserves that would be used to pay benefits in the later, expensive part of the program.

Few people, including businessmen and most of the government's advisors, had wanted to take the fully funded approach. Either for Keynesian economic reasons or reasons related to a mistrust of the government, they did not want the government to hold large funds in reserve for the social security program. They saw little sense in building up a fund for retired people in the future, when the elderly were already in dire need. As the technical committee of bureaucrats advising the Committee on Economic Security put it, "Reserves such as become necessary under a full reserves plan are unthinkable."[49] Instead, the technical committee recommended and the CES accepted a plan that had the double feature of the welfare grants to the states for the relief of the elderly and an old-age insurance progam that called for gradually rising tax rates and an eventual subsidy from general revenues. This plan was stopped only by FDR himself, who realized, at the very last minute, that his old-age insurance plan would develop a deficit in the 1960s. The President ordered Treasury Secretary Henry Morgenthau to make the plan fully financed, without the need for general revenues.

Tempers flared among staff members as the President undid their work. Barbara Armstrong, the Berkeley law professor on the committee staff, refused to believe that Secretary Morgenthau could contemplate a huge reserve plan "without a qualm. The attitude of the Treasury Department . . . was too clearly in the other direction for me to credit that such an opinion could be so easily altered." Armstrong believed that the President's provisions would doom the bill. Democrats as well as Republicans would object to the accumulation of large reserves.[50]

Armstrong correctly anticipated the objections that would be made. Businessmen joined the protest. The Business Advisory Council realized that the President's plan meant higher tax rates than the original plan. The council noted that under the President's plan, the tax rate would reach 6 percent in 1949. At that point, workers would receive less than they might under a private insurance plan. The BAC objected both to the high tax rates and to the large reserves that the President's plan entailed.[51] Despite these objections, the funding provisions of the old-age insurance law formed part of the President's take-it-or-leave-it offer, and the congressmen took it.

A second issue related to old-age insurance stirred even more controversy. That concerned the right of employers and employees who already had old-age pension plans to opt out of the federal law. Presented as an amendment to the bill by Senator Bennett Champ Clark, this proposal passed the Senate and remained in the bill until a conference committee deleted it. Almost alone among the provisions of the Social Security Act, the Clark Amendment caused considerable controversy. Nearly all large companies were nominally in favor of it, and they did what they could to secure its passage. A list of companies known to favor the amendment on July 11, 1935, numbered more than 100 and included, among many others, American Cyanamid, the Borden Company, Eastman Kodak, Gulf Oil, Kimberly Clark, and Standard Oil of Ohio.[52]

Businessmen tended to favor this amendment for at least two reasons. The compulsory nature of the old-age insurance program gave businessmen adamantly opposed to the bill one more reason to oppose it. More moderate business leaders recognized that old-age insurance violated a common feature of American social insurance laws. Unlike workers' compensation or the original versions of the CES proposals, the law did not permit "contracting out" by those companies who wished to provide social welfare services on their own terms. The Clark Amendment would have remedied that apparent defect by permitting an employee to opt for either the federal plan or his employer's private plan, provided that his employer's plan was "not less favorable" than the federal plan. Passage of the Clark Amendment would have have produced competition between private and public systems, and many employers would have welcomed it.[53] It fit in with a welfare capitalist view of the world. Welfare capitalists thought they had done more things—and done them earlier and better—than public-sector officials had.

The federal planners strenuously disagreed. They argued that the Clark Amendment would leave the federal plan with the worst risks to insure: relatively old workers who would not have many years in which to make social security contributions. The private sector could simply refuse to insure such workers and leave the load to the public sector. The public sector would face prohibitive costs. Social security taxes would have to rise to cover the costs, driving more workers away from the system. Support for social security would be undermined by the fact that many workers would have chosen not to participate.[54]

In the end, FDR insisted on the withdrawal of the Clark Amendment for "further discussion." As he did on other aspects of the legislation, the President got his way. On the Clark Amendment, most of the businessmen lost.

SOCIAL SECURITY AS LAW

In August 1935 President Roosevelt signed the Social Security Act into law. Its contents amounted almost to a catalog of America's social welfare programs. First, the bill established a federal-state unemployment insurance program, based on the Wagner-Lewis bill. Second, it initiated federal grants to the states for welfare payments. Money from these titles would be awarded by local welfare departments to needy dependent children, blind people, and elderly citizens. Third, the act granted the states funds for such activities as vocational rehabilitation, infant and maternal health, programs to aid crippled children, and public health programs. Fourth, and most important, the act created an old-age insurance program.

The fourth element in the Social Security Act was the most revolutionary. Unlike the other provisions, the old-age insurance program relied on direct federal provision of a service. It involved no local or state intermediary. The states and localities administered welfare payments; the states administered unemployment insurance; the federal government alone would administer old-age insurance.

The Social Security Act preserved existing institutional arrangements. Unemployment compensation, for example, reflected the previous existence of the Wisconsin law. Federal-state programs of the 1920s that had fallen upon hard times in the 1930s also received explicit recognition in the act. The Children's Bureau, for example, managed to get the old Sheppard-Towner infant-and-maternal-health program written into the Social Security Act. Vocational rehabilitation was almost irrelevant to the country's pressing needs, yet it, too, was mentioned in the act. The welfare portions of the act built upon welfare programs that had already been established in the states and localities. In a sense, old-age insurance represented no exception to this pattern. It also preserved existing institutional arrangements—not a public program in this case, but rather a series of private pension programs.

Although most businessmen opposed the Social Security Act, and it would be difficult to trace a direct business influence on the law, that influence remained. Passed in a time when radical income redistribution was on the agenda, the act, in its old-age insurance provisions, relied upon what authorities called "the contributory-contractual principle." This principle allowed people to equate social security with a private insurance plan where they only "get what they've paid for." As businessmen such as Gerard Swope recognized at the time, the old-age insurance program, like the rest of the social security program, failed to indicate any discontinuity in American social welfare tradition. Businessmen continued to enjoy comparative organizational advantages that allowed them influence over public-sector welfare councils and that led smart politicians like FDR to dress up public-sector programs in as much private-sector clothing as possible.

As if to clinch the point, the Clark Amendment soon became a non-issue. Supporters tried to pass the measure in 1936 and met with little success. In fact, the new version was so complicated that many businessmen realized its futility. Marion Folsom of Eastman Kodak, increasingly regarded as *the* business authority on social security, began as a lukewarm supporter of the

Clark Amendment and then decided that it was hardly worth the trouble. As he explained to an interested researcher, the government plan made little difference to Kodak. "In the future," he said, "the employee will accumulate part of his annuity with the insurance company and part with the government. The total cost to us will be approximately the same as it has been in the past."[55] M. Albert Linton, an important insurance executive and a close advisor to the Republican Party on social security, dismissed the new draft of the Clark Amendment as "impracticable." Business, he said, should simply adjust by allowing the "government plan to cover the basic pensions and then to have additional amounts added on through private agencies."[56] As early as January 1936, an actuary from Connecticut General reported that his company was planning to revamp its pension plans (which it sold to other companies) "in such a way that when [they are] super-imposed upon the Federal plan, the benefits in total will be approximately what they are now."[57]

Early in 1936, officials in the Chamber of Commerce expressed a general sense of the futility of opposing social security. In a confidential note, a chamber staff memo said that no effort should be made to amend the act. If amendments were attempted, the Townsendites might prove just as success-ful with Congress as would the chamber. From that perspective, social insurance looked good.[58]

The law, it became apparent, presented the chamber and other business groups with few immediate challenges. In the spring of 1936, for example, Marion Folsom had spoken before the chamber and delivered a speech that federal officials described as "definitely favorable." Folsom urged business-men to cooperate with the new law. Although some of the businessmen in attendance objected bitterly, they reserved most of their venom for what became the Wagner Act and the "alleged efforts of the administration to set up labor in opposition to management." All in all, the businessmen were less antagonistic than the social security officials had expected them to be.[59]

SOCIAL SECURITY IN OPERATION

The old-age retirement program, for all of its business features, created the beginnings of a distinctively federal social welfare system. Although the new law appeared conservative, it had the potential of expanding the federal government's role in the delivery of social welfare services directly to the people. Whether the Social Security Act contributed to such an expansion would depend on the use to which the act was put—particularly on whether the administrators of the act would successfully amend the legis-lation to accomplish welfare goals.

Before that could be done, the 1935 act needed to be put into operation. In the spring of 1936, for example, the Social Security Board was faced with its first major administrative task, the creation of approximately 26 million accounts for the individuals then eligible to make social security payments. Some leeway was built into the legislation; the collection of payments (the job of the Internal Revenue Service) did not begin until January 1, 1937. Still, it was formidable. No such thing as a computer existed, and what federal officials lacked in sophisticated data processing hardware, they did not make up for in sophisticated personnel. In 1936, the Social Security Board had fewer than 500 employees to undertake its complex assignment.

The board quickly realized that outside assistance was required. Throughout the spring and summer of 1936, it consulted with BAC member Marion Folsom. Folsom, who already ran Kodak's program, asked the advice of other BAC members concerning how the staggering job of beginning Social Security could be accomplished. With the exception of the postal and internal revenue systems, few governmental analogs for social security could be found. After more technical consultation with the BAC, Social Security Board officials concluded that 202 offices would have to be created to begin distributing the 26 million Social Security account numbers and collecting contributions.

Faced with this monumental task, the board decided to secure the full-time assistance of a private insurance company executive. Beginning in May 1936, board chairman John Winant searched for a businessman to administer the operation. In July the board, assisted by the BAC, hired the director of the Industrial Bureau of the Philadelphia Chamber of Commerce to serve as the "czar of registration." In this manner, a private businessmen helped to launch the American social security program.[60] Since old-age insurance relied on a payroll tax, this act only solidified the partnership between businessmen, whose payrolls would fund the program, and bureaucrats, whose administrative skills would direct pensions to those who earned them, in the social security program.

Change still produced its share of friction. Some workers found derogatory messages from their employers in their pay envelopes informing them of "deductions" from their pay starting in January 1937.[61] These employers equated Social Security deductions, like union dues, with theft. These deductions began, conveniently enough, after the presidential election, a fact that hardly escaped the notice of the Republicans. As late as May 1938, employers questioned the need to provide employees with receipts for their social security deductions, since most workers were assumed to be too stupid to understand what those receipts meant.[62]

Despite these hesitant beginnings, the Social Security Board soon began assuming direct administrative control over its operations. In the process it fueled the first significant expansion of federal social welfare staff during the New Deal era. Between 1933 and 1935, the total number of federal employees rose by nearly 50 percent, but emergency or temporary agencies accounted for a substantial proportion of the increase. In NRA's brief life-time, for example, it had gone from employing no one, to employing 5,000 people, and back to no one again.[63]

The Social Security Board, however, existed to provide a permanent welfare service, not a temporary one. In the earliest budget estimates, Social Security Board officials predicted their agency would need a larger staff than NRA had ever had. By June 1941, 12,682 people worked for the Social Security Board and just over 480 regional offices were in operation. Working from a central card index that occupied more than an acre of floor space, employees attempted to cope with the more than 121 million finan-cial statistics that the office received each year.[64] The size of the Social Security Board's operation underscored the fact that it took more people to operate a direct welfare service than it took to administer an agency like NRA that had confined itself largely to ratifying minimum standards formulated by private interest groups.

The Social Security Board provided employment for people whose opportunities had previously been in the private sector. I. S. Falk, a public health expert, had worked for the Committee on the Costs of Medical Care and for the Milbank Memorial Fund. Both of these activities had been funded exclusively by businessmen and by the philanthropic foundations supported by private fortunes. In 1937 Falk found a new place of employ-ment in the Social Security Board's office of research and statistics.[65] When the Committee on Economic Security had wanted to find experts on unem-ployment compensation, it had turned to the Industrial Research Counse-lors Inc.[66] Beginning in 1936, the Social Secruity Board began to acquire its own staff on unemployment compensation; no longer would research on this question be confined to the private sector.[67] The establishment of the Social Security Board provided an important point of transition in social welfare planning form the private to the public sectors.

The technical experts were a new breed of federal bureaucrat. Political nonpartisans, at least in the conventional party sense, they owed their primary loyalties to the service they performed rather than to the group that they served. For many, proper research method mattered more than the uses to which the politicians put their data. In this respect, it was a natural step for people to move from graduate school to federal employment, just as an earlier generation of researchers might have moved from graduate education to a job in a private, business-financed think-tank such as the Na-tional Industrial Conference Board or the National Bureau on Economic Research.[68] By the mid-1930s, the scale of the federal welfare bureaucracy had reached a point where the staff of technical experts employed in Wash-ington were both numerous and well-organized enough to provide a kind of "built-in mechanism for the expansion of the [federal welfare] system."[69]

Perhaps the most important of these technical experts was Arthur

Altmeyer, who succeeded John Winant as the chairman of the Social Security Board late in 1936. Altmeyer was not a charismatic figure. "A successful administrator is about as interesting to the public as cold spinach," he once said.[70] For all of his comparisons with cold spinach, he played an important role in the federal government's change from a passive to an active provider of social welfare.

Altmeyer had made many of the important stops along the public sector's road to maturity. He studied with John R. Commons, worked for the Wisconsin Industrial Commission, and headed the Compliance Division of the NRA. After chairing the technical subcommittee of the Committee on Economic Security, he became one of the first members of the Social Security Board.[71]

Altmeyer represented what may be called a second generation of public social welfare workers. Unlike members of the first generation, such as John R. Commons, he was not a partisan in the sense that he had not spent years lobbying for the creation of a particular law. Workers' compensation, the chief program he administered for the Wisconsin Industrial Commission, had, in fact, originated before he entered college. In addition, his training was far more specialized and labor-market oriented than the earlier generation's had been. Altmeyer supplemented what Commons taught him by studying such things as statistics and even scientific management.[72] In fact, Altmeyer's training resembled that of an actuary or insurance executive working for a private insurance company. His career testified to a growing routinization and professionalization of the public sector—a phenomenon that indicated that the organization gap between the public and private sectors was closing.

At first, Altmeyer and his staff had been worried about the most basic challenges to the program. When the first employees of the research and statistics division were recruited, for example, they worked on the defense of the program before the Supreme Court. On May 24, 1937, the Supreme Court settled the matter in the case of *Helvering v. Davis*. Social security was constitutional. Other challenges were not disposed of so easily.

THE DEBATE OVER FINANCING RESURFACES: THE 1939 AMENDMENTS

The most serious political test of the old-age program continued to be over the way in which it was financed; financing constituted the one facet of social security that still generated controversy. The reasons were not hard to discern. In the first place, the plan would not pay regular pensions to anyone until 1942. That meant people would pay into the system for five years without any real assurance they would ever get anything back. By way of contrast, the welfare programs of many states were ready to pay immediate pensions to the elderly on terms as generous as provided by old-age insurance. In the second place, the reserves required to fund the program still caused considerable stir.

The reserve plan rested on complicated and intimidating computations. In 1937, for example, $511 million went into the Social Security account, only $5 million of which was required for current expenses. In 1937, therefore, most of the social security money rested in what government officials called the "reserve account." In 1967, with the system much further along the road to maturity, the collection of social security taxes would amount to more than $2 billion. For the first time, however, benefits would cost more than the amount taken in, and money from the interest on the more than $38 billion that had accumulated in the reserve account would make up the difference. By 1980 the amount of money held in reserve for social security would reach over 46 billion.[73]

As nearly everyone realized, that was a lot of money. Republican candidate Alfred Landon expressed the fears of many when he said, "We have some good spenders in Washington. With this social security money alone running into billions of dollars, all restraint on Congress will be off."[74] In a rare show of unanimity, the Brookings Institution, the American Federation of Labor, the Chamber of Commerce, the heads of most insurance companies, and the editorial board of the New York *Times* all agreed with Landon on this issue. Even the moderate businessmen who supported the concept of social security deplored the reserves.[75]

Marion Folsom told the Chamber of Commerce that the reserve features of the Social Security Act constituted its "greatest defect." Folsom reasoned that the reserve fund presented two sorts of temptation. One was for the government to spend the money for anything Congress or the President wanted, and the other was to increase the benefits. If benefits were increased, future generations would find themselves with a staggering burden. For Folsom, as for many businessmen, the solution was simple: keep the benefits modest, and do not raise the payroll taxes. Folsom argued that the existing low tax rate (2 percent of the first $3,000 of an employee's wages, half paid by the worker and half by management) would be sufficient at least until 1951. The law called for taxes to rise to 6 percent by that time.[76]

Republican politicians joined a growing chorus of those who wanted to change the old-age insurance program so that the huge reserves did not accumulate.[77] Senator Arthur Vandenberg, the most influential of these politicos, recommended that the payments of benefits should begin sooner than 1942, that the initial benefits should be more generous, and that payroll tax increases scheduled for 1940 should be postponed. Not only were the reserves a "positive menace to free institutions and sound finance," they were financed through a regressive payroll tax that penalized the poor. If the reserves were abandoned, sound finance and more liberal benefits could be achieved simultaneously.

The size of the contemplated reserve proved such an irresistible target because it revealed in stark relief the implications of a federal program that reached over half of the American population. In a labor force of about 49 million workers, social security promised to pay old-age benefits to nearly 27.5 million of them. Even modest pensions paid to such a large number of workers amounted to sums of money that dwarfed previous federal spending efforts in peacetime. To have $47 billion held in reserve for such a program staggered the American imagination. The figure represented eight times the amount of money then in circulation in the United States, nearly five times the amount of money in savings banks—enough money to buy all the farms in the United States, with $14 billion to spare. "Such a treasure—all in one place and conveniently eligible for Congressional raids through the years—is an utterly naive conception," wrote Vandenberg. "That it would remain intact and not suffer periodical depletions is more than human nature in a political democracy can rationally anticipate."

Pressing his political advantage, Vandenberg asked Arthur Altmeyer, at the beginning of 1937, if he would object to a commission inquiring into the matter. Altmeyer had little choice but to agree. This commission tested the political strength of the fledgling public sector, even before the old-age insurance program had really begun.

Altmeyer decided to call the bluff of Vandenberg and the other conservatives. "I think," he wrote the President, "it is possible not only to offset the attacks on the Social Security Act but really to utilize them to advance a socially desirable program." He thought it best to "go off the reserve with our eyes open" and increase benefits without lowering taxes. Altmeyer was aware that even liberal politicians, such as Robert Wagner, were growing restive over social security financing. The Roosevelt recession of 1937-38, which some attributed to the social security taxes being taken out of workers' paychecks, added to the tensions.

When Altmeyer attempted to have supporters of social security appointed to the commission (or advisory council), he met with considerable success. Senator Vandenberg insisted on the appointment of his two close advisors, including M. A. Linton, the actuary and insurance executive who had advised the CES in 1934. Altmeyer named the other employer, employee, and "public" representatives. In selecting the employers, he turned to Marion Folsom for help, and together they agreed on six people who represented the interests of the National Association of Manufacturers, the United States Chamber of Commerce and the National Retailers Association. BAC members Swope, Folsom, and E. R. Stettinius of U.S. Steel were among the businessmen eventually appointed. Folsom served as an unofficial spokesman for this group and as a conduit between the advisory council and the Business Advisory Council. Distinguished labor leaders, such as Sidney Hillman and Philip Murray, and academic enconomists, such as Paul Douglas of the University of Chicago, Sumner Slichter of Harvard, and Edwin Witte of the University of Wisconsin, joined the businessmen.[78]

When the advisory council met for the first time in November 1937, the social security staff prepared background memoranda that enabled the federal bureaucrats largely to determine the subjects under discussion. They controlled the agenda, if not the outcome. The complicated debates, often about what steps should be taken in the present to face contingencies that would arise far in the future, involved difficult calculations: Was a particular feature of the law better or worse than the possible alternatives?

The issues did not neatly fit a public and private dichotomy. Not a single member of the council wanted to repeal the social security legislation and return to a world in which only businessmen, the church, the states, and local charities protected families from destitution. Rather, they argued over which of several public approaches to take and how closely federal programs should follow private models.

In a revealing presentation, Murray Latimer, who had been on the Committee on Economic Security staff and worked for the Social Security Board, pointed out that state old-age welfare laws made average payments "not materially different" from those old-age insurance payments the Social Security Board would begin in 1942. People wondered, Latimer noted, why the returns for contributory social insurance should be no greater than for non-contributory welfare. The argument that social insurance was an earned "right" and welfare required a means test "carries little weight with the man who is paying and sees his neighbor getting substantial sums without so paying," Latimer said.[79]

At the time, some states paid old-age "pensions" to many of their elderly, undermining the notions that assistance carried a stigma and should go only to the needy.[80] Politics often entered the picture. At one point, for example, the governor of Ohio, involved in a political campaign, ordered a flat $10 increase in benefits to all of the elderly on the relief rolls. Not only did such behavior frustrate orderly administration and planning, it also, as Arthur Altmeyer noted, undercut efforts to expand social security coverage. Why should a group, such as farmers, want to be included, if they had to pay for the benefits which were not any better than welfare benefits?[81]

Liberals, such as Lee Pressman of the CIO, scoffed at the idea of orderly social planning. He said that the elderly "wanted to get some money each month to take care of their bread and butter so they can live." The notion of having two separate programs, one a means-tested welfare program and the other a social insurance program, made little sense to him. Like the followers of the Townsend Movement, Pressman believed that the object of social welfare was to get money into people's hands as quickly as possible and not to worry about long-range problems.[82]

Abraham Epstein made similar points when he appeared before the advisory council. By now an outspoken critic of the social security program, Epstein said that the fundamental flaw of the old-age insurance program was its slavish imitation of private insurance. "The entire conception of large reserves is derived from the fact that the framers of the Act have never understood the basic principles of social insurance and have merely adopted a governmental program of private insurance. . . . It is obviously ridiculous to have a governmental plan follow the principles of a private insurance company. Large reserves in a governmental insurance plan only mean double taxation," Epstein said.[83]

In a much more tempered way, R. A. Hohaus, an actuary of the Metropolitan Life Insurance Company, argued along similar lines. He attempted to explain, just as Epstein had, the differences between public and private insurance. Private insurance, he noted, was voluntary and the principle of "actuarial equity" was crucial. The federal government, by way of contrast, had the power to tax and it therefore should emphasize what Hohaus called "adequacy." Hohaus maintained that, "Just as private insurance would collapse if it stressed considerations of adequacy above those of equity, social insurance wil not remain intact if considerations of equity are emphasized more than those of adequacy." The government did not have the private sector's overarching problem of maintaining solvency, and that made all the difference: it could do things beyond the reach of the private sector.[84]

From a different philosophical perspective, economist Alvin Hansen made a similar point: "I don't see any reason why one has to assume that the workers are going to look upon this scheme essentially in the same way as they do upon the private insurance scheme."[85]

Using these justifications, social security officials proposed and the advisory council accepted recommendations that, when adopted by Congress, radically changed old-age insurance. During the April 1938 meeting, Douglas Brown, the former CES staff member and now chairman of the advisory council, unveiled Plan AC-12, which had been prepared by social security actuaries. Unlike previous plans discussed by the council, AC-12 contained provisions for benefits to be paid to the dependent children of a deceased worker. Furthermore, these benefits were to be based on a worker's "average" wages. In the original Social Security Act, all benefits were based on the total wages on which taxes were payable, which, in the jargon of social security, were called "credited wages." Plan AC-12 suggested a radical revision of this concept. In order to pay adequate benefits to dependent children, this new type of benefit would more closely resemble what the worker had been making at the time he died. If he had accumulated relatively little in his social security pension fund because of his youth, the new concept lessened the resulting penalty on his survivors.

The move reduced the similarity in treatment between two workers with the same wage records. The worker who died and left behind dependent children would get back more on his social security investment than would the worker who lived until old age, never married, and never had children. That was because planners now contemplated paying benefits to workers' dependent children, wives, and widows.

The contrast with the earlier law was striking. The 1935 law had featured a money-back guarantee. A worker's estate received a lump-sum payment, based on the deceased worker's contributions into the social security fund. Under the new proposals, workers were entitled to benefits for their wives, for their widows, and for their dependent children. Instead of a lump-sum payment in the event of a worker's death, a family would now receive payments based on the concept of social adequacy. If a man died after he reached retirement age and left behind no wife or children, his social security payments would simply stop, and his estate would receive nothing.

Here then was a shift from equity, the notion of getting back what you paid into the system, to a system that recognized certain social problems as more pressing than others and took steps to solve those problems. The council endorsed this new concept in social security: a concept which began to divorce public-sector social welfare programs from private sector models in a very significant way.

Adopted as part of the 1939 Social Security Amendments, this change in social security met with the qualified approval of the businessmen on the council. As had been the case on earlier councils, businessmen enjoyed an influence beyond their numbers. Simply put, they showed up for meetings and the labor people did not. At one crucial meeting, for example, none of the labor leaders showed up and nearly all of the businessmen attended. As a testy Edwin Witte noted, "With the two labor people invariably absent, the Interim Committee is in control of the anti-Administration men."[86]

Folsom, the principal business spokesman, wanted taxes reduced without extreme increases in benefits. As he told his fellow council members, "We are junking the contributory system for sometime in the future because we are afraid that the [state] old-age assistance is going to get very bad." Politicians, he said, would jump at starting federal Social Security benefits in 1940 and at the payment of benefits to "widows and orphans." The only question, he said, was which politician would take credit for the move.[87]

Folsom's views helped to put the 1939 amendments in perspective. By liberalizing benefits and beginning payments earlier, Congress reduced the size of the hypothetical Social Security reserve account, just as businessmen and others wanted. Businessmen gained an end to the reserve problem and an assurance that America's social welfare system would depend on social insurance rather than welfare alone. Social insurance, although it contained welfare features, still featured the fiscal discipline of payroll taxes paying for benefits. It could be expanded, but not as readily as alternative plans, such as the Townsend Plan. Social insurance also contained contributory-contractual features, in which benefits were based, however tenuously, on participation in the labor force. The administration gained an end to the political embarrassments caused by the reserve, as well as credit for liberalizing the system. It was a nice bit of quid pro quo bargaining, typical of the deals that would be struck in the years that followed.

DISABILITY INSURANCE

Even with much more money coming into the system than was needed, and even in the midst of a severe recession, the 1937-38 advisory council and the Congress still placed limits on the expansion of social security. Disability insurance illustrated just how far the public sector had come and just how far it had to go.[88]

Disability insurance was an implicit challenge to the private sector. Simply put, the provision of permanent disability insurance was beyond the capacity of the private insurance industry. They had tried to supply it and failed. One insurance executive explained that disability was an important risk against which to insure. "We thought we could do it," he said. In fact, permanent disability insurance had a long history within the insurance field.

In the 1920s, insurance companies sold record amounts of disability protection, but in the 1930s problems began to develop. Disability benefits, it became clear, were alternative income sources or tickets out of the labor force. In the 1920s, comparatively few workers availed themselves of this income source because they could make more money by working. When the depression arrived, more workers decided to cash in their tickets out of the labor force. A disability pension appeared attractive to unemployed workers earning nothing.

Of course, insurance companies tried to guard against the payment of many benefits by scrutinizing each claimant to verify disability. The economic hardships of the depression and the subjective nature of disability, however, overwhelmed these efforts. Insurance officials referred to the problem as one of "moral hazard." Not to put too fine a point on it, moral hazard meant that people cheated the insurance companies and claimed disability when they were merely unemployed—and who was to say where unemployment stopped and disability began?[89]

Because of the problem of moral hazard, the insurance companies lost a great deal of money on disability insurance in the 1930s. As a result, the companies refused to sell new permanent disability contracts. The statistics were staggering. In many companies disability claims increased 50 percent from 1929 to 1932 and in some cases 100 percent from 1929 to 1933. Such a high rate of disability caused companies to lose money. To use an example, in 1936 the Travelers Company of New York received $5.8 million in disability insurance premiums but paid over $7.3 million in benefits and other costs. In the twenty years between 1926 and 1946 the ten largest companies lost more than $500 million on disability. By 1946, of course, few companies offered disability insurance. As one actuary explained, "The small amounts of total and permanent disability now being used are on a very restricted basis to favorably selected groups and at relatively high premiums." Disability insurance had become unmarketable. Too few people wished to purchase the insurance at the market price to make it profitable.[90]

Before the late 1930s, the private-sector experience with permanent disability insurance would have warned off the federal government. The thrust of the federal government's social welfare efforts in the 1920s and the early 1930s had been to bring government practice in line with business practice. One clue to a public program's desirability had been its ability to be run along cost-efficient lines. If private insurance could not make disability programs pay, the presumption was that such programs were beyond the federal government's capability. The federal government's function was not to defy the verdicts of the marketplace, but to study those verdicts.

In the late 1930s, the Social Security Board and other planning components of the American social welfare system consciously defied the old wisdom and audaciously proposed a federal permanent disability insurance program. The first step in this process involved determining how much permanent disability there *was* in America. Public health technician I. S. Falk sent canvassers to cities across the country to make this determination. For the first time, federal planners moved ahead of private planners, investigating a problem before private parties had called that problem to the government's attention.[91]

The second step in designing a permanent disability program was to redesign the social security system to pay the new benefits. At the end of 1937 and throughout 1938 the Social Security Board produced a plan for permanent disability insurance programs, as part of its staff work for the advisory council. Like the other plans that the council considered, this one proposed a change of major importance. Specifically, a permanently disabled worker might receive more in benefits than a worker and his employer had paid in taxes. If the plan were enacted, the social security program could no longer be described in passive or conservative terms.[92]

The permanent disability plan forced the federal government to face the same moral hazard problem as the private insurance companies had faced. Not surprisingly, when Social Security officials presented the plan to Linton and the other insurance experts on the council, Linton told them that the plan was unworkable.

The showdown over this matter occurred in October 1938. Attempting to sound confident and reassuring, Arthur Altmeyer and I. S. Falk presented the plan to the council. "You have to go slow on this matter," Altmeyer began. He admitted, however, that the disability insurance plan marked a new departure. He also conceded that the board lacked the ability to predict the exact size of the future disability caseload. His own actuaries' best estimates varied by as much as 20 percent.[93]

Linton spoke after Altmeyer and Falk. If the board wanted to begin a disability insurance program, he argued, it should use the most liberal projections on the number of claimants. Because disability insurance would be the only part of the social security system without an age or means test, it would turn into a "dole." "If you want to adopt a Machiavellian plan to wreck the whole Social Security [system], just put in disability and let it run, especially during a period of depression," warned Linton.[94]

The Social Security Board's answer to Linton revealed the differences between the public and the private sectors. Public officials were not bound by private experience in undertaking new projects. Public social insurance could do things, such as protect against permanent disability, that private insurance could not. Profit considerations were irrelevant in public decisions. Social Security officials responded to institutional, rather than market, signals, and foreign social programs, rather than private American corporations, were the appropriate models for the Social Security Board. Every other country with an old-age insurance program also had a disability insurance program. "There must be some human need," Altmeyer told Linton, "or they wouldn't have coupled it up right from the beginning." Government, not private, plans served as the models.

The council remained unconvinced. On the road to liberal benefits, it stopped at disability. The council thought that disability insurance was too expensive a program to begin so early in the Social Security Board's life. In response to an accusation from Lee Pressman of the CIO that Brown lacked social concern, Douglas Brown said, "It is very simple. I feel that whole report is related to cost. To recommend benefits without some understanding of costs is like saying, 'I want an automobile, but I don't want to pay for it.' "[95] That precisely was the difference between social insurance and the dole. Social insurance related benefits to costs, and the dole did not. Congress apparently agreed with the advisory council. It passed the 1939 amendments with many liberal features, but without disability insurance.[96]

This setback failed to stop the board. After 1939 it continued to experiment with disability insurance and other proposals that extended federal control over social welfare. Federal personnel now saw themselves as practitioners of a distinctly public approach to social welfare programs.

THE NEW DEAL SOCIAL WELFARE SYSTEM

By 1939, with a little imagination, one could detect a clearly organized social welfare bureaucracy in the federal government. It had two centers: an income maintenance center in the Federal Security Agency (FSA) and a minimum standards center in the Department of Labor. The creation of the FSA in 1939, the first of the centers, reflected a long-standing desire to unite the federal departments concerned with social welfare. According to the FSA's own publicity, it was to be run along sleek, functional lines. It would serve "the special needs of people, not as members of diverse groups, but as individuals."[97] To accomplish this difficult task, it would use "the functional groups of constituent agencies for purposes of supervision to effect the greatest possible cooperation among those engaged in similar work."[98]

It sounded like a business merger, and in a sense it was. The Public Health Service came from the Department of the Treasury, the Office of Education from the Department of the Interior, and together with the previously independent Social Security Board they all became the Federal Security Agency on July 1, 1939.

The other center of this brave new bureaucracy, the Department of Labor's Bureau of Labor Standards, was a world removed. This bureau administered the Fair Labor Standards Act, the federal minimum-wage act passed in 1938. In this act Congress summarized and updated the American experience with minimum standard laws. A federal law replaced state laws. After the Supreme Court had declared minimum-wage laws for women unconstitutional in 1923, most states had abandoned them. By 1930 only eight such laws were still on the books and not declared unconstitutional. The depression revived interest in minimum-wage laws in part because some economists viewed such laws as an aid in recovery. Some states, most notably FDR's New York, passed new minimum-wage laws for women. These new laws ran into the old legal snags. In June 1936, the Supreme Court overturned the New York law. Less than a year later the Court overturned itself and declared a Washington state law constitutional. This decision supplied the momentum to the drive for a federal minimum-wage law, a task accomplished in the Fair Labor Standards Act.

The Fair Labor Standards Act differed in three significant ways from previous minimum-wage laws, and the differences transformed it into a new sort of labor law that served a different function than did Progressive Era laws. The first and most important diffrence was that the federal legislation covered men as well as women. Also, the federal law paid minimums that applied to all industries, although (reminiscent of NRA) industry committees could raise that minimum. Third, the federal law penalized employers who made their employees work more than forty hours a week by requiring overtime pay after forty hours. Some federal officials and congressmen thought this provision would help spread employment. The differences meant that minimum standards no longer needed to be localized or molded to the needs of each industry. Instead, a single minimum standard could apply to the entire country and could serve to measure the nation's economic progress. Significantly, the federal government's Bureau of Labor Standards would do the measuring.[99]

Although it looked as though the FSA and the Bureau of Labor Standards provided the nation with a rational bureaucratic structure, closer examination revealed a hollow shell. In the first place, responsibilities were not well articulated between the Department of Labor and the FSA. Programs such as unemployment insurance became battlegrounds between the two agencies.[100]

More important was the fact that the FSA was not the streamlined, functional agency it appeared to be. The major components of the agency—the Public Health Service and the Social Security Board—disagreed over such important matters as the proper financing of health insurance; nor did the FSA even contain all of the many government agencies interested in health. The Bureau of Indian Affairs, for example, continued its health program from within the Interior Department. Creating a new agency failed to erase years of incremental change within the federal government.[101]

In addition to these internal administrative problems, the Social Security Board's welfare proposals suffered from the conventional problems associated with the external political process. The first FSA administrator, for example, was an unannounced presidential candidate who hoped to succeed Roosevelt in 1940. Paul McNutt, a former governor of Indiana, felt no strong loyalty to the social security program. On March 28, 1940, he nearly delivered a speech to the National Industrial Conference Board in which he advocated a Townsend-style old-age pension to replace the social security program and the old-age assistance program. "Needless to say," Arthur Altmeyer wrote the White House, "we in the Social Security Board are shocked at the casual way seven years of planning and progress are brushed aside." Roosevelt killed the speech, but the incident revealed the disarray McNutt's appointment created.[102]

By then Roosevelt no longer worked with an acquiescent Congress. The recession and the court-packing plan decreased his political leverage. The fluid situation of 1935 no longer applied to the New Deal legislative program. No one seriously believed that the President would be able to push a broad new social program through Congress. Congressional opposition to the New Deal stemmed from many of the same sources as business opposition. Social experiment appeared to produce little in the way of substantive result. For all of the legislation, the depression persisted.

These factors slowed the momentum of the Social Security Board's federal social welfare program just as it was being articulated. The threat of war brought it to a dead halt. A conference held on December 19, 1939, revealed the President's mood. Roosevelt wanted to abandon a Social Security Board health insurance proposal and to ask Congress instead for a small hospital construction program to cover rural depressed areas. Despite two messages to Congress, the President failed to get even this small health program.[103]

Between 1933 and 1939, however, America's public sector grew up.

Temporary, emergency programs yielded to permanent ones. A group of influential planners decided to bypass the states and to challenge the private sector with new legislative proposals. But if industrial self-regulation was no longer central to America's social welfare plans, those plans still involved business and government cooperation. Fittingly, the period ended with the liberalization of social security, with its close links to private pension plans, and not with the adoption of a Townsend-style plan.

Furthermore, during the war, the federal government, despite its ambitious agenda for social security expansion, would encounter significant problems. Business and government cooperation would once again prove to be the order of the day.

NOTES

1. Bernard Bellush, *The Failure of the NRA* (New York: W. W. Norton, 1975).

2. Edward D. Berkowitz, *Disabled Policy: America's Programs for the Handicapped* (New York: Cambridge University Press, 1987), pp. 15-40.

3. Arthur Altmeyer, "The Proper Basis for Compensating Permanent Partial Disabilities," (n.d.), p. 5, Arthur Altmeyer Papers, Box 1, Wisconsin State Historical Society, Madison, Wisconsin.

4. *Fifteenth Annual Report of the Federal Board for Vocational Education* (Washington, D.C.: G.P.O., 1931), p. 64.

5. *Fourteenth Annual Report of the Federal Board for Vocational Education* (Washington, D.C.: G.P.O., 1930), p. 2.

6. *Annual Report of the Secretary of the Interior* (Washington, D.C.: G.P.O., 1937), p. 293; *Annual Report of the Secretary of the Interior* (Washington, D.C., G.P.O., 1933), p. 273; *Fifteenth Annual Report*, p. 69.

7. Mary Switzer to Malcolm Bryant, July 7, 1936, July 31, 1936, Switzer papers, Schlesinger Library, Radcliffe College (Cambridge, Massachusetts).

8. Ibid.

9. William E. Leuchtenberg, *Franklin D. Roosevelt and the New Deal, 1932-1940* (New York: Harper and Row, 1963), pp. 121-25.

10. For a general background, see Robert C. Nesbitt, *Wisconsin: A History* (Madison: University of Wisconsin Press, 1973), pp. 399-476, and the Wilbur Cohen Interview, Columbia Oral History Collection, New York, N.Y.

11. "John Bertram Andrews," pp. 32-34, in Walter I. Trattner ed., *Biographical Dictionary of Social Welfare in America*. Westport, Connecticut: Greenwood Press, 1986; Paul H. Douglas, *Social Security in the United States: An Analysis and Appraisal of the Social Security Act* (New York: McGraw Hill, 1936), p. 12.

12. Douglas, *Social Security in the United States*, p. 12.

13. Daniel Nelson, *Unemployment Insurance: The American Experience, 1915-1935* (Madison: University of Wisconsin Press, 1969), p. 128; Roy Lubove, *The Struggle for Social Security* (Cambridge: Harvard University Press, 1968).

14. Paul Raushenbush, "The Wisconsin Idea: Unemployment Reserves," *The Annals of the American Academy of Political and Social Science* 70 (November 1933): 70.

15. Idem.

16. For a revealing glimpse of this rivalry, see Paul Douglas's foreword to the Agathon Press edition of Abraham Epstein, *Insecurity: A Challenge to America—A Study of Social Insurance*

in the United States and Abroad (New York: Agathon Press, 1968), pp. v-xiv. We draw our description of Epstein from this source.

17. I. M. Rubinow. "The Ohio Idea: Unemployment Insurance," *Annals* (November 1933), p. 83.

18. Arthur M. Schlesinger, Jr., *The Coming of the New Deal* (Boston: Houghton Mifflin, 1959), pp. 302-03.

19. George Martin, *Madam Secretary: Frances Perkins* (Boston: Houghton Mifflin, 1976); Frances Perkins, *The Roosevelt I Knew* (New York: Viking Press, 1946), p. 57; Arthur M. Schlesinger, Jr., *The Coming of the New Deal*, p. 298.

20. Schlesinger, *Coming of the New Deal*, pp. 302-03.

21. The elderly have emerged as a central concern of social historians. See W. Andrew Achenbaum, *Old Age in the New Land* (Baltimore: Johns Hopkins University Press, 1978); David Hackett Fischer, *Growing Old in America* (New York: Oxford University Press, 1977); Carole Haber, *Beyond Sixty-Five* (New York: Cambridge University Press, 1983).

22. Deborah A. Stone, *The Disabled State* (Philadelphia: Temple University Press, 1984), pp. 48-51.

23. Kelley Loe, *An Army of the Aged* (Caldwell, Idaho: Caxton Printers, 1936); Committee on Old Age Security, *The Townsend Crusade* (New York: Twentieth Century Fund, 1936); Allen Brinkley, *Voices of Protest* (New York: Vintage, 1982).

24. Wilbur Cohen to Ervin I. Aaron, March 13, 1935, RG 47, Records of the Social Security Administration, National Archives, Washington, D.C.

25. W. Andrew Achenbaum, *Social Security: Visions and Revisions* (New York: Cambridge University Press, 1986), p. 202.

26. Perkins, *Roosevelt I Knew*; Edwin E. Witte, *The Development of the Social Security Act: A Memorandum on the History of the Committee on Economic Security and Drafting and Legislative History of the Social Security Act* (Madison: University of Wisconsin Press, 1963), p. 19; Arthur Altmeyer, *The Formative Years of Social Security* (Madison: University of Wisconsin Press, 1966), p. 11.

27. Altmeyer, *Formative Years*, p. 3.

28. Altmeyer, *Formative Years*, pp. 3, vii-x; Arthur J. Altmeyer, "The Industrial Commission of Wisconsin—A Case Study in Labor Law Administration," *University of Wisconsin Studies in the Social Sciences and History* 17 (1932); Wilbur J. Cohen and Robert J. Lampman, "Introduction," in Witte, *Development of the Social Security Act*, p. xi.

29. Witte, *Development of the Social Security Act*, pp. 4, 16, 23, 48-49.

30. Witte, *Development of the Social Security Act*, p. 112.

31. Ibid., p. 58.

32. "Suggestions for an Advisory Council," (n.d.), Altmeyer Papers, CES File 2, Wisconsin State Historical Society.

33. Witte, *Development*, pp. 48-49.

34. Edwin Witte to Members of the Technical Board, November 9, 1934, Murray Latimer Papers, George Washington University Library Special Collections, Washington, D.C.

35. Altmeyer, *Formative Years*, pp. 21-22; Witte, *The Development of the Social Security Act*, pp. 111-42.

36. Altmeyer, *Formative Years*, pp. 21-22.

37. Douglas Brown, *The Genesis of Social Security in America* (Princeton: Industrial Relations Section, 1969), p. 4.

38. Brown, *Genesis*; "Contributory Old Age Pension Plan: Receipts and Payments," Altmeyer Papers, CES File 1, Box 1, Wisconsin State Historical Society; "The Dead Sea Scrolls of Social Security," in personal possession of Robert J. Myers, Silver Spring, Maryland, contains a detailed list of the various plans that were considered. The government's lack of expertise is illustrated by its need to hire Latimer and nearly the entire staff of Industrial Relations Counselors, Incorporated, which was in the business of designing industrial pensions

for large employers, in order to study unemployment insurance and old age. The use of private organizations to compensate for the lack of research capability within the federal government is clearly demonstrated here.

39. Brown, *Genesis*, p. 8; J. Douglas Brown, *An American Philosophy of Social Insurance: Evolution and Issues* (Princeton: Princeton University Press, 1972), pp. 10-12; Eveline Burns Memoir, Columbia Oral History Collection, p. 52.

40. Brown, *Genesis*, p. 8.

41. Ibid., p. 15.

42. Schlesinger, *Coming of the New Deal*, pp. 302-03; Leuchtenberg, *Roosevelt*, pp. 130-33; Altmeyer, *Formative Years*, p. 3.

43. Wilbur Cohen to Joseph P. Harris, August 19, 1935, RG 47, National Archives.

44. Witte, *Development of the Social Security Act*, p. 40.

45. Witte, *Development*, pp. 88-89; Carolyn L. Weaver, *The Crisis in Social Security: Economic and Political Origins* (Durham, North Carolina: Duke Press Policy Studies, 1982), pp. 64-92.

46. Altmeyer, *Formative Years*, p. 23.

47. *Report to the President of the Committee on Economic Security* (Washington: G.P.O., 1935), p. 34; Witte, *Development*, pp. 93-94; Weaver, *The Crisis in Social Security*, p. 88.

48. Witte, *Development of the Social Security Act*, pp. 78-79.

49. Technical Board on Economic Security, "Minutes of the Executive and Old Age Security Committee," November 22, 1934, in Murray Latimer Papers, George Washington University.

50. Barbara N. Armstrong to Murray Latimer, January 22, 1935, Murray Latimer Papers.

51. Altmeyer to Secretary Perkins, May 9, 1935, RG 47, Chairman's Files, Box 11, National Archives.

52. "Companies Known to Favor Clark Amendment to Social Security Act," in Dr. Rainard B. Robbins, "Confidential Material Collected on Social Security Act and Clark Amendment," July 11, 1935, in Murray Latimer Papers. The list did not include Swope's General Electric, Teagle's Standard Oil of New Jersey, or Leeds's Leeds and Northrup. Leeds, Swope, and Teagle, like Folsom, whose company supported the Clark Amendment, were all BAC members on the CES advisory council.

53. Rainard B. Robbins, "Supplementary Report on the Proposed Substitute for the Clark Amendment to the Committee on Social Security of the SSRC," May 27, 1936, Murray Latimer Papers.

54. Paul Douglas, *Social Security in the United States*, pp. 271-91.

55. Marion Folsom to Rainard B. Robbins, December 18, 1935, Murray Latimer Papers.

56. M. A. Linton to Rainard B. Robbins, December 31, 1935, Murray Latimer Papers.

57. E. C. Henderson, actuary, Connecticut General Life Insurance Company to Rainard B. Robbins, January 9, 1936, Murray Latimer Papers.

58. T. F. Cuneen, Manager, Insurance Department, Chamber of Commerce, to Rainard B. Robbins, January 4, 1936, Murray Latimer Papers.

59. Memorandum for Mr. Winant, April 30, 1936, RG 47, Box 12, File 025, Chamber of Commerce, National Archives.

60. This episode and other formative influences on social security are related in Charles McKinley and Robert W. Fraser, *Launching Social Security: A Capture and Record Account* (Madison: University of Wisconsin Press, 1970), pp. 346-56. See also Caroline Weaver, *The Crisis in Social Security*, pp. 103-06 and Altmeyer, *Formative Years*, pp. 43-73. W. Andrew Achenbaum notes that as late as July 1, 1936, there were only fifty-three employees staffing the Bureau of Federal Old-Age Benefits (*Social Security: Visions and Revisions*, p. 205).

61. Altmeyer, *Formative Years*, p. 69.

62. John Corson to Arthur Altmeyer, May 16, 1938, RG 47, Box 11, Business Advisory Council File, National Archives.

63. *The United States News*, September 2, 1935, in Altmeyer Papers, Box 1, Wisconsin State

Historical Society.

64. McKinley and Fraser, *Launching Social Security*, pp. 33, 39; *First Annual Report of the Social Security Administrator* (Washington, D.C.: G.P.O., 1940), pp. 44, 45.

65. I. S. Falk Interview, Columbia Oral History Collection, pp. 74-76.

66. Witte, *The Development of the Social Security Act*, p. 29.

67. In the middle of congressional consideration of the Social Security Act, Edwin Witte had written Wilbur Cohen, "I am frankly doubtful about any estimates [of unemployment] our people make because they never stick to any one guess." Witte to Cohen, March 11, 1935, RG 47, National Archives.

68. This route was followed by Ida Merriam, who eventually headed the Research and Statistics Division of the Social Security Administration. She was recruited to the Social Security Board by Walton Hamilton, who served as the first research director after having taught at the Brookings Graduate School. For more on think tanks that house experts, see the forthcoming book by James A. Smith on the subject, prepared under the auspices of the Twentieth Century Fund.

69. Gaston Rimlinger, *Welfare Policy and Industrialization* (New York: John Wiley and Son, 1971), p. 232.

70. Laurence C. Elklund, "Mr. Social Security Loses His Job," *Milwaukee Journal*, April 11, 1953, in Wilbur Cohen Papers, Box 47, Wisconsin State Historical Society.

71. See the introduction in Altmeyer, *Formative Years*, and the material in the NRA File, Altmeyer Papers, Box 1—in particular Hugh S. Johnson to Wisconsin Industrial Commission, October 25, 1933.

72. Altmeyer's senior thesis at the University of Wisconsin, "Scientific Management and the Attitude of Labor," (1914) is available in Altmeyer Papers, Box 1.

73. "Cumulative Tax Collections, Benefit Payments, Net Excess of Tax Collections," (n.d.) and "Annual Appropriations, Benefit Payments and Reserves," (n.d.), File 025, RG 47, National Archives.

74. "Text of Governor Landon's Milwaukee Address on Economic Security," New York *Times*, September 26, 1936, p. 31.

75. Mark Sullivan, "Security or Income Taxes," *Washington Star*, November 1937 in File 705, Old Age Reserve 1937, Chairman's Files, RG 47, National Archives; Paul Mellon, "News Behind the News," Cleveland *Plain Dealer*, February 28, 1938; "The Reserve Fund," New York *Times*, September 5, 1938, p. 14; Jay Iglauer to Douglas Brown, March 7, 1938, File 025, RG 47, National Archives.

76. M. B. Folsom, address before Round Table on Industrial Relations, Chamber of Commerce, April 29, 1937, Murray Latimer Papers.

77. The following account of the 1939 amendments is drawn from Edward D. Berkowitz, "The First Advisory Council and the 1939 Amendments," in Berkowitz, ed., *Social Security After Fifty: Successes and Failures* (Westport, Connecticut: Greenwood Press, 1987), pp. 55-79.

78. Altmeyer to Witte, March 29, 1937, Edwin Witte Papers, Box 34, Social Security Correspondence, Wisconsin State Historical Society.

79. Statement of Murray Latimer before Advisory Council, November 5, 1937, in RG 47, Box 12, page 11, National Archives.

80. For a perceptive and well-researched analysis of this point see Blanche Coll, "Public Assistance: Reviving the Original Comprehensive Concept of Social Security," prepared for a conference on social security, Albuquerque, New Mexico, April 1985.

81. Altmeyer, *Formative Years*, pp. 74-78; Statement of Arthur Altmeyer before Advisory Council, October 22, 1938, Box 13, p. 11, RG 47, National Archives; the situation was highly chaotic and varied from state to state. More than half of the senior citizens of Oklahoma were receiving old-age assistance, but only 7.2 percent of the elderly in New Hampshire were—see Achenbaum, *Social Security: Vision and Revision*, p. 31.

82. Statement of Lee Pressman before Advisory Council, Box 12, February 18, 1938, p. 44, RG 47, National Archives.

83. Abraham Epstein, "Statement Before Advisory Council," December 10, 1937, Box 13, RG 47, National Archives.

84. R. A. Hohaus, "Memorandum for Meeting with Social Security Advisory Council," December 10, 1937, RG 47, Box 13, National Archives.

85. Statement of Alvin Hansen before Advisory Council, November 6, 1937, Box 12, pp. 48-49, RG 47, National Archives.

86. Witte to Altmeyer, April 2, 1938, Witte Papers, Wisconsin State Historical Society.

87. Remarks of Marion Folsom before Advisory Council, February 19, 1938, Box 12, pp. 9-10, RG 47, National Archives.

88. For much more on disability insurance, see Edward Berkowitz, *Disabled Policy*.

89. R. K. McNickle, "Editorial Research Report" 11 (1949) in Altmeyer Papers, Box 11; Wiliam G. Johnson, "Disability Income Support and Social Insurance," in *Disability Policies and Government Programs*, ed. E. Berkowitz (New York: Praeger, 1979).

90. E. A. Law, "Experience Under Ordinary Life Insurance," Appendix I to George W. Grange, 'Total and Permanent Disability Benefits Bearing on Extended Disability Benefits Under Social Insurance," Altmeyer Papers, Box 7.

91. I. S. Falk to Josephine Roche, May 23, 1935, RG 47, Records of the Social Security Administration, Accession 62A-82, Container 5, Washington National Records Center (Suitland, Maryland); I. S. Falk Interview, p. 197; George J. Parrott and Rollo H. Britten, "Scope and Method of the Nationwide Canvass of Sickness in Relation to Its Social and Economic Setting," *The National Health Survey: Scope, Method, and Bibliography* (Washington, D.C.: G.P.O., 1950); Britten et al., "The National Health Survey," *Public Health Reports* 55 (1940): 445.

92. The section of the records of the Social Security Administration housed in the National Archives details this matter fully. See, for example, "Specifications for Plan AC-14," November 15, 1938, RG 47, Records of the Executive Director of the Social Security Board, File 025, Box 138, National Archives. For a fuller discussion see Edward Berkowitz, *Rehabilitation: The Federal Government's Response to Disability* (New York: Arno Press, 1980) and *Disabled Policy: America's Programs for the Handicapped.*

93. W. R. Williamson, actuarial consultant, to Altmeyer, October 20, 1938, RG 47, Records of the Executive Director of the Social Security Board, File 025, Box 138, National Archives.

94. This discussion is drawn from the verbatim transcripts of the meetings of the Advisory Council. See also Gerald Morgan to Franklin D. Roosevelt, February 25, 1941, Altmeyer Papers, Box 3.

95. Brown quoted in E. Berkowitz, "The First Advisory Council and the 1939 Amendments," p. 71.

96. Advisory Council on Social Security, *Final Report*, Senate Document 4, 76th Congress, 1st sess. (Washington, D.C.: G.P.O., 1939), pp. 5, 19-21.

97. *Annual Report of the Federal Security Agency* (Washington, D.C.: G.P.O., 1944), p. xv.

98. *First Annual Report of the Federal Security Administrator* (Washington, D.C.: G.P.O., 1940), p. 2; *Second Annual Report of the Federal Security Agency* (Washington, D.C.: G.P.O., 1941), p. 2.

99. The literature on the Fair Labor Standards Act is voluminous, but see the Department of Labor's *Growth of Labor Law in the United States* (Washington , D.C.: G.P.O., 1962), pp. 107-34 for a good summary. Among the contemporary discussions of the law see Robert S. Allen, "Washington Sweatshop," *Nation* 145 (July 17, 1932): 63-64 and the New York *Times,* July 29, 1937, p. 12, and August 9, 1937, p. 3.

100. Edward Berkowitz, "Workers' Compensation and Vocational Rehabilitation," a report to the Interdepartmental Workers' Compensation Task Force (Washington, D.C.: G.P.O., 1975).

101. See the progress report of the Interdepartmental Committee to Coordinate Health and Welfare, January 3, 1936, Altmeyer Papers, Box 3.

102. Altmeyer to Steven Early, March 28, 1940, Altmeyer Papers, Box 4.

103. Arthur Altmeyer, "Health, Medical Care, and Disability," September 18, 1940, Altmeyer Papers, Box 2; Interdepartmental Committee to Coordinate Health and Welfare, "The President's Program for Construction of Hospitals in Needy Areas," January 30, 1940, Altmeyer Papers, Box 3.

7 | DIFFERENT WORLDS OF WAR

World War II produced a permanent change within the American welfare system. The war established the federal government as the major source of funds for social welfare projects. This change occurred without any appeal to political or economic ideology. More than anything else it resulted from the large increase, which accompanied the war, in the size and expense of the federal government. The size of government expenditures during the war years, for example, could only be comprehended by referring to previous levels of federal spending. Washington, as Richard W. Polenberg has noted, spent twice as much from 1940 to 1945 as it had in the preceding 150 years.[1]

Accustomed to regard increased federal expenditures as a temporary phenomenon, neither businessmen nor bureaucrats realized that war was the fiscal health of the state. After every modern war the size of postwar federal budgets never returned to their prewar levels, a trend that had begun with the Civil War. The years after World War II failed to contradict this trend; the only difference was in the magnitude of the change. New Deal spending in the years 1937 through 1941 averaged $9.2 billion a year. By the years 1947 to 1950, however, federal expenditures averaged $37.8 billion. A four-fold increase in government spending had occurred almost unnoticed.[2]

MOBILIZATION

At the beginning of the war mobilization, circumstances appeared to favor federal planners in their attempts to expand social welfare services through federal funds and control. The war mobilization that started late in 1939 came after a six-year period in which federal planners had gained self confidence. By the time of America's entrance into the war federal employees in the Social Security Board and the Public Health Service felt secure enough to recommend congressional passage of federally administered health and disability insurance. Such programs would supplement existing social welfare programs such as the old-age insurance program and the Fair Labor Standards Act. With the beginning of large federal expenditures during the war the fiscal means to accomplish bureaucratic ends bolstered bureaucratic self-confidence.

In this case the appearance of a secure federal bureaucracy was deceptive. Depression, not war, benefited federal welfare planners. The planners emerged during the depression with an appeal to provide security in a time of economic scarcity. Although the return of prosperity made it more possible to finance the security measures, renewed prosperity diminished the appeal of such measures. The very fact that Americans could now afford to finance their own security argued against the desirability of governmental welfare programs. The environment in which welfare programs operated—and in which welfare policies were conceived—had changed markedly.

Not only were social welfare measures in trouble, the war also threatened to destroy the entire New Deal. Roosevelt and other New Deal leaders gained support by appealing to people's fears about the economic situation. When the economic problems disappeared Roosevelt lost political support, as the 1942 elections revealed. In political, as well as social welfare terms, success bred failure.

For businessmen the war produced the exactly opposite situation— the ironies of the transition from depression to prosperity worked to the businessmen's advantage. Throughout the 1930s business disunity hindered efforts to stabilize the economy. The failure of the NRA accented this disunity. As a group, businessmen could agree only on the undesirability of most New Deal programs, and such negative sentiments generated little support from other groups. The war revived the businessmen. Their greatest periods of public success came not in coping with scarcity but, rather, in managing abundance. The return of abundance under wartime emergency circumstances made the businessmen's skills desirable again. These skills included one that had been developing since the beginning of the century—the maintenance of employee welfare.

If the war years revived business interest and ability to deliver social welfare services, they also made businessmen realize that federal funds would play an important role within the modern welfare system. Many of the social welfare issues of the war and postwar years involved a battle between businessmen and bureaucrats over the control of the system. In earlier years this battle had centered over the propriety of federal initiation of social welfare services previously supplied only in the private sector. Beginning with the war years, however, businessmen took the presence of the federal government for granted. The issue now became not who would fund welfare services but who would control the provision of those services. In gaining such control businessmen and members of other private groups enjoyed remarkable success.

Business success began in the early stages of the war mobilization. Faced with preparing the country for war Roosevelt and his advisers searched for ways to keep businessmen from controlling the process. By the end of the 1930s few businessmen enjoyed Roosevelt's unqualified blessings. The president and his administrators continued to consult men whom they regarded as enlightened business leaders. BAC members Edward Stettinius, W. Averell Harriman, and Gerard Swope were prominent within this small group. Other businessmen, however, found invitations to the White House difficult to obtain, in part because they continued to react strongly against what they referred to as the New Deal "experiment." Such men included Henry Ford, Ernest T. Weir, and Tom L. Girdler, joined by managerial capitalists Alfred P. Sloan, Jr. and Pierre S. DuPont. All appeared, in the eyes of the New Dealers, to be partially recovered patients gleefully throwing their crutches at the federal doctor.

The results of the administration's mobilization procedures were politically astute and administratively chaotic. Between August 1939 and January 1942 a bewildering series of mobilization boards appeared. The sequence included a War Resources Board composed entirely of big businessmen that gave way to a National Defense Advisory Commission composed of business and other leaders that was succeeded in its turn by an Office of Production Management (OPM). Added to the OPM a Supply Priorities and Allocation Board further expedited scheduling and delivery of war-related materials. In the crisis atmosphere immediately following Pearl Harbor, President Roosevelt created a War Production Board to serve as the central repository for mobilization efforts. Finally, in May 1943 the president authorized the creation of the Office of War Mobilization that survived the remainder of the war.[3]

Through this maze of agencies ran the thread of business expertise. Government remained dependent upon private businesses to supply the nation with the organizational skill necessary for the successful regulation of a complex wartime economy. In particular, government required the assistance of corporate leaders whose firms were organized well enough to allow them to leave their plants and headquarters for lengthy work in Washington with military, labor, and farm representatives. Businessmen who managed companies with national industrial perspectives proved of special value in this process.

The corporate leaders best able to afford wartime public service and transindustrial outlooks were well represented among the membership of the BAC. The council became a personnel agency for big business expertise throughout the war. The first businessmen called upon to head the early war mobilization agencies were BAC members such as Edward N. Stettinius, Jr. (U.S. Steel) and William S. Knudsen (General Motors). Top managerial staff from other firms long active in the BAC replaced this initial group. Donald M. Nelson of Sears, Roebuck, appointed to direct the War Production Board, exemplified the succession process. Nelson's participation underscored the federal government's dependence upon the management of larger corporations for war mobilization. Businessmen of Nelson's caliber constituted the only existent talent pool of men trained to make intricate allocation and production decisions. Sears, Roebuck's nationwide mail order and retail operations were, indeed, one of the most relevant models for wartime mobilization upon which businessmen and bureaucrats could draw.*[4]

Despite Roosevelt's contrary desires, businessmen controlled the war at home. By early 1942, businessmen streamed into Washington to man the specialized war agencies. A legion of industrial advisory committees sprouted, NRA style, to advise federal administrators concerning the requirements of particular industrial sectors. BAC members such as Sidney J. Weinberg of Goldman-Sachs formulated the membership lists of the boards. Within a shifting, unwieldy, and ultimately baffling series of boards, commissions, and councils representatives of larger American corporations assumed influential positions within the Washington establishment.

The collaboration between the federal government and the larger corporations yielded benefits for both parties. The federal government benefited from increased revenues. Government receipts rose from $7.1 billion in 1941 to $44.5 billion in 1945. Businesses profited handsomely from the fiscal conduct of the war. To insure the production of proper public goods by the private sector the government instituted outright subsidies, low-interest loans, cost-plus contracts (which proved spectacularly successful as devices to spread risk from

---

*The extent to which mobilization procedures were modeled upon the operations of larger private corporations is exemplified by the adoption of the "Controlled Materials Plan" in the summer of 1942. The plan, the centerpiece of the federal government's military mobilization drive, was based upon allocation and forecasting procedures developed earlier by General Motors and other large firms.

business to government), relaxed prosecution of antitrust cases, and accelerated depreciation allowances.

These inducements for business investment in the war helped to modify the nation's industrial structure and to fulfill a longstanding dream of industrial leaders. As a result of favored treatment in the receipt of war contracts the 100 largest American corporations assumed control of a substantially larger share of industrial output. By 1943 these firms accounted for no less than 70 percent of all war and civilian contracts. Between 1940 and 1943 the percentage of the total labor force employed in manufacturing establishments with fewer than 500 workers dropped from 52 to 38 percent. The percentage employed in corporations with over 10,000 workers rose from 13 to 31 percent. In the NRA period business leaders had only dreamed of such economic control. Now, with no special mandate from either the president or the people, the corporations gained that control with relative ease.[5]

THE WAR AND EXISTING SOCIAL WELFARE ARRANGEMENTS

During the war years the tone of government social welfare efforts changed. Conservatives succeeded in dismantling the New Deal programs that had become the domain of groups hit hard by the depression. Others worked to expand old programs by linking demands for increased federal funds with the successful pursuit of victory.. The welfare programs that benefited from these appeals carried either the wartime stamp of emergency or the cost-effective rationales characteristic of the 1920s. Such programs benefited from the war almost as much as the corporations and the federal government.

War made the early phases and the emergency segments of the New Deal irrelevant. Programs such as the WPA, that mobilized the unemployed to man public works projects, made little sense in an economy engaged in the mammoth public works project called World War II. With the eager assistance of Congress, Roosevelt killed WPA in 1942. In the same year Congress added the CCC and the National Youth Authority to the list of war casualties. Young workers had been among the first to be laid off during the depression. The war, however, revived the employment prospects of young workers to such an extent that state authorities reported widespread violations of child labor laws. In New York the number of boys and girls illegally employed increased four-fold. Even such disadvantaged workers as black youths found jobs in wartime.[6]

For the most part the programs that Congress and the president abolished had always been rationalized as temporary programs designed to cope with the depression. Other welfare programs with more permanent authorizations, such as those included in the Social Security Act, fared better during the war. Although welfare (also known as public assistance) payments stood at record low levels, public assistance programs remained on the statute books. Programs designed to improve the public health and to fight the incapacitating effects of disability in local communities not only survived the war but benefited from increased expenditures, and emerged from the war as stronger programs.

The fate of the vocational rehabilitation program revealed how the war could save a welfare program that had neared extinction in the 1930s. Beginning in 1940, reports arrived in Washington telling of new success in placing rehabilitated workers. In Alabama two large shipbuilding corporations had hired many of the state vocational rehabilitation agency's clients. In Arkansas employers eagerly sought the same handicapped workers they had turned down a few months before. During the first year of the war the number of successful rehabilitations exceeded those of the previous year by 60 percent. As one rehabilitation official noted, "The large-scale employment of the physically handicapped is now becoming a reality." Another official attributed "imperative importance" to the hiring of handicapped workers. Their labor was necessary to win the war.

When the changes in employment patterns became clear to the state rehabilitation officials they proposed an expansion of the rehabilitation program at federal expense. Late in 1941 the officials induced a congressman to introduce a bill that asked for increased rehabilitation funds and the creation of a strengthened office of vocational rehabilitation with special responsibility to rehabilitate war casualties.

FSA administrator Paul McNutt and President Roosevelt had even more ambitious plans for the rehabilitation program. Days after the attack on Pearl Harbor, McNutt convened a special conference on rehabilitation programs that was attended by the top echelon of the federal welfare bureaucracy. The conference led to the appointment of a committee that drafted the administration's rehabilitation bill. Congress received this bill in July 1942.

The administration's rehabilitation bill reflected a desire to centralize power within the federal government and to expand the scope of federal social welfare services. The bill broadened the rehabilitation concept. Previously, rehabilitation counselors had used federal money to counsel handicapped clients and to secure jobs for them. The new bill would allow the program to provide medical care for the clients at federal expense. Here was an unprecedented federal subsidy for medical care, although it applied to a limited clientele. The price of the new federal generosity was increased federal control of the program. The bill would allow the FSA administrator, representing the federal government—not the vocational rehabilitation administrators, who represented the state governments—to control the provision of the new medical services. In addition the bill would treat the civilian and veteran disabled population alike. A unified rehabilitation service would deal with both groups. The occupationally oriented federal bureaucracy in the Veteran's Administration would, therefore, lose power to the functionally oriented bureaucracy of the FSA.[7]

In July 1943 Congress passed a civilian rehabilitation bill that completely altered the Roosevelt administration's proposals for federal control of a unified rehabilitation service. The veterans, for example, managed to gain a separate rehabilitation bill with more attractive provisions than those in the civilian bill. The rhetoric of one senator who complained that he had never seen veterans groups so upset "as they are about the proposal to take a simple matter of veterans rehabilitation and pitchfork it into a scheme affecting all of the people of the United States" reflected Congress's perspective on the matter. Further diluting the bill, Congress took the power to control the medical aspects of the rehabilitation program away from the FSA and awarded it to the state rehabilitation officials. The bill, which President Roosevelt signed on July 6, 1943, supplied state officials with more federal funds to provide increased services to the physically handicapped.

Washington, in short, would bankroll welfare programs administered by others, instead of directly controlling programs. By 1944 the federal share of the nation's total expenditures for vocational rehabilitation rose above 50 percent for the first time in the rehabilitation program's history. Within social welfare programs war appeared to increase state power quite literally at federal expense.

In the war and postwar years, then, federal officials repeatedly found themselves in the anomalous position of providing funds for other peoples' projects. It seemed as though federal officials had gained confidence in their ability to plan and administer just when their services were no longer required. The fate of the National Resources Planning Board (NRPB) highlighted the trend.

For the decade after its creation in 1934 the NRPB remained quiet and uncontroversial, undertaking surveys of flood control, soil erosion, and public works projects in an uncoordinated attempt to coordinate federal programs. Composed mainly of academics the NRPB was chaired by Frederick A. Delano, a retired railroad magnate and Roosevelt's uncle. Welfare capitalists Henry S. Dennison and Beardsley Ruml, the treasurer of R. H. Macy Company, sat on the agency's advisory board. The balanced nature of the board's membership and the limited range of its projects kept the board out of the public's consciousness.

When the board ventured into long-term social welfare planning, however, it made more of an impact. In 1939, when the board became part of the newly-created Executive Office of the President, Roosevelt asked it to undertake a long-range study of work relief and social security policy. Although the board conducted the study in its usual plodding style, conservatives feared that the NRPB's recommendations might seek to broaden the scope of the postwar public welfare sector. The board confirmed these fears early in 1943 when it released its report. Largely the product of painstaking research by Columbia University's Eveline Burns, the long report contained more factual reporting than policy recommendations. Among these recommendations, however, was a call for the federal government to become the employer of last resort, particularly for veterans, and "to guarantee, and, where necessary, underwrite, equal access to [social and economic] security, equal access to education for all, equal access to health and nutrition for all, and wholesome housing conditions for all."

Few people paid any attention to the report's ringing phrases—phrases that described goals, rather than specific policies. The report's relative obscurity, however, failed to save it from attacks by congressional conservatives who disapproved of even rhetorical ventures into government social welfare planning. In late 1943 Congress destroyed the NRPB by the simple method of denying it funds. By this time federal planning initiatives lay in complete disarray.

The fate of the Wagner-Murray-Dingell Bill underscored this disarray. First proposed in 1943, the bill embodied legislation to federalize and liberalize the American social welfare system. Under its terms the state unemployment programs would be taken over and administered by the federal government. State workers' compensation programs would largely be superseded by federal temporary and permanent disability insurance programs, and most ambitious of all, the federal government would initiate a health insurance program. Congress reacted with indifference. The bill never came close to passage. Some of its measures, such as disability insurance, did not become law until more than a decade later; others, such as federal temporary disability insurance, never became law.[8]

THE COMMITTEE FOR ECONOMIC DEVELOPMENT
AND VISIONS OF THE POSTWAR WORLD

Through the Committee for Economic Development (CED), organized business quickly filled the gap left by the impotence of federal social welfare planners. The committee was a carefully planned organization. It provided a bridge between two styles of welfare capitalism: the private planning of the 1920s, and the mixture of private and public planning of the postwar era. The work of the CED proved that big business was learning to accept big government as a silent partner in social welfare operations.

The creation of the CED exemplified the process of change within welfare capitalist circles. In January 1942, R. R. Deupree of Procter & Gamble, then serving as the chairman of the BAC, argued that postwar challenges could not be met by a "laissez faire philosophy or uncontrolled forces of supply and demand." This sentiment appeared with such regularity in businessmen's speeches as to become a platitude. Herbert Hoover would have felt comfortable with the line. "Intelligent planning" by businessmen, continued Deupree, was a necessary preparation for the public policy debates that would occur during the "reconstruction period" after the war. If businessmen were to retain their influence in welfare councils they should arrive early, propose consistently, and determine the course of postwar economic policy.[9]

This aspiration to logic persuaded Jesse H. Jones, a conservative Texas banker and Roosevelt's Secretary of Commerce, to invite prominent businessmen for discussions of the postwar economic order. The roster included Owen D. Young, Marion B. Folsom, Ralph Flanders (Jones and Lamson Company), Charles R. Hook, Chester B. Davis, Harrison Jones (Coca-Cola), and James Ford Bell (General Mills). A majority of these men were active or retired members of the BAC.[10]

At the same time three other men were trying to obtain support for the creation of a businessmen's research bureau to forward planning after the war. The three were Paul Hoffman of Studebaker Motors, Robert M. Hutchins, president of the University of Chicago, and William Benton, the founder of a famous advertising agency. Composed of managers from the nation's 100 largest corporations and top-flight academic economists the bureau would become a center for the formulation and dissemination of enlightened capitalist opinion to academic, business, and government leaders.[11]

Secretary of Commerce Jones and the BAC members agreed with the proposal. On September 3, 1942 the CED was legally incorporated to achieve the aims of Hoffman, Benton, and Hutchins. The objectives of the organization included initiating "studies into the principles of business policy and of public policy which foster the full contribution by industry and commerce to the attainment and maintenance of high and secure standards of living for people in all walks of life through maximum employment and high productivity in the domestic economy." No less than 14 of the first 20 trustees of the CED were active members of the BAC at the time of their appointment. Three of the remaining six trustees were apponted to the BAC in short order. Jesse Jones described the membership of the BAC as "in fact, co-sponsors" of the CED.[12]

Like the BAC, the CED was an institutional expression of American welfare capitalism. Although, unlike the BAC, the CED was a private organization, the committee received free office space in the Department of Commerce. The office symbolized the desire of the CED to provide a framework for compromise between businessmen and bureaucrats. For years liberal corporate managers such as Dennison, Folsom, and Harriman had argued that businessmen should concentrate upon controlling the location of power in a mixed system in which both public and private agencies worked to preserve mass social welfare. In early public statements CED leaders expressed support for the employment and old-age pension programs that BAC members had helped to formulate. They accepted the necessity of federal public works spending and they cautiously supported short-term deficit spending.[13]

As in the past, however, welfare capitalists proposed that private welfare systems remain the model for public welfare systems. They created no agenda for new federal welfare programs; instead, they proposed cooperative efforts in which the government relied upon enlightened elements in the private sector to determine what actions to take in the welfare field. Such planning as occurred in the postwar world should supplement, rather than supersede, the market system. The only difference between the CED and earlier welfare capitalists concerned money. The CED tacitly agreed to the propriety of federal spending for appropriate social welfare projects. Washington should finance, but it should not seek to control.*

HARRY S. TRUMAN AND THE END OF EXPERIMENT

The political changes that followed Franklin D. Roosevelt's death in April 1945 helped speed the growth of welfare capitalist influence over the upper levels of the federal bureaucracy. Harry S. Truman proved willing to defend existing public welfare programs, but was unwilling to create new ones. Concerned with the growth of the federal government during 15 years of domestic and international crisis, Truman and his aides generally opposed experiments that would increase the size of the federal bureaucracy.† The American people had been through a lot of experiments,

---

*Gerard Swope and H. S. Dennison were exceptions to this "more federal money, but not more federal control" rule in the late 1940s. Both were considerably more interested in Western European welfare strategies than were their corporate peers. Swope, for example, supported national health insurance by the end of World War II. Both men believed that Scandinavian or Western European-style "welfare state" programs posed no important danger to capitalism. In this belief both men were decidedly "eccentric."

†In 1933, paid civilian employees of the federal government totalled approximately 600,000. By 1940 that number had risen to just over 1 million. When Truman assumed office in 1945 war

Truman remarked privately early in his presidency. They now desired a rest from them.[14]

Acting on these principles the new administration made haste to achieve amicable relations with the big business community. BAC member W. Averell Harriman returned from his post as wartime ambassador to the Soviet Union to become Secretary of Commerce. Fellow BAC member John W. Snyder, a St. Louis banker and Truman's close friend, became Secretary of the Treasury. Snyder, in turn, used his influence with the president to enable the BAC's Thomas B. McCabe (Scott Paper Company) to succeed Marriner Eccles as chairman of the Federal Reserve Board. Meanwhile, BAC and CED members Will Clayton, Paul Hoffman, and Lucius D. Clay assumed important administrative and advisory positions.[15]

The most notable pieces of federal welfare legislation identified with the Truman Era highlighted business-government rapprochement on welfare policy. The "GI Bill of Rights," passed into law with bipartisan support in 1944 provided housing, educational, retirement, and disability benefits to 16 million servicemen and their families. Despite the breadth of the program, businessmen and bureaucrats viewed it in traditional terms. Veterans of World War II who engaged in worthy activities deserved to be reimbursed from the federal treasury for services rendered, as earlier generations of soldiers had been. The GI Bill was, in fact, an extended workers' compensation benefit for those who endured the trauma of war.

The GI Bill possessed the additional advantages of not requiring a large federal bureaucracy to administer it. The federal treasury paid benefits directly to veterans, and federal authorities did little to control the way in which the benefits were spent. As long as veterans enrolled as full-time students in the high school, college, university, or vocational program of their choice they accrued educational benefits. Government, in effect, subsidized the operations of the private educational marketplace. Few businessmen, congressmen, or academicians raised their voices against this large increase in federal welfare expenditures. They failed to perceive the GI Bill as welfare legislation.[16]

The Full Employment Bill of 1946, another of the postwar pieces of social welfare legislation, owed much to the postwar reconversion proposals of the NRPB, but very little to Truman or his top policy advisers. The federal government, the bill's liberal congressional sponsors believed, should guar-

---

had boosted the number to 3.8 million. Demobilization speedily reduced the total to 2.1 million—850,000 of whom worked in a vastly-enhanced/war/defense sector. This postwar situation contrasted sharply with the breakdown of federal civilian employees in 1933. At that time just under one-half of federal employees (287,000) had worked for the post office—and only 100,000 for war/defense-related agencies. By 1948, however, only one-quarter of federal employees worked for the post office (475,000). Twice as many now worked for war/defense agencies. "Other" federal civilian employees had risen from 200,000 (1933) to 700,000 (1948).

antee full employment in the United States. Washington bureaucrats should forecast the yearly performance of the American economy and outline fiscal and monetary strategies useful for achieving full employment. Levels of federal investment, expenditure, and taxation should then be arranged in a manner consistent with this economic goal.

The Full Employment Bill expanded on New Deal welfare precedent by allowing for a clear and continuous federal presence in the management of the industrial economy. Businessmen failed to support this proposed extension of federal welfare responsibility. Smaller businessmen grouped in the NAM and the U.S. Chamber of Commerce reacted viscerally. They spoke of communists in the federal government. Corporate managers who belonged to the BAC and the CED were more sophisticated. They spoke of modifying the full employment proposal. CED leaders Beardsley Ruml and Ralph Flanders cooperated with congressional conservatives to replace the bill with their own proposal.

The CED-backed proposal passed Congress and became the Employment Act of 1946. Federal responsibilities to guarantee full employment were replaced with a call for "maximum" employment of those willing and seeking to work "in a manner calculated to foster and promote free enterprise." The legislation failed to define full employment. The act created a Council of Economic Advisers within the executive branch to advise the president concerning economic policy and to prepare an annual report of the state of the nation's economy. But the law established no machinery for translating governmental proposals into action. In the terms of the legislation, federal administrators "fostered" and "promoted" but failed to act.

Organized business retained the primary responsibility for the creation of the good society, as the welfare capitalists of the CED and BAC had hoped it would. The first two chairmen of the Council of Economic Advisers enunciated glowing visions, to mix a metaphor, of steadily expanding cooperation between business and the federal government to maximize production, income, and profits. These visions, glowing or not, blurred an important point. "Among the industrial democracies of the world," Daniel Patrick Moynihan later concluded, "the United States alone had not instituted a postwar economic policy that gave the first priority to continued full employment. Accordingly, it became impossible to base other social policies on the presumption that all able-bodied persons in need of income would [be able to] obtain it first of all by working."[17]

HEALTH: THE EXCEPTION PROVES THE RULE

In the field of health Truman and his advisers mounted a coordinated effort to expand New Deal welfare procedures. Their efforts to broaden the federal government's role as a health service provider resulted in a further increase in federal expenditures, but no increase in the scope of direct federal controls. Once again Congress upheld the principles of welfare capitalism.

By the end of 1945 health care was among the goods and services in demand by a public anxious to consume the things that had been rationed during the war. Applied technology had improved the quality of medical care during the war and resulted in widespread use of new wonder medicines such as sulfa drugs to reduce battlefield casualties. People reclaimed a faith in technology that had been lost since the 1920s. If American brains, organization, and money could produce an atomic bomb, equally spectacular results could be achieved in saving civilian lives. MIT's Vannevar Bush, administrator of the wartime Office of Scientific Research and Development, posed one of the era's rhetorical questions when he inquired of a congressional committee, "How many penicillins await the touch of scientific genius to bring them to light?" Sensing the comparative political advantages of capitalizing upon this growing interest in medicine Truman proposed adoption of the Roosevelt administration's health program, including medical research, national health insurance, and disability insurance.[18]

The resulting battle was savage. In health, as in no other area of public welfare policy, Truman persisted with his legislative proposals and went farther in support of a comprehensive federal medical insurance program than Roosevelt had ever gone. The American Medical Association (AMA) reacted to Truman's proposals by charging that they formed part of a more general conspiracy against the American way of life. In 1945 the AMA's journal announced that attempts to broaden direct federal control over the medical profession through the creation of a program of compulsory sickness insurance was "the first step toward a regimentation of utilities, of industries, of finance, and eventually of labor itself." This kind of legislation, AMA spokesmen concluded, marked the first step toward fascist totalitarianism and the "downfall of the nation." Unimpressed by such rhetoric Truman and his advisers pushed on anxious, if nothing else, (as Truman confided to an aide) "to scare those doctors and make them do something" by demanding more federal programs than were ever likely to be passed.[19]

Truman lost the battle. His health proposals were shredded by a Congress wary of efforts to expand the public presence in the welfare field. The unsuccessful fight for federal health and disability insurance, however, obscured the fact that other, indirect, forms of federal involvement in the medical field were established in the postwar era and that the medical profession supported those involvements.

Like business organizations such as the BAC and the CED, the AMA recognized the advantages of federal involvement in the health area as long as Washington confined itself to financing programs created and controlled by private interest groups. Throughout the late 1940's the AMA, joined by the American Hospital Association and other medical groups, cooperated with officials of the FSA and the Public Health Service to create legislation that increased federal expenditures but that left the leaders of private medical associations with the primary responsibility of deciding how public money should be spent.

Passage of the National Mental Health Act of 1946, the first major piece of postwar medical legislation, illustrated this process. The act originated when J. Percy Priest, a congressman from Tennessee, approached the Public Health Service for information on mental health programs. Mary Switzer, a bureaucrat who worked for the FSA, presented Priest with mental health legislation that she had drafted with the help of the National Committee for Mental Hygiene, a private lobbying group, and the Menninger brothers, directors of the Menninger Clinic in Topeka, Kansas. The draft bill, later enacted without substantial revision, granted federal money to state health departments to improve mental health facilities. Private nonprofit institutions such as the Menninger Clinic received funds to perform mental health research and train professional personnel. The Public Health Service gained a major new agency, the National Institute of Mental Health, to serve as a center for research and a clearinghouse for information. The powers of federal administrators, however, were limited by the appointment of a National Advisory Mental Health Council composed of recognized private authorities from the field. Mary Switzer, for the FSA, and Karl Menninger, for the mental health specialists, agreed that federal administration of mental health programs was unwise. Instead, federal officials should confine themselves to dispensing funds for progams formulated and administered by state governments or organized medical groups.[20]

Late in 1946 this trend toward federal assistance for organized medicine continued with the passage of the Hospital Survey and Construction Act of 1946 (Hill-Burton Act). The legislation allowed federal funds to be used for underwriting hospital construction. It also created a Federal Hospital Council that reviewed construction plans, awarded money, and helped federal officials set national minimum standards for adequate hospital care. Despite President Truman's insistence that the Federal Hospital Council be limited to advising the Public Health Service, the council, half of whose members represented "fields pertaining to hospital and health activities," possessed binding power over the state plans. Far from fearing the extension of federal power implied by the Hill-Burton Act the AMA commented favorably on the act and claimed credit for its passage.[21]

Federal money, of which the AMA approved, differed from federal control, of which the AMA disapproved. As long as private interest groups maintained primary responsibility for the expenditure of public money they proved willing to cooperate with federal officials to pass legislation to finance worthy welfare activities undertaken by the states, localities, or private groups. By 1950 the National Heart Institute and the National Institute of Dental Research had joined the National Institute of Mental Health in the circle of diseases and medical specialties that benefited from federal largesse. Federal bureaucrats wisecracked about the "disease-of-the-month-club," but financing for medical interest groups continued unabated. By the 1947-48 academic year federal money accounted for one-quarter of all the research funds supplied to private medical schools. In 1949, 6 percent of the $679 million spent to build hospitals came from the Hill-Burton program. With little public fanfare the federal government had become a major force in financing, if not administering, the operations of the American medical profession.[22]

CONCLUSION

In the decade between 1940 and 1950 wartime emergency, the death of Roosevelt, and postwar political stresses undermined the efforts of bureaucrats in the federal government to expand the scope of direct public welfare responsibilities at the expense of the states or organized private groups. Conservative revival at home denied Truman the political leverage necessary to enact Roosevelt's unfilled agenda in the area of health and disability insurance. An unexpected postwar economic boom eased fears of a return to depression conditions and undermined efforts by liberal Democrats to pass full-employment legislation. Wartime mobilization provided corporate managers such as those grouped in the BAC and the CED with a lengthy reintroduction to partnership with federal bureaucrats and allowed welfare capitalism to recover both stature and internal cohesion in the nation's policy councils.

If war provided new legitimacy for the operations of organized business it also produced a vastly expanded federal government. As a result the war cemented a new relationship between businessmen and bureaucrats. The leading edge of business opinion recognized the government's permanent presence in the field of welfare policy. Enlightened businessmen tried to capture federal funds for projects that met with business approval. A project granted that approval typically allowed private discretion over public funds. In the postwar era businessmen enjoyed great success in molding public policy to their own specifications. Within the bureaucracy, however, a growing discontent developed over the course of welfare policy. In the 1950s the bureaucrats would attempt to reassert their control over welfare policy by engaging, if necessary, in what some Washington observers called "bureaucratic hardball."

NOTES

1. Richard W. Polenberg, *War and Society: The United States, 1941-1945* (Philadelphia: Lippincott, 1972), pp. 5-36, 154-83.

2. J.R.T. Hughes, *The Governmental Habit: Economic Controls from Colonial Times to the Present* (New York: Basic Books, 1977), p. 209.

3. Eliot Janeway, *The Struggle for Survival: A Chronicle of Economic Mobilization During World War II* (New Haven: Yale University Press, 1951); Bruce Catton, *The War Lords of Washington* (New York: Harcourt Brace, 1948); and H. M. Somers, *Presidential Agency: The Office of War Management and Reconversion* (Cambridge, Mass.: Harvard University Press, 1950) cover the bureaucratic infighting thoroughly.

4. For specifics of the "Controlled Materials Plan" see Alfred D. Chandler, Jr., "The Large Industrial Corporation," in *Institutions in Modern America*, edited by Stephen E. Ambrose (Baltimore: Johns Hopkins University Press, 1967), pp. 92-94.

5. Janeway, *Struggle for Survival*, pp. 163-66; Carl Monsees, "Industry Advisory Committees in the War Agencies," *Public Administration Review*, 3 (1943): 257-58; John Morton Blum, *V Was for Victory: Politics and American Culture During World War II* (New York: Harcourt, Brace, Jovanovich, 1976), pp. 118-23; Somers, *Presidential Agency*, pp. 40-41; Geoffrey Perrett, *Days of Sadness, Years of Triumph: The American People, 1939-1945* (Baltimore: Penguin, 1974), pp. 64-74, 173-85; Polenberg, *War and Society*, pp. 139-40.

6. Polenberg, *War and Society*, p. 79; Mary E. Switzer, "The Federal Security Agency and the National Defense Program," *National Rehabilitation News* 5 (1940): 5; William W. Alexander, Leonard Outhwaite, and Thelma McKelvoy, "Policy on the Employment of the Physically Handicapped in War Industries," January 17, 1942, OF 504, Roosevelt Library, Hyde Park, N.Y.

7. Edward D. Berkowitz, "Rehabilitation: The Federal Government's Response to Disability, 1935-1954," (Ph.D. diss. Northwestern University, 1976), p. 102.

8. On the National Resources Planning Board, see Charles E. Merriam, "The National Resources Planning Board: A Chapter in the American Planning Experience," *American Political Science Review* 37 (December 1944): 1079-80; Otis L. Graham Jr., *Toward a Planned Society* (New York: Oxford University Press, 1977), pp. 53-57; Patrick G. Brady, "Towards Security: Postwar Economic and Social Planning in the Executive Office," (Ph.D. diss. Rutgers University, 1975). For the developments that led to the proposal of the Wagner-Murray-Dingell Bill see John F. Corson to Regional Directors, March 31, 1940, and Marianne Sakman to I. S. Falk, October 16, 1940, RG 47, Office of the Commissioner, Chairman's Files, 1935-1942, 056.11-056.12, National Archives; Altmeyer, *Formative Years*, pp. 146-54.

9. Robert M. Collins, "Positive Business Responses to the New Deal: The Roots of the Committee for Economic Development, 1933-1942," *Business History Review* 52 (Fall 1978). One of the best sources for business thought and action in the immediate postwar period is the Harry Truman Library in Independence, Missouri. The papers of Louis Holland (especially Box 76), Paul Hoffman (especially Box 40), Will Clayton, and John W. Snyder cover the evolution of the Business Advisory Council and Committee for Economic Development activities in the period.

10. For primary source materials on these developments, see Record Group 40, File 102517/36, National Archives, Washington, D.C. See also Karl Schriftgeisser, *Business Comes of Age: The Story of the C.E.D.* (Englewood Cliffs, NJ: Prentice Hall, 1960), p. 6; Bascom N. Timmons, *Jesse Jones: The Man and the Statesman* (New York: Holt, 1956), p. 280.

11. Collins, "Positive Responses to the New Deal"; Schriftgeisser, *Business Comes of Age*, pp. 13-19; William Benton to Paul Hoffman, September 22, 1941, October 8, 1941, December 22, 1941 in Paul Hoffman Papers, Box 40, Harry S. Truman Library.

12. "Business Leadership for Freedom and Growth: The Committee for Economic Develop-

ment: Purpose, Organization, Accomplishments," (CED, New York, 1958), p. 22; Jesse Jones to S. Clay Williams, June 25, 1942, Record Group 40, File 102517/36, National Archives; David Eakins, "The Development of Corporate Liberal Policy Research in the United States, 1885-1965," (Ph.D. diss. University of Wisconsin, Madison, 1966), chapters 7-11.

13. William Benton, "The Economics of a Free Society: A Declaration of American Economic Policy," *Fortune* 30 (October 1944): 163-65. Liberal BAC members H. S. Dennison, Ralph Flanders, Morris Leeds, and A. L. Filene held CED-style views during the New Deal. See their *Toward Full Employment* (New York: Whittlesey House, 1938). Complete background on the gestation of the book is contained in the Ralph Flanders Papers, Syracuse University, Syracuse, New York.

14. Bert Cochran, *Harry Truman and the Crisis Presidency* (New York: Funk and Wagnalls Company, 1973), pp. 117-20. *Historical Statistics of the United States: Colonial Times to 1970*, vol. 2 (Washington, D.C.: G.P.O., 1976), p. 1102.

15. Alonzo L. Hamby, *Beyond the New Deal: Harry S. Truman and American Liberalism* (New York: Columbia University Press, 1973), p. 295; Robert J. Donovan, *Conflict and Crisis: The Presidency of Harry S. Truman, 1945-1948* (New York: W. W. Norton, 1977), pp. 347-48, 419; Howard Sitkoff in *The Truman Period as a Research Field: A Reappraisal*, edited by R. S. Kirkendall (Columbia, Missouri: University of Missouri Press 1974), pp. 84-88. For critiques of Truman's actions regarding reconversion see Barton J. Bernstein's articles "The Removal of War Production Board Controls on Business, 1944-1946," *Business History Review* 39 (Summer 1965): 243-60; "The Debate on Industrial Reconversion: The Protection of Oligopoly and Military Control of the Economy," *American Journal of Economics and Sociology* 26 (April 1967): 159-72; "The Truman Administration and the Steel Strike of 1946," *Journal of American History* 52 (March 1966): 791-803. For Truman's relationship with Averell Harriman see Box 37, Name File, Postpresidential Papers of Harry S. Truman, Truman Library, Independence, Mo.

16. Perrett, *Days of Sadness*, pp. 338-39. David R. B. Ross, *Preparing for Ulysses: Politics and Veterans during World War II* (New York: Columbia University Press, 1969) is the standard source.

17. Graham, *Toward A Planned Society*, pp. 88-90; Daniel Patrick Moynihan, *The Politics of a Guaranteed Income: The Nixon Administration and the Family Assistance Plan* (New York: Random House, 1973), pp. 94-95; Schriftgeisser, *Business Comes of Age*, pp. 96-97. For a critique of Truman's economic views by the second man that he appointed to head the Council of Economic Advisors created under the terms of the Employment Act of 1946 see Leon Keyserling's Oral History Memoir, pp. 160-61, 203, Truman Library, Independence, Mo.

18. Theodore G. Klumpp, "What Are We Willing to Pay for Health?" New York *Times*, November 18, 1945; Vannevar Bush before the "Joint Hearings of the Subcommittee on Commerce and the Senate Committee on Military Affairs Concerning Post-War Programs for Scientific Research"—both in the General Records of the Department of Health, Education, and Welfare, Record Group 235, General Decimal Series, 1944-1950, 056-60, Box 93, National Archives, Washington, D.C.; Interview by Edward D. Berkowitz with Wilbur J. Cohen, September 20, 1975, Ann Arbor, Michigan; Arthur Altmeyer, *The Formative Years of Social Security*, pp. 153-54. For postwar receptivity to medical research on the part of businessmen see "Beyond the Atomic Bomb," a special supplement to *Fortune's* issue of September 1945.

19. Robert J. Donovan, *Conflict and Crisis*, pp. 125-26.

20. Mary Switzer to Karl Menninger, March 14, 1945, Switzer to Watson Miller, November 15, 1946, Switzer Papers, Schlesinger Library, Radcliffe College; Cambridge, Mass. Interview with Joseph Hunt, December 9, 1974, Washington, D.C.; Watson Miller to Harry Truman, April 1, 1945, November 1, 1945; March 15, 1946, July 1, 1946—all in Record Group 235, General Records of the Department of Health, Education, and Welfare, General Decimal Series, 1944-1950, 011.4; Public Law 487 (The National Mental Health Act).

21. Watson Miller to Harry Truman, October 19, 1945, August 1, 1946; Truman to Clarence F. Lea, January 31, 1946—all in Record Group 235, General Records of the Department of Health, Education, and Welfare, General Decimal Series, 1944-1950, 011.4; Victor Johnson to Mary Switzer, December 20, 1946, Watson Miller to F. J. Bailey, August 7, 1946, Switzer Papers; Public Law 725 (The Hospital Survey and Construction Act).

22. Data on research funds from "Minutes of the Meeting of the National Advisory Health Council," October 22, 1949, Record Group 235, General Records of the Department of Health, Education, and Welfare, General Decimal Series, 1944-1950, 025, Box 33. Data on hospital construction grants from Judith R. and Lester B. Lave, *The Hospital Construction Act: An Evaluation of the Hill-Burton Program, 1948-1973* (Washington: American Enterprise Institute, 1974), p. 16.

8

BACKING INTO THE FUTURE: SOCIAL WELFARE IN THE 1950s

During the 1950s the social welfare system took its present shape. To use the word "system" in this connection may be to imply a degree of cohesion and rationality that was not present in the way that Americans made or executed social welfare policy. For in the 1950s America's system contained two conflicting approaches to social welfare problems. The first of these, a cost-efficiency approach, advocated by businessmen and their allies, viewed the federal government as a financier and expediter of the efforts of states, localities, and private groups. The second, a service provider approach, held by bureaucrats and their allies, perceived the federal government's aim as the provision of comprehensive welfare assistance directly to the populace. When the Eisenhower administration came to Washington in January 1953 it faced the task of determining what, now, was normal in the welfare field. In attempting to answer this complex question the Republicans, as had so often been true of the Democrats before them, backed into the future while looking toward the past.

GOVERNMENT AND THE WELFARE CAPITALIST REVIVAL

Postwar prosperity made possible the corporate profits and tight labor markets that nourished welfare capitalism. The profits could be invested in educational and other measures that made workers more productive and valuable to the firm. The tight labor market made it important to retain workers a company had in its employ, particularly the ones in whom the company had invested money for training. By providing workers with secure working environments and a feeling of creative accomplishment, in other words by engaging in welfare capitalism, this objective could be met.

These considerations led firms such as General Electric, General Motors, and IBM to lead the postwar welfare capitalist revival. The words welfare capitalism had, however, become passé. The modern corporation no longer made use of a term that had originated in a distant era when employers began putting clean towels in washrooms; rather, in a professionalized managerial style, they offered their employees "fringe benefits." The term originated during World War II when federal officials discouraged wage increases but allowed companies to grant nonwage or "fringe" benefits. Among the important fringes that began during the war and continued to be popular after the war were annual vacations, medical care, recreation programs, life insurance, and housing.

Larger firms could afford to be more innovative in their approach toward fringes. In 1948, for example, General Motors started to incorporate cost-of-living escalator clauses in contracts. At the same time General Electric redesigned and widened its employee pension system. IBM put a large number of its employees on a yearly salary and ended worker dependence upon an hourly wage. It was almost as if these firms were consciously demonstrating that the true American welfare state lay within the large and progressive American corporation. Surveying the fringe benefit developed in the postwar decade one commentator wrote that the corporations were on the way to "converting themselves into welfare states."[1]

The fringes extended beyond the tangible economic benefits described above to include efforts to modify worker behavior through industrial psychology. Continuing the work of Elton Mayo and his followers, new researchers investigated the causes of industrial problems such as absenteeism and labor turnover. The number of firms found to be making use of psychological testing techniques, for example, grew from 14 percent in 1939 to 50 percent in 1947. By 1952 the number reached 75 percent. Such behavior modification techniques contributed to enhanced feelings of worker satisfaction with the terms of their employment.[2]

The usual chorus of approval accompanied this welfare capitalist revival. By late 1949 *Fortune* magazine, long a source of enlightened corporate expression, was strongly advocating a renewal of welfare capitalism as an organizational alternative to a further expansion of the welfare state. In the following years the magazine urged larger corporations to establish "human engineering" or personnel management programs based upon those of General Electric or IBM. In 1951 *Fortune's* editors published a special issue of their magazine devoted entirely to the renewal of a welfare capitalist presence in the nation's affairs. Later published as *USA: The Permanent Revolution*, the issue prophesied never-ending capitalist economic and social advance: a non-Marxist revolution in industrial procedures that would produce economic abundance on a scale that would obliterate social conflict.[3]

Feelings of satisfaction applied to unions as well as to management. A vicious wave of strikes had occurred after World War II. Fringe benefits played a large role in the strikes, with powerful unions demanding more health care and job security. John L. Lewis' United Mine Workers and Walter Reuther's United Auto Workers, among others, had won comprehensive health care for their members, and as a result had entered into partnership with management as a social service provider.[4]

The fate of the Truman administration's national health insurance proposal demonstrated how the satisfaction of private parties undercut support for new public welfare measures through which Washington could expand its influence at the expense of private parties. Shortly after Truman's stunning victory in 1948, Arthur Altmeyer of the Social Security Board received surprising news from Michael Davis, a public health expert affiliated with a health insurance lobbying organization whose letterhead celebrities included Gerard Swope and RCA's David Sarnoff. Davis informed Altmeyer that he had just learned that the United Mine Workers would not support Truman's health insurance bill. John L. Lewis preferred the system of private health security that his union had just obtained for itself to a more general system of public health security administered by the federal government. If John L. Lewis led a move away from national health insurance, Davis concluded, "it would be a very serious blow." The blow soon fell, and the Truman administration's efforts to obtain health insurance failed. Satisfied with the fringe benefits that unions had obtained for themselves, key elements of the organized labor movement proved reluctant to attempt to transfer them to the mainstream of the American labor force. The growth of welfare capitalism in the form of fringe benefit programs administered by both labor and management threatened to end the drive to expand the federal social welfare system.[5]

Attempts to expand the federal segment of America's welfare system, however, followed a different dynamic than did efforts to maintain existing public sector welfare programs. In the late 1940s and early 1950s public programs that already existed continued to expand despite the growth of private welfare programs. To borrow an expression from game theory, bureaucrats and businessmen no longer engaged in a zero sum game. The game was much more complicated. At the margin (where the federal system was to be expanded, such as in the field of national health insurance) bureaucratic gains were often businessmen's losses. But behind the margin (within existing public sector welfare programs) bureaucratic gain was often businessmen's gain as well.

The record of the public assistance program illustrated this perplexing phenomenon. When public assistance was first created under the terms of the Social Security Act of 1935 many federal bureaucrats believed that the federal grants-in-aid to the states for the relief of needy children, blind people, and elderly persons would only be a temporary welfare phenomenon. Once the depression ended and old-age retirement benefits began reaching most of the nation's aged citizenry, the public assistance program could be largely, if not completely, phased out.

Public assistance, however, failed to follow the path that welfare experts hoped to lead it down. Rising divorce rates and massive migrations of rural populations to central cities began to pose new types of welfare dilemmas to the postwar United States. Seeking to deal with these dilemmas federal administrators reluctantly began to accept the public assistance program as a permanently necessary "second line of defense" against life's hardships. Indeed, by the late 1940s public assistance payments were costing the federal treasury more than they had in the 1930s. During an unprecedented postwar boom, public assistance payments reached record levels.[6]

Both businessmen and bureaucrats believed that they had an alternative for the public assistance program. The businessmen thought that the employment security provided by the private labor market in a steadily expanding economy would limit the need for public assistance. The bureaucrats, at least those concerned with administering the Social Security Act, argued for an orderly expansion of social insurance as a less costly approach to the problem of need than the unplanned and unmanageable public assistance program. Congress responded to both constituencies. The businessmen benefited from tax policies aimed at accelerating the growth of job openings in private labor markets; and the bureaucrats won their contest to expand their social insurance programs. Public assistance payments, however, continued to grow. In a time of expanding social welfare expenditures all types of established social welfare programs expanded.[7]

The fact that both private and public social welfare expenditures increased was in large part a function of the fact that both systems derived their revenues from the joint business-government venture called the cold war. Disparate government bureaus and many private corporations joined together for the common purpose of conducting an undeclared war against what was perceived of as a global ideological invasion. The change within government engendered by the cold war was expressed in the changed use of the term "security."

In the late 1930s, when the Federal Security Agency was created, people understood the word "security" to apply to social welfare measures. Security meant enough money to eat, to secure shelter, and to purchase health care. As the 1940s progressed, however, the word took on meanings connected with the military. Security now meant freedom from communism or atomic annihilation. When, for example, General Dwight Eisenhower wrote publicly that "my immediate apprehension is that our own people may be inclined to relax in the security effort . . . the indispensable element in progress toward a stable peace," no one thought that he was referring to housing or income maintenance.[8]

Providing security through permanent military mobilization required large government budgets and a continued partnership between business and bureaucrats. Average American military expenditures in the years immediately after World War II were eight times the size of average prewar expenditures measured in constant dollars. In 1949 Washington was spending $13 billion for defense. By 1951 military expenditures totalled $48 billion. For the remainder of the decade, despite repeated efforts to find a way out of the fiscal conundrum, defense costs continued to average approximately $44 billion per year.[9]

Cold and hot wars, the objects of all the military spending, served to tighten the interlocks between businessmen and government officials that had existed since the 1930s. The BAC, for one, used its status as a bridge between the White House and the boardroom to influence the tone of economic policy. Opposition to price controls and excess profits taxes on the part of BAC members Marion B. Folsom, Fred Lazarus (Federated Department Stores), Blackwell Smith (Arthur Kudner, Inc.), and John D. Biggers (Libbey-Owens-Ford Glass) muted the Truman administration's efforts in these directions. Key industries, in particular petroleum, came to enjoy a "formal and apparently permanent return to the inner structure of the federal government."

Quick passage of the Defense Production Act after the outbreak of war in Korea in 1950 highlighted the trend toward partnership between big business and the state. Under the terms of the new legislation the antitrust laws were suspended, NRA-style, for industries connected with the national defense. The law also created a National Defense Production Authority within the Department of Commerce to enroll businessmen in an elaborate system of industrial advisory boards. By the end of 1950, 68 boards had been created. Only two years later a total of 554 existed, most of which are still with us. To reassure businessmen further, Truman did not insist upon labor representation on the defense production advisory boards.[10]

With so many points in common, businessmen and bureaucrats conducted some social welfare projects and experiments together. In the late 1940s and early 1950s many of the experiments involved special efforts to transform public assistance recipients into self-reliant members of the private labor force. Although most of these experiments emphasized the need for local administration of social welfare programs, they applied new technology supplied by the federal government to old welfare programs.

One of the experiments took place in Knoxville, Tennessee, a city with welfare dilemmas of a type encountered in many other localities. In Knoxville the benefits of the cold war took the form of the Oak Ridge atomic energy plant. Despite this high-powered economic boost Knoxville continued to suffer a high incidence of public assistance cases. A local vocational rehabilitation counselor decided to mobilize the community in a campaign to drastically lower public assistance payments. Doctors, social workers, and businessmen joined together to put the old, blind, disabled, and welfare mothers to work. One Washington official said that as a result of Operation Knoxville, as the program was called, the city was "setting the pace for the whole country . . . relief rolls are down, production and employment are up."[11]

Operation Knoxville attracted the support of those who believed in marshaling resources at the local level to put people to work. They saw Operation Knoxville as a constructive alternative to existing federal programs that appeared to them to pay people not to work. Businessmen were well represented among the supporters of this decentralized, efficiency-oriented approach. So, too, were the administrators of public sector welfare programs that had been created before the New Deal. The federal bureaucracy's own Office of Vocational Rehabilitation, a creation of Hoover's New Era, enthusiastically endorsed Operation Knoxville and many similar local welfare ventures.

In 1951 the director of the Office of Vocational Rehabilitation sent a special team to Knoxville that included a wide range of specialists: doctors, social workers, psychologists, and employment specialists. This team interviewed a group of ten public assistance clients who agreed to submit to tape-recorded interviews and to be the subject of local radio broadcasts. The experts worked on the clients' cases for two days. On the third day they turned the clients over to a local team and trained that team how to apply modern psychologically oriented social work, in the broadest sense of the term, to the problems of welfare recipients in Knoxville.[12] Not unlike the cold war itself, Operation Knoxville was an exercise in what many regarded as the best means to secure the country against communism: public officials keeping citizens productive and self-reliant by working together with traditional American institutions such as Kiwanis clubs and local chambers of commerce (the 1920s had, by this time, acquired the patina of tradition). If the armed forces needed complicated weaponry to keep America secure from outside attack, so the social welfare experts needed the wide-ranging methods of psychiatry and labor market analysis to turn back welfare, the persistent enemy that attacked America from within.

Operation Knoxville exemplified a social welfare style that by the 1950s had hardened into a conservative consensus among enlightened business managers and professionals. The consensus rested upon the perceived need for efficiency in the federal government's social welfare operations. Efficiency, to the conservatives of the 1950s, often meant cost reductions by the federal government. An efficient federal welfare program should address the needs of a well-defined constituency and contain incentives to limit expenditures. Programs financed from Washington but administered at the local level were believed to meet these criteria more often than programs administered at the federal level. In businessmen's eyes federal administrators remained vulnerable to demands for the expansion of welfare programs, and expansion meant increased costs. This vulnerability stemmed from the lack of fiscal restraint within the federal government. Federal officials, in short, could buy increasing amounts of political popularity with increasing amounts of welfare expenditures; local officials could not. Local governments, like businesses, needed to maintain balanced budgets; the federal government could run a regular deficit. Freed from the objective of reducing costs, federal officials were extremely likely to mismanage social welfare programs and oversupply welfare services.[13]

The conservative consensus of the 1950s resembled the social welfare attitudes of progressive businessmen in the 1920s, the ones who had applauded federal grants-in-aid for vocational education. By the early 1950s, however, the mainstream of big business opinion had reached the point where liberal entrepreneurs such as Gerard Swope and Henry S. Dennison had been during the New Deal era. Businessmen now accepted the fact of the federal government's continuing presence and responsibility in the field of social welfare. This presence was presumed to be more of a financial than an administrative phenomenon, but presence it was.

The continuing debates over a federal disability insurance program demonstrated how far the conservative mainstream of the 1950s had moved beyond the accepted social welfare wisdom of the Hoover era. Conservatives now spoke of the "over-expansion" of Washington's social security system, rather than advocating the abolition of that system. Instead of merely opposing any form of public action to deal with problems of disability, conservatives now advocated a means of dealing with it that would not expand the scope of direct federal controls in the welfare field. Rather than creating a federally funded and administered disability insurance program, conservatives argued that increased attention be paid to the disabled through the creation of a public assistance program specifically oriented toward them.

Public assistance payments, it should be recalled, were federal grants-in-aid to local governments. While these local governments ran the resulting programs, Washington's role remained that of a passive banker. Such an indirect federal approach to disability, businessmen believed, would keep federal efforts efficient precisely because federal officials would not be the ones determining who was—and who was not—a truly disabled individual. Instead, local officials would perform that crucial administrative function. These officials, in turn, would have the most interest of any element of the public sector in holding "doubtful or fraudulent claims to a minimum." This would be the case because local government officials were most closely analogous to private profit-maximizing and budget-balancing businessmen or so, at least, announced the welfare capitalists appointed to a Social Security Advisory Council in 1948, a group that included the BAC's Edward N. Stettinius Jr. and Albert Linton, the Provident Life Insurance Company executive, who had argued against any form of public sector disability insurance program only a decade before.[14]

The businessmen's logic also persuaded the leadership of the AMA. Since the 1930s, the AMA had consistently opposed a federally financed and administered disability insurance program. If ever Washington bureaucrats involved themselves in providing direct welfare services to the disabled, the AMA's secretary said, it would be but the first step toward a "total national compulsory sickness program." Disability, in short, was the Trojan Horse that could let national health insurance within the gates. "We must always," the AMA official concluded, "oppose any [disability] program which places a brake upon the incentives of the sick and disabled to desire recovery."[15]

A public assistance program oriented specifically toward the disabled met the AMA's need; and the AMA's secretary joined Stettinius and Linton in backing what in technical terms was called "aid to the permanently and totally disabled." Just to make sure that Washington got the point the secretary added that the resulting welfare program "should always be administered on a local level" with federal help only "when a need can clearly be shown."[16] Here, again, was a testimony to the fact that the issue, so far as businessmen and their allies was concerned, was no longer the propriety of federal aid for the disabled, or other classes of welfare recipients. The issue was, instead, the form that federal aid should take. As long as federal welfare initiatives remained as indirect as they were in the majority of public sector welfare programs, businessmen supported these initiatives. But when Washington attempted to expand the scope of its direct power and authority, business opposed its efforts.

THE ADVENT OF EISENHOWER

If the Republicans, who came to power in 1953 on the strength of Dwight Eisenhower's nonpartisan appeal, had a special quality to offer in managing the social welfare system, they believed it was their ability to manage federal programs efficiently along lines suggested by the conservative consensus. The theme of efficient management dominated the early discussions among members of the new administration. Mismanagement of the social welfare system, which had characterized the Truman years, would end during the Eisenhower years. The new administration's confident tone came through in its first budget forecasts. By cutting waste, Republican planners would reduce veterans expenditures almost 10 percent by 1957. Social security and other civilian welfare expenditures would remain approximately the same, even though population was rising fast, because major expenses for public assistance "could undoubtedly be cut by better administration." The Republicans entered office, then, with an optimistic faith in their ability to tame a previously untractable public sector through prudent management.[17]

What constituted good management? Between 1953 and 1956 a Republican answer to this question emerged: Good management began at the top. In place of Truman's tendency to intervene personally in legislative battles and upset bureaucratic planning Eisenhower substituted "an orderly system of operation." Government was to be more businesslike, and less political. Once a problem was identified its solution became the responsibility of an individual, a department, or a special interagency group. The group or individual named responsible then worked through a chain of command until a decision memo reached the president's desk. The approach of Truman and Eisenhower toward health care revealed their different styles. Truman's personal interest in health insurance led him to make health insurance a fiercely partisan issue. Eisenhower stayed aloof from legislative battles and relied extensively on solutions to the problems of health care that his advisors brought to him. Truman's scrappy manner, the Republicans believed, led to the granting of special favors to groups with whom the president sympathized and to uneven, incremental change within the social welfare system. By contrast, Eisenhower's more reserved, non-partisan approach produced rational solutions, well coordinated with existing programs, to social welfare problems.[18]

In the conservative tradition, government left as much as possible to the localities and to private enterprise. Revealing his views to one of his early supporters, Eisenhower wrote of the "great difference between local as opposed to central control . . . local government cannot print and cheapen money in order to cover up or pay for mistakes."[19] Once in office the president expanded on this theme. "We rely," he said, "on the good sense and local knowledge of the community and will therefore decentralize as much as possible. . . . We know that you are far more knowledgeable than Washington as to the nature of your local needs . . . as the local partners in any enterprise, you will be incessantly concerned with efficiency and economy—something which we are promoting in all federal enterprises."[20]

If the government did intervene in local affairs, good management meant that it offered help through services, rather than cash grants. The service approach cost less; encouraged communities to help themselves, rather than depend indefinitely on the federal government; and tended to be less easy to abuse. The service approach was directed at a specific problem. Cash could be used for anything and, therefore, could easily be mismanaged.

Research and development of new products and social welfare techniques was one of the most important services the well-managed government offered its constituents. In an economic report to Congress the administration noted with some pride that, although many federal expenditures were being cut, research and development expenditures continued to grow. "Outlays on the building of new knowledge must continue," the report said, "they are our surest promise of expanding economic opportunities."[21] This statement implied that the federal government played an important role in the economy. It acted as a spark to private enterprise.

In a 1956 book on modern Republicanism, Arthur Larson, an undersecretary of Labor, captured the Eisenhower administration's social welfare style. The administration's talent lay in reconciling opposites. According to Larson the government had a definite responsibility "for the general welfare of people," but it should address this direct responsibility indirectly "with a maximum of private and local content and a minimum of centralized control." This conjunction of opposites led Larson to his synthesis: The new Republicanism combined "provision against . . . personal risk . . . with actual strengthening of both individual values and business vigor." It combined federal aid to education, roads, health, safety and relief with "building up rather than chopping away of state responsibility and stature." Washington might finance, but others administered and controlled.[22]

By 1956, then, the Republicans (or at least the administration) had an intellectual explanation of their social welfare purposes. As the administration's record revealed, however, achieving those purposes was considerably more difficult than stating them. The task required the aid of people with expertise in social welfare programs; not the group that had created the New Deal, but a group that had learned the difference between constructive and destructive government aid. The leaders of welfare capitalism were the logical choice.

The welfare capitalists had not been far from Washington throughout the war and cold war eras, although they retained the most influence over economic and defense production policy. In the Eisenhower administration they gained extensive influence over social welfare policy as well. Perhaps the businessman who mattered most in this area was Marion Folsom. The Eastman Kodak executive began as an undersecretary of the Treasury and then became the head of the newly-created Department of Health, Education, and Welfare (HEW) in 1955. The very existence of this department underscored the businesslike, sensible approach of the administration. Social welfare policy should be the concern of a functionally organized department, and a former personnel officer had just the right sort of expertise to run such a department.[23]

In addition to Folsom the administration relied extensively on two sons of prominent welfare capitalists. The head of the civil service, that entry point into government employment, the government's personnel office, was Philip Young, the son of General Electric's Owen D. Young. The undersecretary at HEW was Nelson Rockefeller, son of John Rockefeller, Jr. It was as if the leadership of government and welfare capitalism was passing to a new generation. Unlike their fathers, the sons had decided to skip the business phase and to begin with the government.[24]

EXPANDING SOCIAL SECURITY COVERAGE

What specifically did the administration do? The answer to this question must begin with what the administration did *not* do: It did not abolish the social security system. The reason for this lack of action involved an important accomplishment of the Truman administration. In 1950, Congress passed the most significant amendments to the Social Security Act since 1939.

As a result of these 1950 amendments, the old-age insurance program became America's most successful social welfare program. That had not been the case earlier. As late as 1940, federal social welfare programs, such as social security, remained relatively small. In 1940, for example, total government spending for social welfare amounted to 9.2 percent of the country's gross national product. Yet in that year the nation spent more than six times as much on state workers' compensation payments as on federal social security. Veterans programs, products of a tradition in which only a select few received benefits, cost fifteen times as much as social security in 1940 and remained more costly until the middle of the 1950s.[25]

In the 1940s, old-age insurance was a money-making machine for the federal government, yet it still encountered serious problems. As the labor force expanded, more people paid into the program. As wage levels rose, more and more workers paid the maximum amount of money into the system. The result was an increase in the amount of money coming into the system, even though Congress refused to raise the level of Social Security taxes and the taxable wage base (the $3,000 limit on a worker's wages subject to the Social Security tax). The amount in the social security trust fund grew steadily during the decade, increasing from $2 billion to well over $13 billion.[26]

Arthur Altmeyer and the people who worked for the social security program viewed their progress in far less sanguine terms. They failed to get what they wanted from Congress in three different senses. Congress refused to make retirement benefits more liberal, to extend coverage to new groups, or to expand the range of benefits beyond old age and into health and disability. By the end of the 1940s, social security administrators spoke in terms of a crisis. In a careful memoir published in 1966, Arthur Altmeyer, who directed the social security program from 1937 until 1953, wrote that the events of 1949 would be "decisive" for the survival of social security as he understood it: a program in which workers and their employers contributed into a fund and "earned" their old age pensions.[27]

With the social security trust fund in such robust shape, why did Arthur Altmeyer worry? His fears were old ones, going back to the Townsend movement and other efforts to expand welfare rather than social security. (The distinction here as elsewhere was between contributory pensions, as in social security, and noncontributory pensions, as in welfare and the Townsend Plan). Jane Hoey, the federal bureaucrat in charge of welfare, had explained the basic problem as early as 1936. She worried that rules that restricted welfare payments to the poor would be liberalized until such payments came to be regarded as basic rights for the elderly. If that happened, then the distinction between welfare (noncontributory) and social insurance (contributory) would collapse, and it would never be possible to put old-age insurance into effect. Altmeyer agreed, concerned that Congress would legislate flat grants—unrelated to worker and employer contributions into a social security fund—to the elderly in the style of the Townsend Plan. If that happens, "we will sink," he said.[28]

Altmeyer's fears persisted in the 1940s. Welfare proved to be at least as popular as social insurance during the entire decade. As no less an authority than Robert Ball, who ran the social security program from 1961 to 1973, has noted, "social security just was not very important." If a senator wanted to gain credit for helping the elderly, he introduced a bill to pay more old-age assistance.[29] As Altmeyer observed, more than twice as many people were on the state welfare rolls, receiving old-age assistance, than were receiving retirement benefits from the federal government under social security as late as 1950.

The reasons had to do with the passage and implementation of the two programs. Old-age assistance covered any needy elderly person; social security limited coverage to industrial and commercial workers who had contributed into the system. Congress refused to raise social security benefits significantly; many of the state legislatures did not hesitate to respond to their elderly constituents by raising the level of old-age assistance. By the end of the 1940s just over a fifth of the elderly received old-age assistance payments and in a few states it was over half. The surprising result was that the average monthly welfare payment was $42 in 1949, compared to an average social security benefit of $25.[30]

America had not yet come to accept social security as its primary means of providing aid for the elderly, and a strong possibility existed that a different form of pension, one based more directly on need, would replace the social insurance principles of social security. That in turn would make it more difficult to extend social security into new areas, such as health insurance. It made little sense to provide health insurance through the social security program when many people were not covered by social security nor interested in being covered. As one of Truman's advisors noted in 1949, the "race between insurance and [noncontributory] pensions" was "nip and tuck."[31] Congressmen echoed these sentiments. "We are at the crossroads," said Representative Thomas Kean of New Jersey. "The [state] old-age assistance program has grown by leaps and bounds." Representative Doughton of North Carolina said that Congress faced a decision "whether the insurance program of the social security system can be strengthened and reinforced against the assaults of [noncontributory] old age pensions."[32]

Responding to this situation, Congress substantially modified the social security program in 1950, choosing to raise the level of benefits and extend coverage. Altmeyer noted with some relief that eight million workers, most of whom were self-employed, were brought into the system and that average benefits were increased by about 80 percent. The social security system picked up almost immediately. The old-age assistance rolls declined as soon as the new social security law went into effect and, for the first time, the number of social security beneficiaries exceeded the number receiving old-age assistance in February 1951.[33]

The battle between public assistance and old-age insurance illustrated how social welfare politics had changed between 1935 and 1950. None of the alternatives in 1950 involved exclusive reliance on the private sector. In 1935, by way of contrast, Congress gave serious consideration to exempting those already covered by a private pension plan from social security. Fifteen years later, both liberal and conservative critics of social security wanted to move to a system that paid flat benefits to everyone. Although they disagreed on how generous the benefits should be, all of the participants agreed on a continuing federal role. Increasingly, social welfare debates involved the question of which level of government should take the lead on the provision of social welfare services, not the question of whether the federal government should be involved.

The Social Security Amendments of 1950 changed the volume of support for federally run programs. Before the postwar era, federal programs embodied the Progressive Era notion that social welfare programs responded to industrialism. They were for factory workers, not farmers. Either they corrected a problem of industrial development, as in workers' compensation, or redressed the imbalance between urban and rural areas of the country—a lack of health care in rural areas for example. By limiting coverage to industrial and commercial workers, social security continued this tradition. In 1985, Senator Daniel Patrick Moynihan, himself an astute student of social welfare programs, acknowledged social security's heritage when he described the program as a response to the problems of urban America.[34] Before 1950, universal coverage had never existed for any federal social welfare program. After 1950, social security held the potential to break the Progressive Era mold and become a universal program.

Extending social security coverage to the self-employed, who worked for themselves and did not receive a check from an employer's payroll, represented the key 1950 breakthrough. Many farmers fell into this group; so did the proprietors of small businesses. Program officials had long realized that incomplete coverage exacerbated the dilemmas of expanding the social security program. It would be difficult, for example, to bring general revenues into the system and ask a farmer to pay taxes to support the pension of a retired steel worker if the farmer were not himself entitled to social security. One social security bureaucrat noted in 1937 that, "If we are going to tax [the self-employed] to pay the subsidy necessary but not include this group in the benefits, I think we are going to find that we will have a very difficult problem on our hands. I think that the problem of providing a subsidy from the general revenue is likely to have a lot of dynamite in it."[35] The solution was to broaden coverage under social security to cover farmers as well as steel workers, the self-employed as well as industrial and commercial workers.

Few precedents existed for collecting a payroll tax from the self-employed who, by definition, had no payroll. The income tax system was one remedy, but not a good one. A 1938 social security advisory council could not determine a satisfactory way of collecting contributions from farmers, self-employed shopkeepers, and others. The United States was not far removed from the world of the twenties in which, according to the Lynds, only 12 to 15 percent of the residents in Muncie, Indiana, reported incomes large enough to make filing income tax returns necessary. World War II marked a watershed in the federal government's ability to collect taxes from almost everyone. In 1948, when an advisory council studied social security, it reported, "The fact that almost all full-time and a large proportion of part-time self-employed persons have for the last few years been required to file income-tax returns has radically altered the outlook for extending coverage to this group. It has been demonstrated that income reports can be obtained from the great majority of the self-employed."[36] The technology of tax collection facilitated the expansion of social security to cover the self-employed; a major bottleneck of the American social welfare system was broken in the process.

THE ADMINISTRATION'S SOCIAL WELFARE POLICY

Because of the 1950 amendments, the Eisenhower administration did not follow the wishes of the Chamber of Commerce. It failed to abolish the social security system. Immediately after Eisenhower's election, chamber members received a policy statement that they ultimately adopted. The chamber urged the substitution of a "pay-as-you-go" plan to replace social security's contributory-contractual principle. Everyone, regardless of his previous social security coverage, would receive $25 a month. Only the amount needed to pay benefits for that year would be collected each year. The plan resembled the old Townsend Plan with much lower benefits. In 1953, $25 a month fell below the level of public assistance in 80 percent of old-age cases. Everyone would be covered by the plan, but just barely. Because everyone would be covered, public assistance would be abolished. In reality the chamber plan was an attempt to place the level of old-age benefits under tighter political control; the government would not be in the position of making long-run guarantees.[37]

The chamber's plan so alarmed Arthur Altmeyer of the Social Security Board that on April 10, 1953, his last day in office, he paid a special call on Marion Folsom. Altmeyer, who disliked the new FSA administrator Ovetta Culp Hobby, was worried about the fact that Hobby had included three

Chamber of Commerce members among a group of five civilian social security advisors. Altmeyer urged Folsom to support the battle against the Chamber of Commerce proposal. Folsom, one of the original business advisors on social security, promised to do what he could. In large part because of his efforts the administration decided to salvage and even to expand social security. The old-age parts of social security and Folsom's welfare capitalism, after all, were not incompatible.[38]

An unwillingness to destroy social security did not amount to a social welfare program. In the summer of 1953 President Eisenhower sent his cabinet members a memo asking for their suggestions. Eisenhower solicited programs that would demonstrate that the Roosevelt and Truman administrations "did not have a monopoly of the goals of a good society." His administration would come up with new programs or rediscover old ones that were inexpensive but constructive.[39]

Confronted with this call to act, Nelson Rockefeller and one of his assistants began to review existing HEW programs and to recommend new ones in the fall of 1953. They soon came upon a program that met the Eisenhower criterion: it was already in existence and not subject to expensive start-up costs, it worked to reduce welfare costs, and it had close connections with an important area of medical technology. In this manner Rockefeller helped the administration to discover vocational rehabilitation, a program that had started in the era of Herbert Hoover and had always appealed to welfare capitalists as the proper alternative to government cash grants.

Masked by the dispassionate analysis that Rockefeller and the other administration managers performed was that the rehabilitation concept fit neatly into the emerging Republican synthesis. It enabled the administration to meet social welfare problems and, simultaneously, to encourage individual self-reliance. The program was a form of positive government action to end America's dependence on the government. For these reasons rehabilitation became the peg on which the administration hung the social welfare it presented to Congress in 1954.[40]

One of the more congenial features of rehabilitation was its compatibility with the styles of businessmen and bureaucrats or Democrats and Republicans. The bureaucrats (and the Democrats) made sure that the administration's program would mean more money for them in the short run, and the businessmen (and the Republicans) contented themselves with the promise of saving government funds in the long run. For some, rehabilitation meant a vital social service provided for the physically handicapped and other public assistance recipients. For others rehabilitation implied an important new approach to social welfare problems that involved weaning people away from the government and into the labor force. In short, the word encouraged the sort of ambiguity that worked to everyone's advantage, an ambiguity that lies at the heart of successful political compromise.[41]

By January 1954 the administration program contained four specific provisions: more money for the vocational rehabilitation program, including money for special grants related to rehabilitation research and training; money to help finance construction of special rehabilitation centers and other nonprimary care centers as part of an expanded hospital construction program; a special amendment to the Social Security Act that enabled a disabled person to receive retirement benefits at 65 even if he had dropped out of the labor force many years before (this was an attempt to imitate the "waiver of premium" provision of private insurance contracts); and a complicated "reinsurance" plan in which the federal government helped private insurance companies finance health insurance. The reinsurance plan died almost before it was born, opposed by both the AMA and the health insurance proponents. If the other parts of the program carried the complicated technical paraphernalia of previously-passed legislation, they were united by the concept of rehabilitation, and this concept held great political appeal.[42]

President Eisenhower presented the 1954 progam to Congress in a series of special messages. All of the messages emphasized rehabilitation as the proper approach to solving social problems. In his Social Security message he noted that the injustice to the disabled should be corrected not only by preserving their social security benefits but also by "helping them to return to employment and lives of usefulness, independence, and self-respect." His special health message spoke of "freedom and individual responsibility" and proclaimed that vocational rehabilitation worked toward those self-sufficient goals. The president noted that 2 million Americans could and should be rehabilitated, but only 60,000 a year were. "Conditions of both humanity and national self-interest" demanded that the situation be changed.[43]

The metaphor of government action as rehabilitation appeared to apply to all of Eisenhower's program. It was as if the nation's inner ear responded to something in the sound of rehabilitation—perhaps it was the assurance that through rehabilitation the government would help people regain control of their lives. In this vein the neighborhoods in which the people lived would be rehabilitated, and the juvenile delinquents who menaced them on the streets would be rehabilitated as well.

Congress enthusiastically endorsed the president's program of rehabilitation, and in August, Nelson Rockefeller, among others, received an invitation to attend the White House signing ceremony for the new vocational rehabilitation bill. For all of the president's verbal inabilities he managed to capture the appeal of rehabilitation in his remarks at the ceremony. Vocational rehabilitation, the former general said, was "a humanitarian investment of great importance, yet it saves substantial sums of money." The statement passed through the room like the Lord's Prayer at a church service. It was part of a litany that included a political paradox capable of sustaining miracles: more money that was less money and more federal power that was less federal power.[44]

THE BUREAUCRATIC COUNTERATTACK

If Eisenhower thought he could sidestep battles between businessmen and bureaucrats through a middle of the road rehabilitation approach to welfare problems, he soon learned differently. The vocational rehabilitation bill of 1954 had been passed. For the rest of his presidential tenure, however, Eisenhower was called upon to defend his administration's welfare policies against repeated bureaucratic counterattacks. The aging general lost as many battles as he won.

The reasons for the war are not hard to find. A triumph of a rehabilitation approach threatened important elements of the existing federal welfare bureaucracy with occupational suicide. To expect these bureaucrats to preside over their own disappearance reflected a flaw in the Republican administration's analysis of social welfare policy. As systems managers who were concerned with current problems, key Eisenhower aides tended to assume an identity of interests between the heads of federal departments and the departments themselves. In corporations, after all, workers produced what management ordered them to produce. Compensation and working conditions were negotiable, but no union would ask General Motors to make cupcakes. Nor would automobiles be mysteriously transformed into steam turbines in the blink of an administrative eye. What applied to the employees of private companies, however, failed to apply to the federal civil service. Government was not big business carried on by other means. Corporate bureaucrat Marion B. Folsom, on leave from Eastman Kodak, had interests far different from the career-minded civil servants who worked under him in the Department of Health, Education, and Welfare. When Folsom advocated a gradual decrease in federal welfare expenditures and employment nothing guaranteed that his subordinates would agree with his views. Because the Eisenhower rehabilitation approach meant the federal welfare bureaucracy would have cut its own throat, there was every reason for a disjunction of interest between the career civil service and the executive branch.[45]

The separation of the bureaucracy and the executive branch had been evident as early as 1939, when the Social Security Board wanted to pass a national health insurance bill and the President wanted to wait. Now, with a Republican administration in power in Washington, the gap between the bureaucracy and the president widened.

The widening of the gap might have come even if Adlai Stevenson had won the 1952 election. In the late 1940s, frustrated with continuing congressional unwillingness to pass health and disability insurance, members of the federal welfare bureaucracy began to practice a more sophisticated form of politics. Instead of presenting the elected representatives of the American people with legislative proposals that they regarded as being the correct approach to the problems of health care and income maintenance, bureaucrats began formulating new, less ambitious, proposals consciously designed to attract a political following. Previously, bureaucrats had recommended an all-inclusive program of health and disability insurance. Now, however, they separated their health insurance proposals from their disability insurance proposals. Remembering the political clout that the nation's elderly had exercised in the Townsend Movement of the 1930s federal bureaucrats went further and health insurance became health insurance for the elderly alone, rather than for the population as a whole. Tailoring their proposals to specific interest groups, federal welfare bureaucrats took on the duty of lobbying for programs that they themselves would administer. In the process they acquired a new degree of independence from the executive branch.[46]

Despite this new independence, federal bureaucrats—particularly those working for the Social Security Board—owed their existence to Democratic presidents. The transition to Eisenhower and the Republicans was a crucial test of whether there would be a continuity of principle and practice within Washington's welfare bureaucracy. The Republicans were pressured to replace the leaders of the bureaucracy with loyal party members, some of whom had been waiting for a post in Washington for 20 years. Even the director of a conservative (that is, pre-New Deal) program like vocational rehabilitation, a woman who had once worked as a special assistant to Herbert Hoover's Secretary of the Treasury Andrew Mellon, faced the threat of being replaced by the chairman of the California Republicans for Nixon Committee. The woman saved her job, but other leading bureaucrats such as Arthur Altmeyer, the chairman of the Social Security Board, symbolized the New Deal with too much clarity to survive the transition. Altmeyer left. Jane Hoey, the director of the public assistance program, left. The principles of social security survived. So did the agenda for increasing the number of direct federal welfare services.[47]

New Deal agenda and approaches remained intact because of a shift in the location of social welfare expertise that had occurred since 1935. In the beginning of the New Deal the Roosevelt administration had been forced to depend mainly upon businessmen for advice concerning the problems involved in providing welfare services to national constituencies. Since 1935, however, an increasingly specialized public bureaucracy had mastered the basic process and had translated social welfare concepts and policies into a special rhetoric of which they, and not the businessmen, were the masters. When it came to public assistance categories and other technical matters the bureaucrats possessed valuable skills (if only in translating the jargon that they had created) and a lengthy institutional memory that made them the experts upon whom any new administration had to primarily depend to frame social welfare proposals. If Arthur Altmeyer paid the price of visible leadership by losing his job, other welfare bureaucrats on the Social Security Board who were equally knowledgeable and equally partisan stayed on to advise the new Republican president and his chief aides.

The Eisenhower appointee as director of the Social Security program, for example, relied on the advice of Wilbur Cohen. Once a special assistant to Arthur Altmeyer, Cohen now worked in the research department of the Social Security Administration. According to one inside report the new Social Security chief told his boss (the secretary of Health, Education, and Welfare) soon after his arrival that he "couldn't get along" without Cohen and Robert Ball, another holdover.[48] Cohen and Ball worked to keep the Eisenhower administration's legislative proposals consistent with long-range social security plans issuing from within the federal welfare bureaucracy itself. Their efforts tested all of their newfound political skills. In 1954 Cohen complained privately to Altmeyer that "We do not know what the guide lines and policies [of the executive branch] are—so we work in the dark—we are holding the fort, it is true. But the expenditures of energy are tremendous."[49]

Work, however, had its programmatic rewards. In 1954 amendments were made to the Social Security Act. The nuances of these amendments added up to a victory for the forces of continuity in federal welfare procedure. In the long-disputed realm of disability, for example, Wilbur Cohen persuaded the administration to back what technocrats referred to as a "disability freeze." Under the terms of this plan a worker who became permanently disabled (and, therefore, unable to contribute further into his old-age pension piggy bank account) would enjoy increased benefits when he reached the minimum retirement age of 65. In effect the worker's retirement benefits would be calculated and paid out to him as if he had been paying into his retirement account for all of his working lifetime at the level that he had been contributing previous to the time when he had become permanently disabled. The federal government, in short, would subsidize the disabled worker's social security piggy bank so that when it was eventually broken for the worker upon his retirement the worker would have enough monthly income to live a decent life.[50]

Cohen's proposal for a disability freeze interfaced nicely with the rhetoric of Eisenhower administration advisers such as Nelson Rockefeller. One of Rockefeller's assistants remarked that Cohen's plan "seemed eminently fair. It seemed humane. It didn't cost much." In addition, the disability freeze proposal blended with the administration's emphasis upon rehabilitation. Once a worker was declared permanently disabled (that is, disabled for a lengthy period) he became a candidate for rehabilitation. In this manner the disability freeze became "a great, huge recruiting system for rehabilitation," in the mind of the Eisenhower administration. Severely disabled workers would, in this view, be guaranteed a minimum level of income once they reached age 65. This, in turn, would improve their morale and, not unimportant, keep them from believing that they were receiving some form of discretionary dole from public funds. The disabled, then, would be more likely to cooperate with interested welfare officials to surmount their afflictions and return to the labor force. If they did, well and good—federal expenditures would fall. If they proved unable to reenter the labor force, however, they would not suffer unnecessary hardship, and public expenditures would not rise in an ad hoc fashion; rather, federal retirement subsidies would be fixed at a level determined by the worth of the worker as measured by the private marketplace at the time when that worker had suffered his disability.[51]

The Eisenhower administration might see the disability freeze as a logical extension of marketplace capitalism. To the bureaucrats of the Social Security Administration* the freeze represented something very different. Wilbur Cohen, for one, realized that the disability freeze marked a crucial first step toward a disability insurance program, a program in which federal officials supplied welfare services directly to the population without benefit of intermediaries. To participate in the disability freeze program, Cohen realized, a worker had first to be declared permanently disabled. The program that Cohen constructed, therefore, put federal officials in the new business of making disability declarations.

Cohen also appreciated the virtues of programmatic gradualism. Like the Roman General Fabius, he moved slowly, in the hope that incremental movement would accomplish what the grand programmatic leaps of the past, such as the Wagner-Murray-Dingell Bill of 1943, had failed to accomplish. From federal subsidies for social security retirement accounts to even more direct federal disability benefits paid to the people at the onset of their disability was a relatively short step once the principle of allowing federal officials to define an individual as disabled was conceded.[52] Considered in this light, then, Wilbur Cohen's successful attempt to get the Eisenhower administration to first sponsor and then pass into law the disability freeze program was an act of consummate political skill, one that advanced the scope of direct federal welfare controls by playing upon the ambiguities of the rehabilitation approach to social welfare problems.

Back home in Madison, Wisconsin, Arthur Altmeyer listened to President Eisenhower announce the 1954 amendments to the Social Security Act with a sense of relief. Not only had the Republican administration rejected the abolitionist schemes of the U.S. Chamber of Commerce, it had also widened the scope of direct federal welfare controls. Dismissing Eisenhower and his top aides as secondary, Altmeyer credited Wilbur Cohen with the real victory. The administration's acceptance of the fundamentals of the New Deal approach to social welfare was a personal triumph for Cohen. "Not only have you translated the technical material into understandable

---

*The Social Security Board was renamed the Social Security Administration in 1946.

form," Altmeyer wrote his protégé, "but you have enabled the administration to understand and take into account the attitude of interested groups and public relations generally. I shudder to think of what might have happened if you had not been there to facilitate the thinking and bridge the transition."[53]

THE PASSAGE OF DISABILITY INSURANCE

During the crucial transition from Democratic to Republican rule bureaucrats such as Wilbur Cohen held the fort. Programs that allowed the federal government to provide welfare services directly to the people had not been abolished, and a small number of gains in the scope of direct federal controls had been made in a relatively uncongenial political environment. Democratic victory in the congressional elections of 1954, however, encouraged the bureaucrats and their allies to become even bolder. In the years that followed they made a final push for the enactment of a disability insurance program administered by the federal government. By now a strong prodisability insurance lobby matched the antidisability insurance lobby led by the AMA, the U.S. Chamber of Commerce, and the NAM. The pro lobby had two leaders: Wilbur Cohen, who left the federal government in 1955 to take a job at the University of Michigan, and Nelson Cruikshank, who directed organized labor's Department of Social Security. From outside the government Cohen maintained his close relationships with social security personnel and with influential Democratic congressmen such as Wilbur Mills and Lyndon Johnson. The only difference his departure from the government made was that he acquired more freedom to engage in partisan politics. Early in 1956, for example, he advised Edwin Witte to write to Senator Walter George of Georgia. Cohen's letter revealed his political competence: George "is for it [disability insurance] but a statement . . . from the former Executive Director of the Committee on Economic Security and Secretary of the Wisconsin Industrial Commission will help him. He will have to buck Senator Harry Byrd and several other members of the Senate Finance Committee and . . . your support of the administrative feasibility of disability insurance would be very helpful." As for Cruikshank, the significance of his position lay in the fact that he lobbied on behalf of a newly-merged AFL and CIO, with strong political clout.[54]

The House passed a disability insurance bill for people over 50 years of age in June 1955, as it had done once before, and passage of a disability insurance program depended on the Senate, which had never passed the program. For the first time, however, the bureaucrats neared passage of a key element of their legislative program despite the presence of an unsympathetic president. Just as the 1938 Social Security Advisory Council meetings concerning permanent disability insurance marked a point of discontinuity within the American social welfare system, so the Senate battle for passage of disability insurance in 1956 represented something new. The fight in the Senate symbolized the political maturity of the social welfare bureaucracy, and it gave the bureaucrats a strong claim to parity with businessmen.

Hearings in the Senate Finance Committee began in February. Welfare capitalist Marion Folsom, ambivalent concerning the desirability of disability insurance, postponed his committee appearance. Over the years Folsom had reversed his position on disability insurance. In 1944 he had chaired the social security committee of the Chamber of Commerce and backed permanent disability insurance. In 1948 and 1949 he had advised the Senate Finance Committee and opposed the measure. Now, in 1956, he had to comment on the proposed program once again—this time as the secretary of Health, Education and Welfare. He listened to people with views on both sides of the question. Wilbur Cohen, who realized that "a lot will depend on what Secretary Folsom says," visited him three times. In March, Folsom reached a decision. Appearing before the Senate Finance Committee he spoke against disability insurance, a pronouncement that meant the administration would use its powers to oppose the House bill.

The Senate Finance Committee, picking up its cue, reported a social security bill in May that lacked provisions for permanent disability insurance. It was a bad political omen for the prodisability forces. Senators, who depended upon the Finance Committee for passage of special tax legislation, rarely opposed the committee's wishes. Nonetheless, Cohen and Cruikshank began to speak to interested senators about staging a floor fight.

Coached by Cohen, Senator Walter George offered an amendment to the Finance Committee's bill, asking that disability insurance be included in the Senate's final social security bill. The Democrats, who were disciplined by majority leader Lyndon Johnson and mollified by a compromise created by Oklahoma's Senator Kerr (which established a separate trust fund for the permanent disability insurance program; an apparent move to protect the financial integrity of the old-age, survivors program) held firm enough to force a close vote. The climactic moment came on July 17, 1956. By a one-vote margin the Senate voted in favor of permanent disability insurance for all Americans over 50. The vote prevailed in conference committee and withstood the threat of presidential veto. The federal welfare bureaucracy had enacted a major piece of the reform agenda that they had formulated almost 20 years before.

Writing a report a few months later, Nelson Cruikshank decided to delete a section in which he prophesied that Congress would someday soon extend protection against disability to all age groups, not just those over 50.[55] To have included this section would have been indiscrete, but it also would have reflected the truth. As Cruikshank understood, the existence of a law was an invitation to its liberalization. Other amendments made to the

Social Security Act in 1956 also testified to the validity of this bureaucratic truth. Among other things the law extended coverage of existing federal welfare programs such as old-age retirement to new elements of the population and raised the federal share of public assistance payments to the states. The trick within the American social welfare system was to get a law passed creating a new federal welfare program. The expansion of the program would follow. The passage of permanent disability insurance, then, acted as a guarantee that the program would someday be extended and liberalized. In fact, "someday" arrived soon. By 1960, disability insurance coverage had been effectively extended to the entire population. The modified New Era welfare ideology of the 1950s had been made to serve New Deal welfare ends.[56]

In the 1950s the language of psychiatry came to describe more and more of American life. In the terms of this language the American social welfare system was schizoid. One of its personalities, the product of businessmen and their allies, was fiscally conservative, concerned with cost-efficiency, and conceptually oriented toward "rehabilitating" people to make them less dependent upon the government. The welfare approaches of the executive branch throughout the Eisenhower years exemplified this side of the system. The other side of the social welfare system, the product of bureaucrats and their allies, worked to provide broad protection against life's hazards by increasing the direct-service-provider role of the federal government. The efforts of men such as Wilbur Cohen and Arthur Altmeyer to create a federally administered disability insurance program represented this other personality of the system.

The twin personalities of the American social welfare system, in other words, were not integrated. Little or nothing in the long history of the public sector's involvement in the welfare field provided hope that the federal government would get clear of its problems or even make an intelligent synthesis of its twin personalities. The programs of businessman and bureaucrat alike could be expected to benefit from the trend to liberalize existing welfare programs. In the future the American welfare system would get regularly snarled in programmatic cross-purposes and more weighted down with the jargonized ideas of businessman and bureaucrat alike. The need for a decision of which of the two general approaches to adopt or for a reintegration of the entire system grew yearly. Unfortunately, the type of "systems analysts" necessary to accomplish this task, to shift to the language of the 1960s, proved hard to find.

NOTES

1. Godfrey Hodgson, *America in Our Time* (Garden City, N.Y.: Doubleday, 1976), pp. 18-19; Eric F. Goldman, *The Crucial Decade and After, America 1945-1960* (New York:

Random House, 1960), p. 269; Jules Backman, *The Economics of the Electrical Manufacturing Industry* (Albany, N.Y.: University Press, 1962), pp. 231-32, 242; John Brooks, *The Great Leap: The Past Twenty-Five Years in America* (New York: Harper & Row, 1966), pp. 53-54; Thomas J. Watson, Jr., *A Business and Its Beliefs: The Ideas that Helped Build IBM* (New York: McGraw-Hill, 1963); Milton Derber, "The Electrical Manufacturing Industry," in *How Collective Bargaining Works*, edited by H. A. Millis et al. (New York: Twentieth Century Fund, 1942), pp. 744-59.

2. R. Alan Lawson, *The Failure of Independent Liberalism, 1930-1941* (New York: F. P. Dutton, 1972), pp. 52-54; Loren Baritz, *The Servants of Power: A History of the Use of Social Science in American Industry* (Middletown, Conn.: Wesleyan University Press, 1960), p. 155.

3. "USA: The Permanent Revolution," *Fortune* special issue (February 1951); Russell W. Davenport, "The Greatest Opportunity on Earth," *Fortune* 40 (October 1949), p. 65. See also Krooss, *Executive Opinion*, and W. H. Whyte and the editors of *Fortune*, *Is Anybody Listening?* (New York: Simon and Schuster, 1952).

4. Edward Berkowitz, "Social Welfare in the Post World War II Era: The United Mine Workers and Rehabilitation," in *Research in Economic History*, edited by Paul Uselding (forthcoming).

5. Michael Davis to Arthur Altmeyer, November 24, 1948, Altmeyer Papers, Box 10.

6. Arthur Altmeyer's statement before the Senate Advisory Committee on Social Security, March 14, 1948 in "Addresses by Arthur Altmeyer," Department of Health, Education, and Welfare Archives, Washington, D.C.; "Monthly Payments for Social Insurance and Related Programs . . . 1935-1954," *Social Security Bulletin* 18 (August 1953): 4. For a provocative, if speculative, analysis of the rise in public assistance payments see Frances Fox Piven and Richard Cloward, *Regulating the Poor* (New York: Random House, 1968).

7. The piece of legislation that illustrates this point most clearly is the Social Security Amendments of 1950. *House Report 1300*, 81st Congress, 1st sess.; *Senate Report 1669*, 81st Congress, 2d Sess.; Arthur Altmeyer to Oscar Ewing, March 24, 1947, RG 235, General Decimal Series, 1944-1950, 500-700, Box 26; Wilbur J. Cohen and Robert J. Myers, "Social Security Amendments of 1950: A Summary and Legislative History," *Social Security Bulletin* 17 (October 1950): 3-15.

8. President Eisenhower to Leonard Finer, July 30, 1953, Official File 154 G-4, Eisenhower Papers, Dwight D. Eisenhower Library, Abilene, Kan.

9. Bert Cochran, *Truman and the Crisis Presidency* (New York: Funk and Wagnall Co., 1973), pp. 285-90.

10. Edward S. Flash, Jr., *Economic Advice and Presidential Leadership: The Council of Economic Advisers* (Cambridge: Harvard University Press, 1965), pp. 54-55, 66-67; Cochran, *Truman*, p. 340; Robert Engler, *The Politics of Oil* (Chicago: University of Chicago Press, 1976), pp. 274-75.

11. Mary E. Switzer, "Year of Progress in Rehabilitation," *The Georgia Vocational Rehabilitation News*, December 1951, Switzer Papers, Schlesinger Library, Radcliffe College, Cambridge, Mass.

12. "Story of 'Operation Knoxville,' " July 27, 1951, RG 290, Accession 62A-190, Container 4; "Community Organization for Vocational Rehabilitation—Here's How to Do It," 1952, RG 290, Accession 62A-190, Container 4, Washington National Records Center, Suitland, Md.; James Garrett to Mary Switzer, March 7, 1952, Donald Covalt to Switzer, March 25, 1952, RG 363, Accession 71A-1382, Carton 107, Washington National Records Center.

13. See, for example, "You and Socialized Medicine—The Basic Facts and a Call to Action," 1949, RG 235, General Decimal Series, 1944-1950, 011.4, National Archives, Washington, D.C.

14. M. Albert Linton, "Should Total Disability Be Included in a Federal Old Age Security Program?" March 2, 1948, Edward M. Stettinius Collection, University of Virginia Library, Charlottesville; U.S. Advisory Council on Social Security, *Permanent and Total Disability Insurance*, Senate Document no. 162, 80th Congress, 2d sess.

15. A. Palmer Deering to Arthur Altmeyer, December 29, 1947 and American Medical Association's Secretary Letter no. 131, December 19, 1949, RG 235, General Files, Office of the Administrator, Federal Security Agency, Alphabetical Series, 1944-1950, American Medical-American Society.

16. *Idem.*

17. Special Republican Study Group to Nelson A. Rockefeller, November 10, 1951, Official File 107-13, Eisenhower Papers.

18. Robert L. Branyan and Lawrence H. Larsen, *The Eisenhowr Administration: A Documentary History* (New York: Random House, 1971), p. 8; Robert J. Donovan, *Eisenhower: The Inside Story* (New York: Harper & Row, 1956), p. 35; Charles C. Alexander, *Holding the Line: The Eisenhower Era, 1952-1961* (Bloomington: Indiana University Press, 1975), p. 38.

19. General Eisenhower to George Sloan, March 1, 1952, Personal Files of General of the Army Dwight D. Eisenhower, 1916-1952, Eisenhower Papers.

20. "The Administration's Goals and Accomplishments," January 4, 1954 in *Public Papers of the Presidents: 1954* (Washington: G.P.O., 1960), pp. 2-6.

21. "Economic Report to the Congress by President Eisenhower," January 28, 1954, Official File 99-G-7, Eisenhower Papers.

22. Arthur Larson, *A Republican Looks at His Party* (New York: Harper & Row, 1956), p. 1, 10, 198.

23. Marion Folsom Oral History Memoir, Columbia Oral History Collection, Columbia University, New York, N.Y.

24. Branyan and Larson, *The Eisenhower Administration*, p. 53; Sherman Adams, *Firsthand Report: The Story of the Eisenhower Administration* (New York: Harper & Row, 1961); Theodore P. Kovaless, "Business and Government in the Eisenhower Era," (Ph.D. diss. New York University, 1972).

25. *Social Security Bulletin: Annual Statistical Supplement, 1981* (Washington, D.C.: Department of Health and Human Services, 1981), pp. 53, 54.

26. Ibid., p. 79.

27. Altmeyer, *Formative Years*, p. 169. See also Christopher Leman, "Patterns of Policy Development: Social Security in the United States and Canada," *Public Policy* 25 (Spring 1977): 261-90.

28. From Blanche Coll, "Public Assistance: Revising the Original Comprehensive Concept of Social Security," unpublished paper prepared for New Mexico Conference on Social Security, April 1985.

29. Robert Ball, "The Original Understanding of Social Security: Implications for Later Developments," unpublished paper prepared for the Yale Conference on Social Security, April 1985.

30. Altmeyer, *Formative Years*, pp. 169-70; Mark H. Leff, "Historical Perspectives on Old-Age Insurance: The State of the Art on the Art of the State," in Edward Berkowitz, ed., *Social Security After Fifty*, p. 42.

31. Staff Comments, "Expansion and Extension of the Social Security System," February 14, 1949, Charles Murphy Papers, Harry S. Truman Library, quoted in Leff, "Historical Perspectives on Old-Age Insurance," p. 41.

32. Both of these October 4, 1949, speeches from the *Congressional Record* are quoted in Edward Berkowitz, "Introduction: Social Security Celebrates an Anniversary," in Berkowitz, ed., *Social Security After Fifty*, p. 20.

33. Altmeyer, *Formative Years*, p. 185; Achenbaum, *Social Security*, p. 45.

34. Senator Daniel P. Moynihan, *Congressional Record*, June 19, 1985, p. S 8347. When we speak of social security here and elsewhere, we mean old-age and survivors insurance and not the programs authorized by the Social Security Act of 1935: social insurance, not welfare. Welfare, it can be argued, did cover nonindustrial workers before 1950, but it was highly selective in its coverage and applied to people outside of the labor force, such as children, the elderly, and the blind.

35. Wilbur Cohen to Arthur Altmeyer, February 10, 1937, RG 47, Records of the Social Security Administration, Box 98, Chairman's Files, File 705, National Archives.

36. *Old Age and Survivors Insurance*, Summary, Report to the Senate Committee on Finance from the Advisory Council on Social Security, 80th Congress, 2nd Session, 1948, in *Readings in Social Security* (New York: Prentice Hall, 1948), ed. William Haber and Wilbur Cohen, pp. 250, 266-67; Robert S. Lynd and Helen Merrill Lynd, *Middletown: A Study in Modern American Culture* (New York: Harcourt, Brace and World, 1929), p. 84.

37. Arthur Altmeyer, "Social Security, the Republican Party and Eisenhower," in Wilbur Cohen Papers, Box 47; Altmeyer, *Formative Years*, pp. 213-19.

38. Altmeyer, *Formative Years*, pp. 214-15.

39. Dwight Eisenhower to Oveta Culp Hobby, July 30, 1953, RG 235, General Decimal Series, 1951-1955, 011, Box 12, National Archives; H. Alexander Smith to Hobby, October 28, 1953, RG 235, General Decimal Series, 1951-1955, 011, Box 7, National Archives, Washington, D.C.; Roswell Perkins Oral History Memoir, Columbia Oral History Collection, Columbia University, New York, N.Y.

40. Address by Oveta Culp Hobby before Air Force Officers Wives' Club, October 18, 1953, and "A Frontal Attack on Disability," both in RG 290, Accession 62A-190, Box 7, Washington National Records Center; "Problems Analysis Notebook," 1953, vol. 1, pp. 8-10; RG 235, General Decimal Series, 1951-1955, 011, Box 10, National Archives, Washington, D.C.

41. Martha Derthick, *Uncontrollable Spending for Social Service Grants* (Washington, D.C.: Brookings Institution, 1975), p. 21.

42. "A Frontal Attack on Disability"; Nelson Rockefeller to Roger Jones, December 28, 1953, RG 235, General Decimal Series, 1951-1955, 011 (1953-1954), Box 12, National Archives, Washington, D.C.; Arthur Altmeyer to Wilbur Cohen, August 10, 1953, March 18, 1954, Cohen Papers, Box 47.

43. Dwight Eisenhower, "Special Message . . . on Old Age and Survivors Insurance and on . . . Public Assistance," January 14, 1954, and "Special Message on the Health Needs of the Nation," January 18, 1954, both in *Public Papers of the Presidents: 1954*, pp. 62-76; Donovan, *Eisenhower*, pp. 143, 171, 172, 223-31.

44. Oveta Culp Hobby to Honorable General Wilton B. Persons, RG 363, Accession 71A-1382, Box 137; Eisenhower statement, August 3, 1954, RG 363, Accession 71A-1382, Box 65, Washington National Records Center, Suitland, Maryland.

45. Daniel P. Moynihan has examined this general problem in two books: *Maximum Feasible Misunderstanding: Community Action in the War on Poverty* (New York: Free Press, 1970) and *The Politics of a Guaranteed Annual Income* (New York: Random House, 1973).

46. James L. Sundquist, *Politics and Policy: The Eisenhower, Kennedy and Johnson Years* (Washington, D.C.: Brookings Institution, 1968), pp. 111-55, 287-322.

47. Mary Switzer to Stephen Gibbons, April 19, 1953, Switzer Papers, Schlesinger Library, Radcliffe College, Cambridge, Mass.; interview with Dr. Howard Rusk, March, 1975 (New York); interview with Charles Schottland, September 20, 1978 (Waltham, Mass.).

48. Arthur Altmeyer to Wilbur Cohen, November 18, 1953, Cohen Papers, Box 47.

49. Cohen to Altmeyer, November 5, 1953, Cohen Papers, Box 47.

50. Wilbur Cohen, *Retirement Policies Under Social Security: A Legislative History of Retirement Ages, the Retirement Test, and Disability Benefits* (Berkeley: University of California Press, 1957), p. 54; "NRA Memo," July 14, 1952, National Rehabilitation Association Papers, National Rehabilitation Association, Washington, D.C.; "Preservation of Benefit Rights for the Disabled," September 27, 1953, RG 290, Accession 62 A-190, Box 8, Washington National Records Center, Suitland, Maryland.

51. Roswell Perkins interview, p. 25.

52. Wilbur Cohen interview (Ann Arbor).

53. Altmeyer to Cohen, January 15, 1954, Cohen Papers, Box 47.

54. Cohen to Edwin Witte, February 22, 1956, Cohen Papers, Box 7; Nelson Cruikshank to George Meany, June 12, 1956, Nelson Cruikshank Papers, Box 11-A, Wisconsin State Histor-

ical Society, Madison; Charles Schottland interview.

55. This section derives heavily from Nelson Cruikshank, "Disability Insurance in 1956," unpublished manuscript in Cruikshank Papers, Box 11-A, Wisconsin State Historical Society, Madison; Schottland interview; Edwin Witte to Wilbur Cohen, July 27, 1956, Cohen Papers, Box 7.

56. The expansion of the disability insurance program is covered in such modern documents as "Disability Overview" briefing memo for secretary of Health, Education, and Welfare, August 7, 1975, privately held; Rutgers University Bureau of Economic Research, "An Evaluation of the Structure and Function of Disability Programs," (New Brunswick, N.J., 1975).

9
AMERICAN WELFARE PRACTICE: PATTERNS OF CONTINUITY AND CHANGE

In 1956, with the passage of disability insurance, the basic terms of the American social welfare system were set. The federal government funded programs that took three broad forms.

In the first instance, the programs provided old-age and disability pensions through the social security system. Private employers used the federally administered pensions as a base on which to build private pensions. To this base, the employers often added health insurance and such measures as sick leave, all considered to be the responsibility of management in an enlightened capitalist economy.

In the second instance, the federal government sent money to the states and localities for programs in aid of those who were, in effect, excused from the labor market. The definition of just who should be allowed not to work shifted over time. Nearly always, however, the old and the handicapped were included on the list. So were young children.

In the third instance, the federal government funded programs that attempted to liberate welfare recipients from a life of dependence on government handouts. These programs often were identified as "investments in human capital" or as "seed money" or as "rehabilitation" measures. Whatever the label, the programs nearly always traded on the promise of saving government money in the long run as a rationale for spending it in the short run. The process of government intervention resembled jump-starting a car. According to this analogy, the government entered the scene, offered help to a worthy individual such as a ghetto youngster or a person in a wheelchair, and then went on its way. The person who had received the help joined the work force and had no further need of the government. In this way, people who consumed taxes as welfare recipients were transformed into tax payers.

Fashions in social welfare changed between 1956 and 1986, as the mood of the nation shifted. Through the euphoria of the sixties, the pessimism and confusion of the seventies, and the conservative resurgence of the eighties, however, the basic terms of the social welfare system remained the same. Thirty years after the passage of disability insurance, the system contained all of the approaches to social policy that have been described in this book, including minimum standards, social insurance, and welfare capitalism. All remained active, vigorous parts of the scene in 1987, and with the trends toward singing the praises of the free market and denigrating the accomplishments and abilities of federal bureaucrats, welfare capitalism appeared to be undergoing yet another revival.

In what follows, we attempt to bring our story up to date and to show that this history of public and private social welfare programs remains relevant to modern policy concerns.

SUCCESS OF THE SOCIAL INSURANCE MODEL

By any measure, social insurance became the nation's largest and most successful social welfare technique in the period between 1956 and 1986. The very concept of social security, for example, was synonymous, in most people's minds, with the Old-Age, Survivors, and Disability insurance program run by the Social Security Administration. (Therefore, in this chapter the phrases "social insurance" and "social security" are used as synonyms.) The sheer volume of social security operations was impressive. By the middle of the 1980s, the Social Security Administration operated 1,300 offices and maintained ten regional headquarters. The employees in these locations sent 432 million checks to social security recipients per year and met with countless individuals who wanted information about the program.[1]

In terms of the money spent, social insurance dwarfed the other federal social welfare programs. In 1955, for example, federal outlays for Aid to Families with Dependent Children remained below $0.5 billion and federal outlays for welfare payments to the permanently and totally disabled, the blind, and the elderly amounted to $1 billion. Social insurance, by way of contrast, cost $4.3 billion, and the disparity between it and other social welfare programs widened over time. In 1965, the welfare programs cost $3 billion in federal outlays and the social insurance program $16.6 billion.[2]

Social security's success came gradually. The program did not begin operations until 1937 or pay its first pensions until 1940. As late as 1950, welfare to the elderly cost more and reached more people than did social security. Soon afterwards, however, social insurance skyrocketed ahead of the other programs.

Ideology played a part in social insurance's success but so too did more mundane factors related to the economy, politics, and demography. No less an authority than Robert Ball, who piloted the program through the years of its greatest success as Commissioner of Social Security, captured the ideological appeal of the program when he referred to its "self-help approach." In social insurance, Ball noted, people demonstrated something "positive—that they have worked sufficiently to be eligible and thus have an earned right to the payment." Welfare forced applicants to prove something "negative—that they do not have enough to get along on."[3] The positive program garnered more political support and more federal funds than the negative program; it violated America's preference for private over public action less than did blatant income redistribution through welfare. Social insurance was not the dole, and it deserved everyone's respect. It was, in short, a middle-class entitlement, a respectable version of an insurance program for the worthy poor. As one academic put it, social security "helped incorporate not only the industrial working class but the broad middle spectrum of American society into an institutionalized and long-term relationship with the state."[4]

The striking thing about social insurance was that it achieved its unprecedented success painlessly. It harnessed the growth of the American economy to its advantage. Paul Samuelson made this point to the readers of his *Newsweek* column in 1967. He called social security the "most successful" program in America's welfare state because it was based on "the eighth wonder of the world—compound interest." Other commentators echoed Samuelson's faith in the program. Edwin Dale wrote in the New York *Times* in 1972 that, "unless the world blows up or the country goes bankrupt, it is highly likely that current workers will get back from Social Security more than they paid in."[5]

These commentators understood the full implication of America's recovery from the depression. When the Social Security old-age insurance program began in 1937, experts expected many old people and relatively few young people to be in the population in the second half of the twentieth century. They failed to foresee the prosperity of the war and postwar eras and the baby boom that accompanied this prosperity. The combined result of these events was more money coming into the system than predicted. With unemployment down, more workers paid into the system; fears about the system's future were eased by the realization that, beginning in the middle of the sixties, the children of the baby boom would begin to enter the labor force and pay into social security accounts. No wonder, then, that Congress decided to increase social security benefits and hold down social security taxes, as benefit increases in 1952, 1954, and 1958 illustrated.

A second, less widely understood phenomenon also accounted for social security's success. It was forever young. In 1940, as we have discussed, relatively few of the nation's retired citizens could benefit from social security. Too few of them had paid into the system, and most had retired before social insurance began. In 1950, many of the nation's self-employed entered the social security system. That meant, for exactly the same reason, another period of more people paying in than were receiving benefits. In 1951, for example, relatively few of the self-employed who were retired received social security pensions but many of the self-employed were paying into the system. In this manner, the system received an early windfall—not once, but each time a new group received social insurance coverage. Since the greatest single expansion of coverage occurred in 1950, the system received a great boost in the 1950s.

A third and final reason for social insurance's success was its exemption from many of the political stumbling blocks that inhibited other programs. Most programs operated under two sorts of limits. Congress had to authorize that money be spent on the progam in a particular year, and then Congress had to agree actually to spend the money. A program might therefore be authorized for five years, but during each of those years, program administrators would have to appear before appropriations committees and defend the program. If the President wanted to cut the budget, he might well decide to reduce the appropriations below the level Congress had authorized. Alternatively, Congress might take offense at a program and refuse to appropriate money for it. As a form of social insurance, social security, almost alone among social welfare programs, was excused from this political exercise. It operated outside the routines of the federal budget and federal appropriations committees. It operated as an entitlement, in which benefits were mandated by law, and money to pay for it came from payroll taxes that were automatically collected.

After the early 1950s, few members of Congress wanted to change the system. Social insurance conferred its benefits on people who lived in every congressional district in the nation. Congressmen appeared content to allow the tax committees in the House and Senate, in close cooperation with the employees of the Social Security Administration, to handle the many details of the program. Then, once these committees prepared a bill that more often than not contained a feature that would make the program more generous, most members of Congress voted for it. Congressmen quibbled over details, such as the treatment of the blind under disability insurance, but accepted the general principles of the program. It appeared to bring them votes at relatively little cost.

Political appearances to the contrary, social security's success was not without cost. Because the social security program was so successful, policymakers utilized it to handle many social welfare problems. In this manner, for example, the problems of disability became subsumed under the disability insurance program. As part of social security and using a model provided by old-age insurance, the disability insurance program paid pensions to the disabled on the condition that they retire from active employment. Just as the elderly who worked beyond 65 had to wait for their old-age pensions, a disabled person who wished to remain in the labor force got nothing. Retirement helped the disabled become financially secure, but it did little to foster a sense of independence among them.[6]

In this case, as in so many others, social security cast a halo over the nation's social policy. The "social insurance" model enabled large social programs to be cast in a golden light. Whether social insurance represented the best solution to the various problems remained in doubt. The truth was, however, that a lifetime of benefits for, say, attendant care to the handicapped was a difficult matter to negotiate politically. People regarded such proposals as special favors. Disability pensions for those same handicapped people, through social insurance, proved much easier to obtain. People regarded them as earned rights.

SOCIAL SECURITY'S GREAT CRASH

Social security's halo also hid many of its inconsistencies that might be called defects. The program benefited from its ideological image as a force for self-reliance, a form of insurance that employers and employees paid for themselves. In fact, however, the program operated as a tremendous source of income redistribution, from the working to the retired, from the living to the dependents of the dead, from the healthy to the sick, from the able-bodied to the disabled. Unlike private insurance, social security did not function on what the experts called a "purely actuarial basis." Instead, need and politics entered the picture: some people received more from their social security contributions than others because social policy makers had decided that some people were needier than others. Some received more than others for political reasons. In 1950, for example, the self-employed were covered under a provision that enabled them to pay three-quarters of the combined employer-employee rate for the same benefits. The provision made sense because it seemed "fair" and made social security more attractive to the self-employed. If a private insurance company operated under that notion, however, it would soon go out of business.

No one objected to these social insurance features of social security so long as everyone continued to receive more from the program than they had paid into it. It was a painless program, the "eighth wonder of the world," that brought benefits at little cost; it was not a welfare program that asked people to donate their money to the "undeserving" poor who had not contributed anything to their own salvation. When the economy began to slow and the birthrate to decline, however, a crisis arose in the social security program. The costs of social security began to become visible, and it no longer looked as though the invisible process of economic growth, with its rising salaries and expanding labor force, would cover the increasing costs automatically. Economic crisis reminded people that social security was not just another private insurance policy that the government required all workers to have. It was a public social insurance program that required financial sacrifice for the public good. Viewed in that light, social security's golden halo no longer shone so brightly. The program survived and remained the keystone of America's welfare state, yet it was no longer immune from criticism.

The crisis in social insurance took a long time to arrive. As early as 1939, Social Security Administration bureaucrats had realized that a day would come when the system would spend more in benefits than it received from payroll taxes. In 1939, the advisory council asked that Congress recognize the need for general revenues to supplement worker and employee contributions. In the 1940s, worried about a possible post-war depression, Congress even wrote this principle into the law, yet it soon thought better of the idea and repealed a provision that called for the federal government to make up deficits in the program through general revenues.[7] In the affluent 1950s and the 1960s, no one much cared. Crisis appeared to be a long way off and could be averted through careful planning and timely increases in payroll taxes. In the meantime, the program continued to collect windfalls through new groups entering the system and through larger-than-expected increases in wages, which increased total employer and employee contributions into the social security accounts.

The crisis in social security occurred in the 1970s. In that decade, Congress made a fateful decision to end the bidding to raise social security benefits before elections and to increase benefits in a scientific way. Led by conservative members who wanted to contain social security costs, Congress decided to "index" the program to the rate of inflation. If prices rose, then benefits would rise. It seemed a safe bet for the program's solvency since conventional wisdom held that wages, which determined money coming in, always increased faster than prices, which would now determine money going out.

It seemed a safe bet until stagflation changed the conventional economic wisdom. The consumer price index, which contained costly items like housing and gasoline, increased faster than average wages. Since social security benefits were tied to the consumer price index, their cost began to rise at a faster rate than expected. Adding to the problems, unemployment rose at the same time as prices did, a near impossibility in the standard economic analysis. That meant less money came into the system than expected. The result was a crisis. As one Social Security official explained, "Our 1972 estimates turned out to be very wrong, very quickly. But if we had predicted what actually happened in the 1970s, we would have been practicing in an asylum."[8]

At last social security had come of age, and, beginning in the Ford administration, presidents scrambled to keep the program solvent. After a painful political battle, Jimmy Carter convinced Congress to raise social security taxes in two senses. The percentage of the social security tax and the amount of income subject to social security taxes were both raised. After this legislation in 1977, the Carter administration had hoped to go further and actually to cut benefits. Congress refused to grant the administration's request, agreeing with one social security loyalist that "reducing benefits" would represent a "breach of faith" between the government and social security contributors, acclimated to the idea that none of them were getting more out of the system than they had put into it.[9]

Inflation continued into the Reagan administration. When the President tried to correct the problems of inflation with a tight money policy, a severe recession broke out. Inflation fell, all right, but widespread joblessness brought new problems to an already troubled social security system and led to further loss of confidence.

By now, the social security halo was severely eroded, and people began to question the solvency and even the desirability of social security. The affluent young—or yuppies, as they came to be called—had particular reasons to doubt the need for social security. In an era of high interest rates, social security suffered a double burden that diminished its appeal. The high interest rates were symptomatic of inflation and high prices; inflation raised social security benefits and increased the financial strain on the system. That in turn raised the question of social security's solvency and caused young people to wonder if it would survive to see *their* retirement. These questions arose just when alternative private-sector investments, such as the much-touted Individual Retirement Accounts, appeared particularly attractive because of the high interest rates. Those with money in their pockets looked beyond social security for financial help. They compared private-sector plans to a public-sector plan they were accustomed to think about in private-sector terms. Predictably, they found the latter wanting. It became fashionable to "zero it out" in sessions between the young and their financial advisors.

A June 1983 issue of *Newsweek* captured the growing disenchantment with social security. The story mentioned that the social trust funds were losing $20,000 every minute of every day. If things continued along the same course, thre would be no money left to mail social security checks on July 3, 1983. The elderly and disabled would discover a new meaning for the word independence day. Social security would crash. Some of the commentators cited by *Newsweek* did not think this to be much of a tragedy. A conservative critic wrote a column in which he argued that, "Social security is at once a bad deal, a lie, and a national obstruction." Another economic analyst called the program "institutionalized pickpocketing of the young." This analyst noted that the present generation of retirees received all of its investment in social security, with interest to spare, in 2.8 years. Baby boomers would have to wait 15 years to get back their investments, provided they lived that long. Viewed this way, social security became an intolerable burden on the backs of the young.[10]

Business groups joined in the growing condemnation of social security, but in a restrained manner. They knew, if many an academic analyst did not, that a social security retirement account was not equivalent to a private annuity. In 1981, for example, the influential Committee on Economic Development issued a report on "Reforming Retirement Policy." The report sharply criticized the nation's retirement policy as being "uncoordinated" and "shortsighted" and too loosely linked with the nation's other economic concerns, such as increasing investment and maintaining economic growth. The report featured what had become a standard criticism of the nation's public policy: that Congress simply piled program upon program without much thought to the system being created. The report spared social security from extensive criticism, however, and never once suggested that social security be abolished.[11]

Despite the growing criticism of social security, Congress and the administration joined forces to "save" the program in 1983. The Republicans had learned the potency of the social security issue in 1981, when the President had proposed cuts in the program and, at the height of his popularity, received a resounding defeat. Social security became a major issue of the 1982 elections and caused the Republicans to lose seats in Congress. It appeared that, even though some of the program's popularity had been diminished among the young, it still enjoyed a strong core of support from the elderly and from others who realized the organic links between the generations. The elderly were not just any old (so to speak) interest group. Instead, they were also young people's parents and grandparents. The message was clear: politicians tampered with social security at their own peril. This knowledge made the Republicans wary of taking the lead on a program to save the social security system; they refused to move to reduce benefits, decrease program eligibility, or increase taxes without the full cooperation of the Democrats.

In December 1981, President Reagan had appointed a bipartisan commission to propose solutions to the social security problem and report to the President at the end of 1982. The announcement of this commission hardly made Washingtonians very optimistic. Such commissions traditionally served as convenient means to sweep difficult problems under the rug. As one commentator put it, "Such commissions seem to come and go in the nation's capital with the frequency of tourist buses, and with about as much political effect."[12]

This commission did better than most. For their own reasons, representatives of each political party wanted to "save" social security. Daniel Patrick Moynihan, the ebullient New York senator who served on the commission, argued that the key was getting the Republicans to agree that social security could be saved through "a combination of relatively modest steps." These included raising the tax rates and reducing some future benefit increases.

The alternative of a bankrupt social security system was intolerable to Moynihan. He despaired over the fact that polls showed that half of the nation did not think it would receive social security benefits. Moynihan asked the readers of the *Washington Post* to think of what such a default implied: "that government is lying. That government is stealing. That government cannot be trusted. . . . We began to accept the idea that there are fundamental issues that our system cannot resolve. . . . We have got to stop that. There is a center in American politics. It can govern."[13] Democrats Moynihan and Congressman Claude Pepper worked with Republicans Robert Dole and Congressman Barber Conable and, together with administration figures such as James Baker, the White House Chief of Staff, and David Stockman, the budget director, fashioned a compromise.

Each side sacrificed something. The Democrats, led by such respected figures as Robert Ball, agreed to such things as a one-time omission of the cost-of-living adjustment. The Republicans acquiesced to increased social security taxes.

For all of that, the 1983 compromise left the program largely intact. Essentially, the Democrats convinced the Republicans that the problem was a temporary deficit that would take care of itself in time. In the 1990s, they argued, the system would enjoy a breathing spell. The retirement of the depression generation and the continued employment of the baby boom generation would generate an impressive surplus in the program. The retirement of the baby boomers, everyone admitted, posed serious problems, but those problems lay far in the future, beyond the exquisitely present-minded concerns of the politicians. As David Stockman put it, "I'm not going to spend a lot of political capital solving some other guy's problems in 2010."[14] Viewed that way, the commission's problem was to find enough money to get through immediate financial problems. The commission did just that, making temporary adjustments, accelerating already-scheduled tax increases, and bringing new groups like new federal employees into the system. Crisis was averted. As the National Commission expressed the matter, it believed that "the Congress in its deliberations on financing proposals, should not alter the fundamental structure of the Social Security program or undermine its fundamental principles."[15]

The work of the commission represented an impressive political exercise. Nonetheless, some damage had been done to the integrity of the public sector. Social security had, after all, nearly gone broke, and only last minute heroics saved it. The situation suggested a parallel between the public sector in the 1970s and 1980s and the private sector in the 1920s and 1930s. Both systems had come perilously close to collapse. Both episodes eroded public confidence and caused people to reevaluate their commitments. This parallel was easier to make because the fundamental differences between public sector and private sector had never been clear in America and because, by the 1980s, it was fashionable to equate a good private-sector with a good public-sector program—the Progressive and New eras all over again.

The truth was, however, that no one seriously entertained dismantling social security in the 1980s any more than the notion of ending free enterprise was given credence in the 1930s. In both instances, too many people had a stake in the status quo for it to be altered beyond recognition.

As we have implied, businessmen as well as bureaucrats wanted to preserve social security. The most important reason for this desire concerned the design of employee benefit programs. Businessmen used social security as a base on which to provide additional employee benefits. Ever since the days of Marion Folsom, public social insurance programs and private welfare capitalism had been interlocked.

A technical example from the field of disability helps to illustrate this point.[16] In 1982 an estimated 23,316,000 workers were covered by private long-term disability insurance policies. Over 17 million of these workers received these policies from their employers rather than by purchasing the policies themselves. Although these fringe benefits were not universal, at least 20 percent of America's workers had this form of disability protection. Of 21 million workers in the nation's largest and medium-sized companies, two-fifths had long-term disability insurance, according to a 1983 Department of Labor study.

The link between these private disability plans and social security disability insurance was quite direct. All private long-term plans require a person to apply for social security disability benefits; some will not provide benefits to people who are not receiving public benefits. In this way, the private companies use the public sector to enforce the public sector's strict definition of disability in their contracts. Furthermore, the private insurance companies encourage and even require applicants to appeal the decision should the applicant be rejected for public benefits. Under the rules of social security, denied applicants may request an initial reconsideration, then a hearing before an administrative law judge, and ultimately may take their case to federal court with full right of appeal. Beginning at the administrative law judge hearing, many applicants hire lawyers to plead their cases, even though legal counsel is neither required nor encouraged. General Motors, to name just one large corporation, requires its employees to appeal denied social security cases. Many insurance companies gladly pay the cost of the lawyer.

Insurance companies pay for lawyers because they want to shift the costs of disability from the private to the public sector. As rehabilitation expert Donald Galvin notes, "Risk management consultants routinely advise their . . . clients to engage in cost-shifting." In this spirit, some long-term disability contracts promise the replacement of 60 percent of an employee's pre-disability income as a result of payments from *all* sources. More than a quarter of the plans written today specify that all private and governmental disability payments be considered in computing a disabled worker's benefits, although it is more common for benefits to be offset only against income from public programs. Without exception, today's insurance policies stipulate that private benefits be reduced to reflect benefits paid by Social Security; without exception, Social Security becomes the first payer. The economics of these offset rules is not subtle: the more that other sources pay, the less the insurance company pays.

In this way, and in many others, public social insurance and private fringe benefits work together. For this reason, business hesitates to demand radical cutbacks in social security. If Congress were to cut back on disability insurance, for example, the costs of private employers would almost surely rise. The federal deficit might be reduced, but employers would not be better off. Because the public and private sectors cooperate in this manner, social security through social insurance appears destined to remain the nation's largest and most important social welfare program.

WELFARE

The obvious social security program to compare with social insurance is noncontributory welfare. Unlike social insurance, welfare has come under severe attack and withstood those attacks less well. Welfare, unlike social security old-age, retirement or disability insurance, lacks a ready comparison between it and private-sector activities. For all that politicians like to think otherwise, welfare represents a handout, pure and simple. As a handout, welfare has many political vulnerabilities that politicians, eager to save federal funds, have exploited.

The most important fact governing the history of welfare concerns the rise of Aid to Families with Dependent Children (AFDC) as the most important welfare program. Between 1935 and 1950, the elderly received the bulk of federal and state welfare funds. That fact tended to diminish the distinctions between "unearned" welfare and "earned" social insurance. The elderly could not easily be classified as shiftless. As late as 1955, the federal government spent twice as much on welfare for the permanently and totally disabled, the blind, and the elderly as it did on welfare for dependent children and their families. Two years later, the nation reached an important milestone: there were more recipients of AFDC than of any other type of welfare. By 1970, the costs of AFDC were consistently greater than those of all the other welfare programs combined. Welfare, which once meant aid to the elderly, now meant aid to dependent children of unmarried, divorced, or abandoned women.[17]

As early as 1957, signs pointed to great future growth in the AFDC program.[18] Poor people were moving from areas with low welfare benefits to areas with high welfare benefits, from the agricultural South to the urban North. If all other factors remained equal, welfare expenditure would rise. In the 1960s, too, many young people would themselves have children and create a larger pool of potential welfare applicants.

Then changing sexual and marital mores further complicated the numbers. By the late 1950s and early 1960s, the AFDC caseload, as the social workers referred to it, no longer consisted of widows, dependent children, and orphans. Instead, it contained increasing numbers of single mothers, many of whom had never married, and of illegitimate children. A study commissioned by the Eisenhower administration gingerly recognized these facts in 1960, stating that AFDC made financial assistance available for the protection and care of 2.3 million "homeless, dependent, and neglected children . . . found not only where a parent is dead or physically incapacitated, but also in families where there is desertion, divorce, or, indeed, where there was no marriage."[19]

With the realization that the nature of the AFDC caseload had changed came a new concern over the breakdown of the family and community structures. Thoughtful individuals realized that the AFDC program did little to deal with family or community breakdown—if anything, the law encouraged families to separate. A larger group of the poor found that a mother and father living separately could do better financially than could a family living together. If the parents were separated, AFDC allowed the parent with the child to collect welfare; the family that lived together had less access to public aid.

Although expansion in the welfare rolls alarmed Americans, they still regarded welfare as primarily a local responsibility and as a means to aid the "deserving poor." Nonetheless, the notion began to gain currency that the federal government had to redesign the programs to encourage people to form and preserve families and to foster work. The Kennedy administration, in the optimistic spirit of the times, hoped to reach welfare recipients through social services that would remove the barriers that prevented them from working. The administration did in fact undertake two significant reforms. In 1961 the program was amended to add a provision for unemployed parents. The next year Congress passed a measure that added rehabilitation services to AFDC.

These measures represented a substantial intellectual change. In the past, welfare had gone to people who had been excused from working because they were too old, too young, or too sick to work. With the shift in the welfare population, welfare began to go to people who had children under their care but who were neither too old, too young, nor too sick to work. In response, policymakers, who expected welfare mothers and fathers to work, widened the differences between welfare and social security. Social security went to the truly deserving—widows, orphans, and the elderly who were excused from work. Welfare now went to the less than totally deserving who were expected eventually to work. Social security represented an entitlement that in most cases would be paid for life; welfare became a penalty for failing to hold a job or for having an illegitimate child, and no one was encouraged to remain on the welfare rolls.

The Kennedy measures made little real difference in the growth of the welfare rolls. The unemployed-parent provisions revealed the weaknesses in the combined federal-state approach to public welfare. Instead of limiting AFDC to one-parent families, coverage was extended to two-parent families, provided that the primary wage-earner was unemployed. States were not required to participate in this part of the AFDC program, however, and half of them did not. The laggards were the same states from which the poor were fleeing. Requirements in all states were stringent. To qualify the family for aid, one of the parents had to be unemployed; to be certified as unemployed, the primary wage-earner must have worked six of thirteen calendar quarters prior to applying for welfare. Once on welfare, that recipient was forbidden to work more than 100 hours a month. Not surprisingly, enrollment in the unemployed-parents part of the AFDC program remained low.[20]

The 1962 amendments, which emphasized the rehabilitation of welfare recipients, also proved to be a disappointment. Ellen Winston, appointed to serve as Commissioner of Welfare in 1963, said it was her aim to emphasize constructive programs with more stress on services to help people to help themselves, as contrasted with money payments.[21] Welfare recipients would become more independent and self-reliant and in the process be released from a culture of poverty. Once in the labor force, these people would benefit from the same rising tide of economic growth that lifted all Americans. Despite generous terms from the federal government, in which the federal government paid 75 percent of the cost of rehabilitative and preventive services, social services proved to be a poor match for the forces that were helping to swell the welfare rolls.

Congress and the Johnson administration tried again in 1967, this time with something called the Work Incentive Program or WIN. Under WIN, all able-bodied adults were given the opportunity to acquire vocational skills and work experience. Again, nothing much happened. Disappointed, Congress passed the Talmadge Amendments in 1971; all able-bodied AFDC recipients without responsibilities for children under age 6 were now *required* to register for WIN services, and program administrators were *required* to spend one-third of their budgets on subsidized training and employment. The trouble was that employment was in short supply, particularly for single mothers without a high school diploma. Again, nothing much happened.

When, for example, the Ford administration prepared a briefing paper for the President in 1975, it needed to look hard to find good things to say about the WIN program. The data for fiscal 1974 showed 1,811,446 people registered; the program in that year and for the years to follow acted as an inefficient funnel to place the registrants in jobs. For one reason or another, only 534,885 people reached the stage of program participant, only 177,271 obtained employment, and only 51,627 left welfare.[22] The cost-to-benefit ratio of such an effort left the Ford and Carter administrations with little to cheer about. WIN had proved to be a loser.

The Nixon administration had tried and failed to end what people referred to as the "welfare mess" in a different manner, yet the new approach also ended in disappointment. Where the Kennedy and Johnson administrations had emphasized service programs to promote opportunity, Nixon attempted to consolidate the nation's many programs and substitute cash for services. The vehicle he chose to accomplish these results was called the Family Assistance Plan, or FAP.

FAP reflected an effort to initiate a new style of social welfare. Instead of social workers counseling the poor, the new approach relied on intellectual guidance from economists who set about to improve the efficiency of the nation's programs. The drive toward efficiency took many forms, but two of them were particularly important. One involved a shuffling of governmental responsibilities, reassigning them to the level of government best able to administer them. An old idea of which Eisenhower would have approved, this initiative became known as the New Federalism. It involved proposals for block grants from the federal government to the states, which the states could use for specified purposes. The other form of efficiency centered on building work incentives into welfare programs.

The basic insight here came from what economists called the theory of labor supply. According to this theory, a person faced a choice between working and leisure. If he were given money not to work, he might well prefer leisure over working, providing the financial sacrifice were not too great. Welfare represented money that was paid to people who agreed not to work. If a person decided to go to work anyway, he often found his welfare grant reduced by the amount of his wages. Under such a system, the economists reasoned, it made little sense to work. In the economists' jargon, the marginal tax on a welfare recipient's earnings was too high. The solution, then, was to lower the marginal tax rate and in that manner encourage a welfare recipient to work. In the academic haunts of the economists, this idea was called the "negative income tax." Outside of academia, people referred to the idea as a "guaranteed annual income."

FAP was a proposal for a guaranteed annual income. In place of AFDC, there would be a minimum cash payment to all families with dependent children. The proposal and those that followed it for the rest of the decade could be illustrated as follows: Suppose there were a guaranteed benefit of $2,000 and a 50 percent tax on earnings. A family with no earnings would receive the guarantee of $2,000 from the government. A family that earned $2,000 would receive the guarantee and keep half of its earnings; the guarantee of $2,000 and the after-tax earnings of $1,000 total $3,000, so the government would give $1,000 to this family. A family that earned $4,000 would receive the guaranteed $2,000 and retain half of its $4,000 in earnings for a total of $4,000; this family would neither receive money from the government nor owe the government money.

The idea had the intellectual purity and logic of the economist, yet the economists' hour in public policy yielded comparatively little in the way of substantive programs. After a succession of guaranteed annual income proposals from Presidents Nixon, Ford, and Carter, only two programs emerged. One, called "Supplemental Security Income" or SSI, brought the principles of a guaranteed income to the elderly, blind, and disabled. The other, called food stamps, operated as a "disguised" form of guaranteed income.[23]

As one official expressed the idea, food stamps owed their appeal to their name. It was food stamps, not beer stamps, and it had the virtue of supplying aid that was limited to the purchase of essentials. Food stamps, like SSI, had a substantial political following that united urban liberals concerned about the problem of hunger and rural conservatives concerned about the disposition of surplus agricultural commodities. For all of that, food stamps represented cash payments to the poor that were linked to income and that followed the economists' precepts about preserving work incentives. If, for example, an AFDC family received $20 in food stamps and already spent more than $20 on food, then the food stamps increased the cash at the family's disposal. SSI, for its part, owed its popularity to the fact that it conferred its benefits on the "worthy" poor. Some of these worthy poor, such as the elderly, commanded a considerable political following.

More ambitious aspects of the welfare reform proposals, such as a guaranteed income for the working poor, failed. One reason was that the proposals demanded sacrifices from groups that fared relatively well under existing programs, such as veterans and the blind. Welfare programs that accommodated such special interests retained their appeal because they concentrated benefits upon a readily identifiable group, a seemingly sensible tactic in a small welfare system. Under modern conditions, this practice blocked systematic reform by creating groups that had nothing to gain from such reform.

The guaranteed annual income proposals also failed because the legislators had few opportunities to acquire a comprehensive view of the social welfare system. Committee structures helped to lock legislators into a program-by-program view of social policy. Control over income maintenance, for example, was divided among more than sixty congressional committees and subcommittees in 1980.[24] Perhaps that explained why a recently widowed mother of several children, one of whom was disabled, could apply to seven federal programs for aid. In a typical jurisdiction, she would have to go to at least four different offices, fill out at least five different forms, and answer 300 separate questions. Fourteen hundred pieces of information might be needed just to determine the level of the woman's income.[25] Not surprisingly, legislators decried the conflicting terms and unforeseen results of the system, even as the committee system reinforced their natural loyalties to the programs that they had helped to design or pass. When it came time to trade those programs for a guaranteed income, they abandoned their loyalty to *their* programs only reluctantly.

WELFARE UNDER PRESIDENT REAGAN

When President Reagan came into office, he abandoned the guaranteed income strategy altogether. To the advisors close to Reagan, the previous plans had failed as much for economic reasons as political ones. Robert Carleson and Martin Anderson, two of Reagan's domestic advisors in his first term, have argued that the guaranteed annual income presents a logical puzzle with no good solution, a Rubik's Cube that looks easy to twist into place but never quite comes together. The idea relies on a decent level of income for those who cannot work and must depend on the government (the government's guarantee), on low tax rates as welfare recipients begin to work and make money (the marginal tax rate) and on an implicit political promise of reasonable cost. Each of these three things depends on the others. Halving the tax rate doubles the amount of income at which the government continues to pay benefits and therefore increases the cost of the plan. In short, "There is no way to achieve all of the politically necessary conditions for radical welfare reform at the same time." To this bit of logic, the conservatives have added pieces of empirical evidence that cast doubt on the negative income tax and the guaranteed annual income. The Seattle-Denver negative income tax experiments of the 1970s revealed, for example, that a guaranteed income increased the rate of divorce among the working class.[26]

Martin Anderson's rhetoric on the subject of a guaranteed annual income captures the conviction and fervor of the Reagan forces. "A small, largely liberal, intellectual elite" who have been seduced "by simplistic beauty" favor a guaranteed annual income. The members of this elite reside in the favored liberal haunts: "the universities, the welfare agencies that administer the program, the government, and the welfare rolls." Perhaps because of the privileges they enjoy, they have a desire to be free "of the constraints of reality, to soar off into the dream land of unlimited plenty." These "neo-romantics" believe that people "basically like to work . . . and that even mild incentives will encourage them to leave the welfare rolls." Those who oppose the idea see the world "as it is" and have a "realistic, traditional view of life." They recognize that people with a guaranteed income will "simply cease working and loaf." They accept the conditions of a world of unequal income, wealth, power, beauty, and talent, a world in which "people need help from others and by this very fact are dependent." It is no wonder then, that Anderson describes a central objective of the Reagan administration as "not to propose any disguised guaranteed income programs."[27]

Reagan welfare reform, enacted in 1981 and 1982, centered on providing aid to what the administration described as the "truly needy," by "purifying" the welfare rolls and forcing as many welfare recipients as possible to work. This change in the style of welfare reform coincided with a change in government's attitude toward the poor. The Kennedy, Johnson, and Nixon administrations tended to treat the poor somewhat the way adults treated children. The poor were not flawed, so much as they were inexperienced. To enter the mainstream, they needed to be taught about the value of work and to learn other social lessons. In the Reagan years, intellectual discourses that guided policy portrayed the poor as flawed, as lacking in civility, and as victims of government benevolence. The poor were a race apart who could best benefit from what previous generations had called self-help and benign neglect.

Where previous analysts had tended to ignore the racial characteristics and family structures of welfare recipients, the new conservative analysts of the Reagan era often highlighted these characteristics. They asked the nation to take what they called a "realistic" look at the poor. For example, George Gilder, an influential writer on social welfare, painted a sordid picture of life in black ghettos that, unlike previous pictures, focused far more directly on the ghettos' inhabitants than on the external forces that created the ghettos' bad environment.

In Gilder's portrait, the ghetto family lives on welfare. The man of the house, only sometimes present and not the father of all the children in the apartment, spends his time drinking beer and watching television. At times, he gets nasty and drunk and argues with the women in the house. The teen-age boys in the house are out of control, and they carry guns and knives. The 15-year-old girl in the house longs to flee and knows that on her 16th birthday she can gain her freedom, but only by having an illegitimate child and going on welfare. In this way, the government becomes the ghettos' true pimp and promotes illegitimacy.

For Gilder, the moral of this highly moralistic tale illustrated what he called the "limits of public assistance." We must, he urged, "abandon the idea of completely eliminating poverty by distributing money to the poor." Welfare reform could not eliminate poverty because, as support approached an adequate level, it subverted "the male role as provider and promoted family breakdown."[28]

Other conservative social commentators believed that the liberals had it backwards, continuing to talk about what government owed the poor when they should instead focus on what the poor owed society. Lawrence Mead, a professor at NYU, argued that it was time to think about "obligations rather than rights." "We have to use welfare," he wrote, "to set some standards for the recipients." Mead recommended requiring as a condition of support that they "fulfill social obligations and especially that they work."[29]

In this manner, the logic of the economist yielded over the course of a decade to the morality of the philosopher. As usual, subtleties became lost in the heat of the moment. Here, for example, is how two congressional staffers summarized the influential work of Charles Murray, author of the widely cited *Losing Ground*, in a memo for their conservative congressman. Murray, they wrote, suggests that economic growth in the 1960s might well have ended poverty among the working-age population within a decade. "However, once the welfare reforms were implemented, people receiving benefits came to the realization that they did not have to work to attain self-sufficiency as did the rest of the population. Consequently, a trap was benevolently and ignorantly set which ensnared millions of Americans and has not allowed them to escape poverty."[30] The moral was clear: be kind by being cruel.

This background discussion gave a sense of legitimacy to the Reagan efforts to cut the level of AFDC benefits and to institute strict work requirements. It led to further differences between welfare recipients and social security beneficiaries. The former got exposed to the social theories and techniques of the moment; the latter cashed their retirement checks every month.

Yet, for all of the harsh rhetoric, the welfare reform debate continued to be conducted along well-established lines. In a recent round, the nation's governors wanted to change the welfare system from an income maintenance program to a work and training program. To accomplish this result, the governors, acting through the National Governors Association, proposed that every employable welfare recipient, defined as someone who is able-bodied and whose child is at least 3, receive training, job-search assistance, child care, and medical care. The governors estimated the expense at one billion dollars, of which they wanted the federal government to pay at least 80 percent. The Reagan administration soon countered with a program of its own, based on its report on welfare called, *Up from Dependency*, a marvelously resonant title that emphasized the administration's point: welfare is a form of slavery. The administration proposed the GROW program, which consisted of a work and training program run by the states with matching federal funds. All AFDC recipients with children aged *6 months* or older would be required to participate in a program preparing them for work, and teenage parents without a high school degree would be required to participate in an education program.[31]

The governors and the administration differed on how generous the federal government should be and on how old a child should be before its mother should be asked to work. Still, they agreed on a broad outline of a program. As one publication noted, a consensus appeared to be forming early in 1987. Liberals accepted the notion of a work requirement; conservatives recognized that government had a responsibility to help provide education, training, and child care.

If there was a consensus, it was an old-fashioned one. The liberals wanted to add job training services to the nation's social welfare arsenal permanently. The conservatives wanted to wean people from the government. The same consensus had sustained the rehabilitation programs of the 1920s and of the 1950s. The rhetoric of investment could still be heard on both sides. Congressman Jim Wright of Texas, the Speaker of the House, defended an increase in government spending in these words: "Of course, it cannot be revenue neutral in its first year if it is to achieve the objective. But if people move from welfare, where they are consuming resources, to jobs where they are paying taxes, it becomes not only revenue neutral but revenue positive."[32] The jargon about "revenue neutral" had changed a bit; otherwise the words could have been spoken by a New Era bureaucrat from the vocational rehabilitation program.

HEALTH INSURANCE

National health insurance became the central social welfare issues of the 1970s and 1980s. Its history clearly illustrates modern developments in social welfare policy and the close alliance between the public and private sectors in the provision of social welfare services. Welfare concerned business only peripherally; as welfare recipients were weaned from the rolls, business and the private sector were expected to take up the slack. Although organizations like the CED lent their support to measures such as the negative income tax, welfare remained the bureaucrat's arena. Health care, by way of contrast, was a matter of vital concern to professional providers, such as doctors and hospital administrators, and to organized consumers, such as private employers. If income security formed the keystone of the welfare state, health care was the most important component of modern welfare capitalism.

The debate over national health insurance was as notable for what was not discussed as for what policymakers did discuss. After the 1930s, for example, no congressman seriously entertained the idea of what, for want of a better description, might be called "true" national health care. By this term, we mean health care paid for and provided by the government under a system in which doctors work for the government. Instead of socializing medicine, government tried to reach accommodation with organized medicine through measures such as the 1946 Hill-Burton Hospital Survey and Construction Act (discussed in Chapter 7) in which federal dollars went to projects that hospital administrators approved and controlled.

Meanwhile, as it became clear in the 1940s and 1950s that the government would not enact a law to pay for health care, collective bargaining agreements became vehicles for the provision of employer-based health care. The growth of what came to be called private social security paralleled that of public social security. As early as 1954, for example, unions were responsible for purchasing one-quarter of the nation's health care. In that year, some 12 million union members and 17 million dependents enjoyed union-provided health coverage.[33]

As private organizations staked their claims to the health insurance turf, government worked the edges. First, it received authority to pay for the health care of welfare beneficiaries. This process began during the New Deal and continued in 1960 with the passage of a law that allowed the states to subsidize health care for the elderly on welfare. In 1965, the process reached its climax with congressional passage of Medicaid—federal money to pay the health costs of *all* welfare recipients, not just the elderly. Nothing about these laws challenged the primacy of private health care providers. They simply allowed the states to reimburse these providers when they took care of welfare recipients.

Next, the federal government grudgingly won permission in 1965 to pay for the medical care of people who had retired and were receiving social security benefits through old-age insurance. Passage of this program, referred to as Medicare, demonstrated social security's halo effect. Unable to secure any form of national health insurance, social security bureaucrats decided to limit their efforts to securing coverage for people *already* retired, rather than for the working population. Medicare, like so many other aspects of the welfare state, became an extension of social insurance coverage.

Medicare passed in the heyday of the Great Society, when it was almost certain that some form of health insurance would be passed. One observer characterized the atmosphere as one of "political certainty."[34] Even the American Medical Association, a traditional enemy of the Social Security Administration on health insurance, felt the need to produce a proposal. Called "Eldercare," the AMA bill would have permitted the elderly to receive hospital and medical benefits. But the bill would have covered only the poor and would have been administered by the states.

Wedded to social insurance models, social security officials, such as Robert Ball, were quick to denounce the AMA bill. It was public assistance—welfare, not social insurance. "Any assistance program is unsatisfactory," Ball told Congressman John E. Fogarty of Rhode Island. "Public assistance," Ball said, "helps older people meet their healthcare costs only after their resources are depleted to the point that they cannot afford these costs." Social insurance, by way of contrast, prevented dependency by allowing people to make contributions during their working lifetimes and have hospital protection beginning at age 65.[35] It was familiar rhetoric applied to a new field.

Ball and his colleagues denounced welfare schemes but offered Congress only very limited health insurance proposals. The administration wanted to pay the hospital bills, not the doctor bills, of the elderly who had retired and were receiving social security old-age insurance. As HEW Secretary Anthony Celebrezze put the matter to one of his friends at the beginning of 1965, "We feel that private and private non-profit insurance plans offered to younger Americans through various collective bargaining agreements, group health and individual insurance plans have largely met the needs of working Americans during their early years and that the Federal Government need not get involved in this area."[36]

In essence, Celebrezze and the social security officials who guided his actions envisioned a three-layered system. For the poor, there would be subsidized medicine to welfare beneficiaries, administered by the states; for workers, there would be union and welfare capitalist health plans; and for the retired, there would be federally financed hospital insurance.

Congressman Wilbur Mills, who knew how to count votes, prepared to move a health insurance bill out of his Ways and Means Committee in 1965. Master politician that he was, he responded to all of the parties at interest and produced a measure that contained three major provisions. One, as already discussed, was Medicaid, subsidized medicine for welfare recipients. Another was hospital insurance, as Ball had favored, or Medicare. A third was the supplementary program that paid the doctor's bills, known among the Washington insiders as "Part B of Medicare." This third program was optional, and beneficiaries had to pay extra for it.

In the Medicare program, then, the federal government used social security funds to reimburse hospitals and doctors for medical care. The program intruded very little on the existing systems of providing and paying for medical care, except to pump more money into the systems and bid up costs. Where doctors had previously prided themselves on treating some of the elderly for free, now Medicare stood ready to pay the bills at "customary" rates over which the federal government had little influence.[37]

The mechanics of the legislation indicated its accommodation of powerful forces in the health field and its strict reliance on insurance principles. The Medicare law allowed groups of hospitals the option of nominating "fiscal intermediaries," instead of dealing directly with the Social Security Administration. These intermediaries were to provide financial services such as billing, and the federal government was to pay the bills. As expected, the overwhelming majority of hospitals and other institutions nominated private organizations to be their fiscal intermediaries. The government paid the hospital according to the hospital's costs, not according to some predetermined schedule. The more a hospital spent, the more money flowed from the government. In a similar way, private health insurance organizations served as the intermediaries between the federal government and the doctors. Quite literally, then, the federal government simply bought into the health system, using the politically convenient cover of the social security system. That was the American version of national health insurance: federal money and private control.

Liberal toward the hospitals and the doctors, the Social Security Administration took a more conservative attitude toward the elderly who received the care. More than other parts of the social security program, health insurance followed strict insurance principles, which hit the elderly in their pocketbooks. Mechanisms in which the consumer shared some of the costs, designed to discourage frivolous use of health care, were built into the program, just as they were in most private health insurance plans. Medicare consisted of reimbursement for up to ninety days of hospitalization for each "spell" of illness, and it featured initial charges before Medicare "kicked in," plus additional charges as a patient's illness progressed. The law required the patient to pay $10 per day after the sixtieth day of hospitalization, for example.[38]

In this manner, Medicare continued trends that had begun with disability insurance. Both relied on reassuring analogies from contributory social insurance to extend the boundaries of the welfare state. One paid for disability insurance; one built up a fund that purchased health insurance. Both conferred rights that people had "earned." Yet there were important differences between retirement benefits and the health and disability benefits that came along later. The retirement benefits could be paid for by building up a fund that would be spent later. Disability and hospital care posed more difficult problems. How much money should one set aside for disability, which might never happen, or for ill health? No one really knew. Neither ill health nor disability was certain to occur in an individual's case. Aging was inevitable, but how could you be certain that someone was disabled or ill? No one really knew that either. To cope with these problems and to appease opponents who doubted the federal government's competence, the Social Security Administration turned over the administration of both programs to outsiders. For disability, they chose state rehabilitation agencies; for health insurance, they opted for private health insurors. That was the nature of the American welfare state: federal money and state or private administration.

HEALTH INSURANCE AFTER MEDICARE

After the Great Society and the passage of Medicare, the prospects of expanding the federal government's presence in health care finance diminished. The health insurance issue passed through many of the same phases as welfare reform, with the same discouraging results. It was one thing to expand social insurance and pass Medicare. Those on disability insurance, for example, received Medicare benefits in 1972 without a congressional whimper. It was quite another thing to allow the federal government into the system that financed medical care for workers and their families.

As in the field of welfare, cost soon became the predominant issue in discussions of health insurance. Rising health costs could be traced to many sources, including the Medicare law itself. Certainly, the passage of Medicare coincided with the beginning of an era in which health care costs went out of sight. Reciting those statistics can become numbing, but one might reflect on the fact that between 1966 and 1980, Medicare and Medicaid costs *doubled* every four years. Medicare cost $7.1 billion in 1970, $35 billion in 1980, and $70 billion in 1987. Medicaid cost $2.7 billion in 1970, $19 billion in 1980, and $26 billion in 1987. The rate of growth in the cost of medical services rose from 3.2 percent a year in the seven years before Medicare to 7.9 percent annually in the five years after. By 1985, the nation spent more than 10 percent of its GNP on health care.[39]

No wonder, then, that the terms of the policy discussion shifted. No longer was access to medical care the paramount worry in Washington. In the 1970s, people worried far more about how to contain health care costs. The welfare discussion took a parallel course. It went from concern over how to provide opportunity to the poor during the Great Society (access, in other words) to moaning about the "welfare mess" (cost, in other words). Joseph Califano, Carter's Secretary of HEW and as trendy a follower of social welfare politics as could be found, put the matter in a 1978 memo to Jimmy Carter, "We need a national health program, not just national health insurance."[40] Federal money had to be accompanied by greater federal control over expenditures.

Liberals and conservatives had tried and failed to pass national health insurance for the working population in the 1970s. In 1970, for example, Senator Edward Kennedy and Representative Martha W. Griffiths of Michigan called for a comprehensive program of free medical care, replacing all public and private health plans in a single, federally operated health insurance system. The plan would have required hospitals and doctors to operate within budget constraints that, at that point, did not exist; health care would have been "free." If you had to go the hospital, your bills were paid. Richard Nixon, a conservative president in a liberal era, countered with his own health insurance plan in 1971 that would have required *employers* to provide health insurance benefits. In effect, President Nixon wanted to mandate welfare capitalism. Neither the President nor the former President's brother brought their versions of national health insurance to America; neither could "thread the political needle," in Kennedy's phrase.[41]

Nixon, for his part, set the health care debate off in new directions by treating health care as he had welfare reform. He asked the economists to come up with a way to make the health care system more rational. As they had with the welfare system, the economists proceeded to discover "disincentives" built into American health care. They were not hard to find. Because the government paid the bills on the basis of "reasonable costs," it was profitable for hospitals and doctors to jack up their prices.

Nixon's search for a better way ended with the rediscovery of "prepaid group health," an idea that had been widely discussed in health reform circles since the late twenties. It had, in fact, been one of welfare capitalist Edward Filene's interests in the last stages of his life.[42]

Here is how prepaid group health worked: Payment in advance, or "prospective payment" as it was called, provided an incentive to keep costs within agreed-upon limits. Doctors only got a fixed amount per patient, and as a result they had an incentive to keep the patient well and out of the hospital. Group practice ended the practice of trooping from specialist to specialist in the interest of getting well. In a group practice, all of the specialists were housed under one roof and could work together in an efficient manner.[43] Together, the doctors could cut down on the hospital admission rate. It paid them to do so. The more people they admitted to the hospital, the less money they made. A permissive system of hospital care would be replaced with a controlled system.

Further, nothing about prepaid practice restricted access to health care, particularly if the government decided to pay the costs for its special clients: the elderly and the indigent. These arguments persuaded health experts to put a new label on prepaid group practice and call it the health maintenance organization (HMO).

The Health Maintenance Organization Act of 1973 mandated that employers of twenty-five persons or more who were subject to the federal minimum wage must offer a prepaid group practice plan to their employees as one of their health insurance choices, provided that such a plan was operating in a particular area. To assist in the creation of such plans, the government provided loans and grants to HMOs that met federal requirements. The rationale behind this part of the legislation hinged on creating competition in the health care market; the large private health insurance carriers would no longer enjoy a near monopoly in the health insurance field. At the same time, however, the law acted as a force for social uplift by setting strict standards for plans certified as HMOs.

Community rating was one such requirement. It meant essentially that one size would fit all. The idea here was to apply the same rates to high-risk, under-served groups as to other groups and, in a sense, to use the HMO as a way of subsidizing medicine for the less advantaged. A black family living in Harlem would pay the same rate as a white family living in Scarsdale. In this way, the proprietors of HMOs would not be able to "pick off" the young and the healthy and refuse to serve groups with potentially greater problems.[44]

The health maintenance organization, in other words, was both liberal and conservative, in much the same way that the welfare programs of the twenties swung both ways, depending on the predilections of a particular proponent. On the one hand, health maintenance organizations served as forces for social uplift and means of bringing medical care to the poor and the elderly. On the other hand, health maintenance organizations were forces contributing to the efficiency of the health care system and a means of reducing health care costs. As such, they served as a means of limited compromise in a troubled area of social welfare at a time of congressional leadership.

It was similar to workfare; both were proposals that exemplified the political least common denominator. Although a person's point of view could shift at any point in the process and cause a retreat from support for workfare or health maintenance organizations, both sorts of programs provided structures on which to rest political compromises.

In both cases, furthermore, the federal government sought a means of controlling the costs of its own programs. Passage of legislation and the implementation of programs marked responses to problems created at least in part by previous legislation. In this sense, an era of federal activism that might be described as liberal led to a new era of federal activism that might be described as conservative. New programs arose both in times of prosperity and in times of austerity, in times of presidential and of congressional leadership.

By the late 1970s, it looked as though legislation on HMOs and on aid for medical education would be all that the President or the former President's brother would be able to get on health care. President Carter's proposals bore a resemblance to the welfare capitalist plans of the early 1930s. He wanted to require employers to furnish private insurance for their employees and to create a public corporation to provide insurance protection for those not covered by private insurance.

WELFARE CAPITALISM: THE SEQUEL

In the middle 1980s, even Senator Kennedy conceded that employers would have to remain the nation's major providers of health care. He no longer believed that the federal government should make major efforts itself. Instead, he took the position that Presidents Nixon and Carter had before him and advocated requiring employers to provide health insurance. It amounted to nothing less than a return to the minimum standards proposals common in the Progressive and New Deal eras. The federal government would set standards and give the private sector the freedom to meet them. The corporation was to be the focal point of social action, if it obeyed Washington's rules.

Not surprisingly, the debate over Kennedy's health proposal resembled earlier debates over minimum wages. In speaking before Senator Kennedy at a June, 1987 hearing about the notion of "mandating" health insurance,

Robert Crandall, the head of American Airlines, said that it would help to create a "level playing field." He noted that Continental Airlines could compete unfairly by virtue of having "abrogated its labor contract," and not paying health insurance. Crandall supported Kennedy's bill because it would bring "unfair employers like Continental up to a decent level."[45]

Walter B. Mayer, the head of the employee benefits division of Chrysler, made similar arguments. He noted that about $300 per car was spent on health benefits and that some manufacturers failed to pay health benefits. In effect, that meant that Chrysler and other affluent companies were paying other companies' health care costs. Chrysler endorsed the Kennedy bill.

Some, like Senator Dan Quayle of Indiana, wondered about the wisdom of mandated benefits. How far would you go, the Senator asked the businessmen. Would you mandate pensions? Yes, said the representative from Chrysler. As Robert Crandall of American Airlines expressed the matter, "There are some free riders out there," and he wanted to eliminate them. It was a line Gerard Swope might have used in the 1920s and 1930s.

To be sure, the Kennedy proposal was not a product of the Progressive or New Deal eras. For one thing, the world had grown more complicated. The Kennedy proposal, for example, would preempt existing *state* laws in the health insurance field which, according to Philip Briggs, a Vice President of the Metropolitan Life Insurance Company, had raised costs. For another thing, Kennedy envisioned a quid pro quo: get small employers to buy insurance, but create large pools from which they could get insurance. The quid was coverage for employees in small companies, and the quo was reduced premiums for small employers. In an activist state, it became possible to rig the market and regulate private actors. A third and final difference was that businessmen and bureaucrats both now looked to Washington for the solution of policy problems; the federal government was firmly at the center of policy initiatives.

At the same time, welfare capitalism remained alive and well, even in this new and complex policy environment. Fifty years after the passage of the Social Security Act, private employers still provided vital social services; they, rather than the federal government, took the lead in supplying health care for their employees. Health care, as the representative from Chrysler had noted, represented a large investment. To protect that investment and keep employees productive, a new generation of welfare capitalist efforts arose. The labels and some of the contents were different, yet corporate efforts marked logical extensions of methods begun a century ago by Nelson O. Nelson and other business pioneers.

To get the flavor of modern welfare capitalism, consider the following examples from the health and disability fields.[46]

Johnson and Johnson, a pharmaceutical company, initiated a program called "Live for Life" which was typical of modern welfare capitalist efforts. The goal was to improve employee health by achieving specific improvements in nutrition, weight control, physical fitness, cessation of smoking, and management of employee stress and blood pressure. A committee drawn from top- and middle-level managers and labor leaders launched the voluntary plans. Benefits available to employees included an assessment of their current health status, and a "life-style seminar." There followed what the company called "action programs" in smoking cessation, weight control, stress management, nutrition, exercise, and dealing with high blood pressure. The company claimed that the program led to a 15 percent reduction in sick days.

Another example of modern welfare capitalism was called the Pennsylvania Buy Right Strategy, an updated version of the activities that used to be conducted by the National Civic Federation. With information provided by the Pennsylvania Business Roundtable, companies initiated for their employees an education program on health care cost reduction.

Medical care cost increases at a compound annual rate of 17 percent between 1979 and 1984 at Air Products and Chemicals, Inc. prompted the introduction of a redesigned medical plan in 1985. The company's health care cost management strategy involved, among other things, corporate introduction and sponsorship of wellness, fitness, and safety programs for employees and their families. Recently, the company completed construction of a fitness center at its headquarters.

In the field of disability, companies began to experiment with what corporate personnel officers called "disability management at the workplace." As with many corporate trends, the words had no precise meaning. Disability management was a highly heterogeneous movement that owed its prominence to the evangelical zeal of corporate managers. It derived from many of the same impulses toward enlightened self-interest as had motivated corporate leaders like Edward Filene and Henry Dennison to improve working conditions at the beginning of this century. Intelligent selfishness, both men had called it—welfare capitalism that paid dividends.

To illustrate how disability management works, consider the case of the Minnesota Mining and Manufacturing Company (3-M), a large company with over 50,000 employees. By 1980 this company found itself with 583 active long-term disability cases and decided to take measures to reduce the costs that such a large caseload implied. It responded by creating disability program coordinators and putting them in charge of monitoring the disability caseload and preventing more people from entering the caseload. The coordinators attempted to build an element of accountability into what had been a very fragmented operation within the company. They made sure that every effort to find work for an employee was expended before the employee retired and left the labor force as a disabled worker.

In a representative case, a 30-year-old laborer in a heavy manufacturing job sustained a work injury that left him unable to do lifting. Unable to do his former job, the man was placed in a different position which matched his physical capabilities. Although he received rehabilitation benefits from the company's long-term disability policy, he never entered the rolls on a permanent basis.

The program, although it has just begun, has achieved a measure of success in reducing disability expenditures. It owes much of its success to the way in which it creates incentives to prevent disability. When a person acquires a disability at 3-M, his disability maintenance costs become a responsibility of that man's department. That gives the department a bottom-line reason for taking steps to keep the man employed. Even if the man can no longer work for his original department, he may still be able to work elsewhere, and it may be economical for the original department to pay part of the man's salary.

At base, the disability management approach marks an attempt to reduce the costs of disability benefits by keeping people at work. In nearly all cases, keeping people at work means retaining them within the employ of the original company. Some companies have pursued this objective very aggressively, as the example of Boise Cascade illustrates.

Boise Cascade became involved in disability management in 1979 when it discovered that 250 of its employees at a Minnesota plant were disabled and drawing workers' compensation. Management grew concerned over the cost of maintaining these workers, particularly since workers' compensation costs were rising and showed no signs of abating. The company called in a consulting psychologist who studied the physical requirements of each job and determined that many of the jobs could be modified in a way that would permit the disabled people to return to work. Eventually 100 of the 250 went back to work, reducing the company's workers' compensation liability from $13 million to $3 million. The company also increased the size of its medical department and became actively involved in the rehabilitation of injured workers; it even prepared a special training film to make supervisors sensitive to the problems of working with handicapped workers. It was as though Elton Mayo had joined forces with Dr. Joyce Brothers to create a new generation of welfare capitalism.

Other companies take similar steps to keep injured workers employed. At Omark Industries, which makes tools for the lumber industry, a physician treating an injured worker receives a description of the worker's job. If the physician thinks that the job should be modified or redesigned to accommodate the functional limitations of the worker, and if it is possible and financially feasible to do so, the job modification will be made. David R. Evert goes so far as to mention an "absolute return-to-work job guarantee to every disabled employee" as a policy of the Control Data Corporation.

In an America where private-sector criteria are once again applied to public-sector programs, the private sector is where the action is in social welfare policy and programs.

CONCLUSION

As these examples make clear, businessmen and bureaucrats had both come a long way. By the beginning of the twentieth century larger American corporations discovered the nation as an arena over which to manufacture and distribute products. This discovery led to complex administrative and social problems, and, as part of their attempt to solve such problems, big businessmen began fashioning functional bureaucracies to organize and control their industrial operations. The role of national leaders fell to them naturally, because there were few other takers. Consequently, the businessmen engaged in the practice of welfare and personnel work as part of the process of bureaucratic restructuring; this was work previously undertaken only by local institutions such as the courts or the church. The work progressed to the extent that by the end of World War I giant firms such as General Electric had evolved individualized, but national, welfare states for their employees.

With businessmen leading the way, federal and state bureaucrats sponsored some legislation, such as minimum wage laws, and expedited other legislation, such as workers' compensation. Workers' compensation laws illustrated the state of relations between businessmen and bureaucrats in the Progressive Era. Working with state officials, enlightened employers created sets of minimum standards, in this case minimum amounts of money for compensating injured employees. Instead of dealing with the old locally-oriented institutions such as the courts that had previously handled such matters, employer and employee came to enjoy the benefits of a no-fault insurance approach to industrial accidents through workers' compensation. It was one of the first bureaucratic intrusions on business power in the social welfare field, but it was a minimal one. State workers' compensation boards were created to administer the workers' compensation insurance funds, but state money was not used to finance the funds. Private employers paid for the increased costs, if any. In a sense, workers' compensation laws functioned automatically, allowing injured workers to receive their compensation without any intensive process of state intervention. State compensation officials, therefore, confined their efforts to forwarding efficient and humane procedures among businessmen in their respective states. Federal officials, in turn, sought to persuade state workers' compensation boards, where possible, to use standard administrative, actuarial, and financial procedures.

Throughout the 1920s larger American corporations remained the major models for the provision of welfare services. This dominance, exemplified by the rise of a welfare capitalist ideology in business, academic, and political circles, was less the product of a conscious corporate conspiracy than it was a testimony to the comparative organizational advantage the corporate sector held over the government. In an era when interested Americans believed social welfare to be a matter of social engineering, corporate leaders were presumed to be the ones best able to accomplish the task.

War had also increased the scope of federal welfare initiatives, but public welfare programs remained modeled upon private programs. By 1921 the states received modest amounts of federal funds to maintain infant and maternal health, to rehabilitate disabled workers, and to create vocational education programs. For the first time, Washington indirectly financed welfare programs aimed at a larger clientele than Indians and Eskimos.

Although Washington had begun to finance indirectly, it made no efforts to control directly. All the formal federal welfare programs created during the 1920s gave money to the states. The states, not the federal government, then used the increased public appropriations to provide temporary advisory, training, and medical services to welfare clients. Federal efforts were not aimed at providing citizens with continuing protection against the hazards of life; instead, they demonstrated the social effectiveness of welfare activities to interested groups in the state and localities. These groups, it was assumed, had the responsibility of following through upon the federal initiatives.

Depression provided a severe shock to both the private and public welfare programs created during the 1920s. Corporate and community welfare plans operated upon the principle of accumulating funds for use in case of emergency. During the extended emergency called the depression, contributions to the funds decreased and payments from the funds increased until the assets dwindled to nothing. Suspicion grew that businessmen possessed neither the wisdom, will, nor funds to solve social welfare problems on their own.

Established public welfare programs suffered as badly as private programs. Rationalized in terms of cost-efficiency these public programs were complements to private activities and private labor markets. When the private labor market collapsed, so did the efficiency rationale for rehabilitation, health, and education services that lay at the heart of the public programs. Exceedingly confused about what to do, federal bureaucrats were being asked to do something.

Initially the federal efforts did little to change the traditional structure of America's welfare system. When Roosevelt entered office in 1933 he followed Hoover's lead and used a government agency to lend money to banks and business firms in the hope that the loans would spur economic recovery. This type of program, one that simply granted money to businessmen and asked them to work themselves out of the depression, was only as strong as the businessmen's ability to invest money in profitable ways. In 1933 few outlets for such profitable investment existed.

Some of the leaders of Roosevelt's administration realized that Hoover's procedures were simply not enough. They went further and gave business-men increased opportunities to get together and solve national problems under loose federal sponsorship. The NRA was the institutional expression of this attempt at enhanced cooperation between big business and the state. Its sponsors aimed to nationalize the welfare capitalist order.

Businessmen, however, were unable to organize themselves sufficiently to solve welfare problems. By the middle of 1934 the failure of the NRA was obvious—a victim of both internal and external factors. The inability of the BAC to agree upon a labor policy during the months of 1933 and 1934, for example, reflected a lack of cohesion among the corporate leaders them-selves. At the same time, the rise of the CIO, the Townsend Movement, and Huey Long's "Share Our Wealth" scheme created external challenges to the effectiveness of the NRA over which businessmen or their bureaucratic sponsors had little or no control.

As the NRA disintegrated, the Roosevelt administration tried to formu-late some plan of action to replace it. Businessmen, aware that their own failure invited strengthened governmental efforts to solve welfare problems, moved away from their earlier insistence that they alone control social welfare programs. Federal officials, however, failed to exploit this opening immediately because they lacked clearly defined models upon which to proceed. The notion that welfare programs be modeled after programs in other countries, not after the programs of private corporations, arose very slowly among these officials.

The Social Security Act of 1935 marked the first, hesitant step toward a distinctly federal social welfare program. Washington provided direct services to the people under the old-age segment of the legislation—the part that people referred to as Social Security. Even this part of the legislation was not completely divorced from the private sector. A person's old-age pension reflected his wage in the private labor market, and the entire scheme was consciously based on life insurance provided by the private insurance industry. The other sections of the act were even less federal operations or federal creations. The unemployment insurance aspects of the Social Security Act were run by the states with federal aid; so were the wel-fare or public assistance components of the act.

Gradually, in the years after 1935, federal bureaucrats gained experience and confidence in their abilities to define welfare needs and dispense welfare services themselves. They began to see themselves less as expediters of enlightened cooperation among private groups and as financiers of worthy activities undertaken by the states and more as administrators of welfare programs that provided welfare services directly to the people. After 1937 the bureaucrats worked to pass an agenda of federal welfare legislation that included such items as national health insurance and disability insurance.

As if to signal the change, the bureaucratic structure of the federal welfare establishment was restructured along lines that made it resemble more closely the functional organization common in large American corporations. By 1940 the FSA, the Fair Labors Standards Act of 1938, and the Social Security Act of 1935 stood as the pillars of the federal welfare sector.

War further accelerated the growth of federal influence within the American welfare system, but it did so in a way that established the primacy of federal money, rather than the primacy of federal control. By 1943 it was becoming clear to many big businessmen that the federal government would never shrink to the size it had been in the 1920s. The leading edge of big business opinion, exemplified by the BAC and its new organizational sibling the CED, recognized also that Washington had become a permanent factor in the area of welfare policy. Such enlightened entrepreneurs, who no longer equated the federal government with sin, moved to condition debate regarding public sector welfare policy in ways that allowed them to capture federal funds for projects of which they approved. In this effort they were very successful. The structure of the medical programs passed into law during and immediately after the war underlined this fact. As long as Washington confined itself to financing programs created and controlled by private interest groups such as the AMA, federal welfare initiatives were welcomed. When federal bureaucrats attempted to broaden their exercise of direct administrative controls, however, as in the original Full Employment Act of 1946, their efforts were strongly opposed.

Federal bureaucrats were not happy with the resulting welfare system and pressed more strongly for further discretionary powers over welfare operations. For its part, Congress did little to resolve the resulting stalemate. It granted funds to well-organized private groups and maintained the public welfare programs enacted in the 1920s and the 1930s, but it took no policy initiatives. Lacking the spur of domestic economic emergency that had allowed Roosevelt the opportunity to push through the original Social Security Act, the Truman administration was only able to pass programs upon which both businessmen and bureaucrats agreed. This fact accounted for the dominance of the rehabilitation approach to social welfare problems throughout Truman's two terms in office. Rehabilitation, a variation of 1920s welfare procedures, with a new federal twist, was rationalized in the traditional language of cost efficiency and provided federally subsidized services that in theory, made Americans less dependent upon the government.

When Dwight Eisenhower came to power, federal bureaucrats were working to pass disability insurance and other federal welfare programs, as they had been doing for 15 years, and businessmen and their administrative allies were countering with programs that emphasized rehabilitation. The Republicans made the first move and passed legislation that enabled disabled workers to obtain retirement benefits even if these workers had not put enough into their social security piggy banks to earn the benefits. The bureaucrats supported this legislation because they realized it marked the first step toward enactment of disability insurance. Two years later the effectiveness of this strategy was revealed by congressional passage of disability insurance. Unable to beat the businessmen in a stand-up fight, federal bureaucrats had joined them just long enough to add another program to their welfare arsenal. New Era welfare strategies had been made to serve New Deal welfare ends.

Looking toward the past, the Republicans stumbled into the future. To make sense of the growing number of federal subsidies and federal grants-in-aid and to cut the costs of existing federal programs Eisenhower authorized the creation of a new cabinet level department: Health, Education, and Welfare. Significantly, the department was organized along the functional lines common in corporations, not the occupationally-oriented lines common in the federal bureaucracy. Just as the Department of Defense spurred efficiency by subjugating the special interests of the services to the function of providing defense against foreign invasion, so the Department of Health, Education, and Welfare brought order out of a sea of interest groups and programmatic circumstances. Not surprisingly, Marion Folsom, a noted welfare capitalist member of the BAC and the CED, was picked to transform the department from a granter of special favors to a provider of coordinated services.

With the creation of HEW the continued existence of federal welfare programs was insured. In the future the question would not be whether the federal government should be clearly and continuously involved in the formulation and implementation of social welfare policy; instead, it would be: What amalgamation of public and private power should accomplish social welfare ends? Americans had created a mixed system based largely upon welfare capitalist precedents and federal administrative initiatives. In this system, businessmen and bureaucrats shared power in a symbiotic relation.

NOTES

1. W. Andrew Achenbaum, *Social Security: Visions and Revisions* (New York: Cambridge University Press, 1986), p. 4.

2. Edward D. Berkowitz, "Changing the Meaning of Welfare Reform," in John Weicher, ed., *Maintaining the Safety Net: Income Redistribution Programs in the Reagan Administration* (Washington, D.C.: AEI, 1983), pp. 23-24.

3. Robert M. Ball, "The Original Understanding on Social Security: Implications for Later Developments," unpublished manuscript.

4. Gary P. Freeman, "Voters, Bureaucrats, and the State: On the Autonomy of Social Security Policymaking," unpublished paper.

5. Samuelson and Dale, quoted in Achenbaum, *Social Security*, pp. 54, 61.

6. For more on this point, see Edward D. Berkowitz, *Disabled Policy: America's Programs for the Handicapped* (New York: Cambridge University Press, 1987).

7. Mark H. Leff, "Speculating in Social Security Futures," unpublished paper.

8. Paul Light, "The Politics of Assumptions," unpublished paper. See also Paul Light, *Artful Politics: The Politics of Social Security Reform* (New York: Random House, 1985), p. 50.

9. Achenbaum, *Social Security*, p. 69.

10. "The Social Security Crisis," *Newsweek*, January 24, 1983, p. 22; Walter B. Williams, "A Skeptic's Challenge," Ibid., p. 26.

11. *Reforming Retirement Policies: A Statement by the Research and Policy Committee of the Committee for Economic Development* (New York and Washington: CED, 1981).

12. Quoted in Achenbaum, *Social Security*, p. 80; about the commission, see also Light, *Artful Politics*.

13. Daniel Patrick Moynihan, "More Than Social Security Was at Stake," *Washington Post*, January 18, 1983, p. A-17.

14. Quoted in Edward Berkowitz, "Social Security Celebrates An Anniversary," in Berkowitz, ed., *Social Security After Fifty: Successes and Failures* (Westport, Connecticut: Greenwood Press, 1987), p. 15.

15. Quoted in Robert Ball, "The Original Understanding on Social Security."

16. The following example comes from Edward Berkowitz and Monroe Berkowitz, "Incentives for Reducing the Costs of Disability" (CED background research paper, January 1986).

17. Edward Berkowitz, "Changing the Meaning of Welfare Reform," pp. 23-24.

18. This discussion of AFDC is drawn from President's Commission for a National Agenda for the Eighties, *Government and the Advancement of Social Justice, Health, Education and Civil Rights in the Eighties* (Englewood Cliffs, New Jersey: Prentice Hall, 1981), pp. 55-74.

19. President's Commission on National Goals, *Goals for Americans* (Englewood Cliffs, New Jersey: Prentice Hall, 1960), p. 257.

20. James R. Hosek, "The AFDC-Unemployed Fathers Program: Determinants of Participation and Implications for Welfare Reform," unpublished paper.

21. Remarks of Ellen Winston quoted in "Bureau of Family Services, Minutes of the Meeting on Medical Matters, October 3 and 4, 1963," RG 363, Accession 74-30, Box 3, Washington National Records Center, Suitland, Maryland.

22. "Briefing Paper: The Work Incentive Program," April 25, 1975, pp. 2-4, in Spencer Johnson Papers, Box 12, WIN File, Gerald R. Ford Library, Ann Arbor, Michigan.

23. U.S. Congress, Joint Economic Committee, Subcommittee on Fiscal Policy, "Income Security for Americans: Recommendations of the Public Welfare Study," (Washington, D.C.: G.P.O., 1974).

24. Testimony of Senator David Durenberger (Minnesota) before the President's Commission for a National Agenda for the Eighties, 1980.

25. U.S. Congress, General Accounting Office, "U.S. Income Security System Needs Leadership, Policy, and Effective Management" (Washington, D.C.: G.P.O., 1980), p. 22.

26. Martin Anderson, *Welfare: The Political Economy of Welfare Reform in the United States* (Palo Alto, California: Hoover Institute Press, 1978), pp. 135-48.

27. Ibid., pp. 68, 70-80; Martin Anderson, "The Objectives of the Reagan Administration's Social Welfare Policy," unpublished paper.

28. George Gilder, "Welfare Spurs Family Breakdown," *Insight*, June 23, 1986, pp. 68-69.

29. Lawrence Mead, "Prospects for Welfare Reform," *Policy Forum*, November 1986 (mimeo).

30. Memorandum from Dave and Eli to Congressman [name withheld to preserve confidentiality], March 25, 1987, privately obtained.

31. Ron Haskins, Assistant Minority Counsel, to Republican Members of Congress, February 27, 1987, privately obtained; Julie Rovner, "Governors Jump-Start Welfare Reform Drive." *Congressional Quarterly*, February 28, 1987, pp. 376-78.

32. Wright, quoted in Rovner, "Governors," p. 377.

33. Paul Starr, *The Social Transformation of American Medicine* (New York: Basic Books, 1982), p. 313.

34. See Theodore R. Marmor, *Politics of Medicare* (Chicago: Aldine Publishers, 1973).

35. Robert Ball, "Report for Representative John E. Fogarty about the American Medical Association's Eldercare Program," n.d. RG 235, Accession A-1793, Box 53, Washington National Records Center.

36. Celebrezze to Dr. C. Norman Sheely, January 18, 1965, RG 235, Office of the Secretary, Accession-1793, Washington National Records Center.

37. Achenbaum, *Social Security*, pp. 161-78; Theodore R. Marmor, *Politics of Medicare*. The source that dominates the field of health care is Paul Starr, *The Social Transformation of American Medicine*.

38. In addition to Starr, *Transformation*, and Marmor, *The Politics of Medicare*, see Richard Harris, *A Sacred Trust* (New York: New American Library, 1966), pp. 55, 69-72.

39. These statistics are drawn from Paul Starr, *Social Transformation*, p. 384 and from Committee for Economic Development, *Reforming Health Care: A Market Prescription* (Washington, D.C.: CED, 1987).

40. Joseph A. Califano, Jr., *Governing America: An Insider's Report from the White House and the Cabinet* (New York: Simon and Schuster, 1981), p. 103.

41. Starr, *Transformation*, pp. 394-97.

42. The following section is derived from Edward Berkowitz and Wendy Wolff, *Group Health Association: A Biography of a Health Maintenance Organization* (Philadelphia: Temple University Press, 1987).

43. See Daniel M. Fox, *Health Policies, Health Politics: The British and American Experience, 1911-1965* (Princeton: Princeton University Press, 1986), pp. 21-36.

44. Lawrence D. Brown, *Politics and Health Care Organizations: HMOs as Federal Policy* (Washington, D.C.: Brookings Institution, 1983), pp. 296-97.

45. These statements derive from notes taken by Edward Berkowitz at a hearing of the Senate Committee on Labor and Human Resources, June 24, 1987.

46. These examples are drawn from background research done for the CED project on the costs of medical care.

BIBLIOGRAPHIC ESSAY

The following essay makes no attempt to list every source consulted in the research undertaken for this book. Readers interested in access to more exhaustive listings are referred to other locations.

CHAPTER 1

Three manuscript collections have provided specifics regarding the welfare capitalist innovations with which this chapter deals. The Edward Albert Filene papers in the Bergengren Memorial Museum Library of the World Council of Credit Unions in Madison, Wisconsin are both extensive and well arranged. Bound speeches, correspondence, and diaries provide useful background concerning Filene's reform and business philosophy. The Nelson Olsen Nelson papers at the Missouri Historical Society in St. Louis and the Henry S. Dennison papers (recently deposited by the Dennison family at the Baker Library of the Harvard Graduate School of Business Administration) are less complete, and need to be supplemented by the numerous periodical and other writings that the two men produced over the course of their respective careers. Specific citations of the holdings of the three collections are contained in Kim McQuaid, "Henry S. Dennison and the 'Science' of Industrial Reform, 1900-1950," *American Journal of Economics and Sociology*, vol. 36 (January 1977); idem, "An American Owenite: Edward A. Filene and the Parameters of Industrial Reform, 1890-1937," *American Journal of Economics and Sociology*, vol. 35 (January 1976); idem, "The Businessman as Social Innovator: N. O. Nelson and the Consumer Cooperative Movement," *American Journal of Economics and Sociology* vol. 34 (October 1975); idem, "Businessman as Reformer: N. O. Nelson and Late Nineteenth Century Social Movements in America," *American Journal of Economics and Sociology* vol. 33 (October 1974).

In recent years a number of useful publications surveying business thought and action in the late nineteenth and early twentieth century have appeared. All supply necessary background on the contexts out of which early welfare capitalist innovations evolved. Alfred D. Chandler, Jr., *The Visible Hand: The Managerial Revolution in American Business* (Cambridge, Mass., 1977) is a refreshingly well-written overview primarily concerned with patterns of administrative change within technology-intensive corporations during the period 1850-1920. David F. Noble, *America By Design: Science, Technology, and the Rise of Corporate Capitalism* (New York, 1977) attempts to place the growing emphasis upon 'scientific' management technique within a "revisionist" historical context. The book is particularly valuable for its coverage of the increased influence of engineers in corporate bureaucracies during the period from 1880 until 1920. Noble, however, proves contradictory relative to the type of relationship that existed between what he terms "liberalism" and "corporatism" in the period. On occasion said relationship is stated to be "always tenuous," but Noble later appears to conclude that it was direct, immediate, and compelling. Daniel Nelson, *Managers and Workers: The Origins of the New Factory System in the United States, 1880-1920* (Madison, 1975) provides a necessary supplement to the Chandler volume in that this book seeks to explain how the interaction between employer and employee combined to influence the timing and direction of industrial change. Chandler, in spite of his many virtues, all too often writes of businessmen as if they were isolated in an industrial universe in which labor's position was entirely that of a dependent variable. Jonathan R. T. Hughes, *The Governmental Habit: Economic Controls From Colonial Times to the Present* (New York, 1977), focuses upon the evolution of nonmarket economic controls on the local, state, and national levels. His argument is that analysts who seek to understand the operations of industrial and economic actors without comprehending the legal environment(s) in which such action takes place are engaged in a futile exercise, at best. Stuart D. Brandes, *American Welfare Capitalism, 1880-1940* (Chicago, 1977) and Milton Derber, *The American Idea of Industrial Democracy, 1865-1965* (Urbana, 1970) provide a catalog of welfare capitalist innovations and a typology of such activities previously only available in dated—but still exceedingly useful—volumes including John R. Commons, et al., *History of Labor in the United States, vol. 3* (New York, 1935), W. Jett Lauck, *Political and Industrial Democracy, 1776-1926* (New York, 1926), and Robert Dunn, *The Americanization of Labor* (New York, 1927).

Other published sources of substantial but less direct importance include Robert H. Wiebe, *Businessmen and Reform: A Study of the Progressive Movement* (Cambridge, 1962)—a study that should be augmented by Wiebe's later *The Search for Order, 1877-1914* (New York, 1967) and *The Segmented Society* (New York, 1975). Edward C. Kirkland, *Dream and Thought in the American Business Community, 1860-1900* (Ithaca, 1956) is a workmanlike study of mainstream corporate opinion on the eve of the welfare capitalist era. Robert Ozanne, *A Century of Labor-Management Relations at McCormick and International Harvester* (Madison, 1967), makes use of internal company records of matters usually not preserved for historical scrutiny. Samuel P. Hays, *The Response to Industrialism, 1885-1914* (Chicago, 1957) and Thomas C. Cochran and William Miller, *The Age of Enterprise: A Social History of Industrial America* (1942, revised edition: New York, 1961) are two extremely well-written texts that have caused more than one generation of long-suffering college students to wonder why all historians cannot write as succinctly and well as authors like these. Reinhard Bendix, *Work and Authority in Industry: Ideologies of Management in the Course of Industrialization* (New York, 1956) is a classic treatment chiefly valuable for its comparative approach to patterns of managerial thought in England, Russia, and the United States. Gerald Grob, *Workers and Utopia: A Study of Ideological Thought in the American Labor Movement, 1865-1900* (Chicago, 1969); Louis Filler, *Crusaders for American Liberalism* (New York, 1938: and many times reprinted); Charles M. Destler, *Henry Demarest Lloyd and the Empire of Reform* (Philadelphia, 1963); and James Weinstein, *The Corporate Ideal in the Liberal State, 1900-1918* (Boston, 1971) are all worthwhile treatments of labor and reform thought and action during the period in which welfare capitalism was taking root in the United States.

Contemporary government reports and periodical articles are also an indispensable source for welfare capitalist activities in the period before World War I. The "essay on sources" in Stuart Brandes' *American Welfare Capitalism*, pp. 187-202, is the best single listing.

CHAPTER 2

The accounts of progressive era minimum standards and social insurance laws come from two sets of periodicals. One set consists of contemporary journals of which the *American Economic Review*, the *Proceedings of the Conference on Charities and Corrections*, and the *Journal of Political Economy* are the most useful. As many historians know already, these journals provide an amazingly comprehensive review of contemporary legislative developments. The second set of periodicals are recently-initiated historical journals, particularly *Labor History*. This journal has gone on to take a deep interest in workers' culture and other esoteric items, but it began with a deep interest in trade unions and labor legislation.

The account of minimum wage legislation comes from the publications of the state agencies that held the responsibility to administer such laws. The publications of the Massachusetts Minimum Wage Commission are particularly detailed and, therefore, useful for gaining an understanding of how the laws actually operated. The secondary literature holds a brilliant article by William Graebner, "Federalism in the Progressive Era: A Structural Interpretation of Reform," *Journal of American History* (September 1977). This article goes beyond the individual case study and makes some important generalizations of the relationship between state and federal government in the Progressive Era.

The literature concerning workers compensation is vast. The best place to begin is to obtain the pamphlets written in the various states that investigated the industrial accident problem, such as the *Report of the Connecticut State Commission on Compensation for Industrial Accidents* (Hartford, 1911). The researcher should then turn to some of the competent articles written recently concerning this subject. From these articles will be gained a sense of the dollars-and-cents considerations that motivated the passage of the laws. Articles worth the time are Robert F. Wesser, "Conflict and Compromise: The Workmen's Compensation Movement in New York." *Labor History* (Fall 1976); Richard A. Posner, "A Theory of Negligence," *Journal of Legal Studies* (January 1972); Joseph F. Tripp, "An Instance of Labor and Business Cooperation: Workmen's Compensation in Washington State," *Labor History* (Fall 1976); and Robert Asher, "Radicalism and Reform: State Insurance of Workmen's Compensation in Minnesota, 1910-1933," *Labor History* (Winter 1973). Posner and Asher both contain striking data, which can be used for more general and less ideological purposes than the authors manage.

CHAPTER 3

Any investigation of welfare capitalism during and immediately after World War I ends up owing substantial debts to a small group of writers who have made this a subject of their study.

Samuel Haber, *Efficiency and Uplift: Scientific Management in the Progressive Era, 1890-1920* (Chicago, 1964), and Milton J. Nadworny, *Scientific Management and the Unions* (Cambridge, 1956), analyze the depth and direction of "scientific" management thinking and the impact of Taylorism on middle-class reform clientele. Loren Baritz, *The Servants of Power: A History of the Use of Social Science in American Industry* (Middletown, Connecticut, 1960), treats the evolution of the personnel management and human engineering elaborations of the scientific management impulse. Herman Krooss, *Executive Opinion: What Businessmen Said and Thought on Public Issues, 1920's-1960's* (New York, 1970) is a thorough treatment of the spectrum of "enlightened" (and unenlightened) entrepreneurial opinion. Joan Hoff Wilson, *American Business and Foreign Policy, 1920-1933* (Lexington, Kentucky, 1971), traces the ways in which domestic welfare capitalist opinion influenced—and was influenced by—the nation's ad hoc involvement in international political and economic affairs. The same author's *Herbert Hoover: Forgotten Progressive* (Boston, 1975), more overtly revisionist in tone, seeks to interweave programmatic dynamics of welfare capitalism with the social psychology of the nation's political leadership—exemplified, of course, by Hoover. Robert C. Cuff, *The War Industries Board: Business-Government Relations during World War I* (Baltimore, 1973); Melvin I. Urofsky, *Big Steel and the Wilson Administration* (Columbus, Ohio, 1969); and Robert F. Himmelberg, *The Origins of the National Recovery Administration: Business, Government, and the Trade Association Issue, 1921-1933* (New York, 1976) provide an institutional treatment of the internal nuances of corporate-governmental "cooperation" during and immediately after the war. The Cuff and Urofsky volumes are especially readable. These studies do not show any coherent big business line to have existed in the period. But, unfortunately, revisionist and mainstream historians continue to talk past one another regarding the issue of the growth of corporate influence in the United States as a result of World War I. Alfred D. Chandler, Jr., *Strategy and Structure: Chapters in the History of American Industrial Enterprise* (Boston, 1962) remains the best single source for larger corporations' internal organizational dynamics. The prose style, however, requires dedication from the reader. Peter Collier and David Horowitz, *The Rockefellers: An American Dynasty* (New York, 1976); F. A. McGregor, *The Fall and Rise of MacKenzie King* (Toronto, 1962); and Irving Bernstein, *The Lean Years: A History of the American Worker, 1920-1933* (Boston, 1960) are all good for the Rockefeller initiatives. The McGregor book is particularly useful for the influence of John D. Rockefeller, Jr.'s brand of welfare capitalism on the managements of companies in which the Rockefeller family had substantial interests. Collier and Horo-witz's book has spawned a crop of imitators in the comparatively few years since its appearance. But, thus far, the various volumes that have appeared on the Mellon, Guggenheim, and other families have proved disappointing.

David Brody, *Steelworkers in America: The Non-Union Era* (Cambridge, 1961); John R. Commons, et al., *History of Labor in the United States, vol. 3* (New York, 1935); Graham Adams, *The Age of Industrial Violence, 1910-1915* (New York, 1966); and Herbert Gutman, *Work, Culture, and Society in Industrializing America: Essays in American Working-Class and Social History* (New York, 1976) provide background regarding employee responses to employer initiatives. David Brody's fine essay "The Rise and Decline of Welfare Capitalism" in *Change and Continuity in Twentieth Century America: The 1920's* edited by John Braeman. (Columbus, Ohio, 1968) is also required reading.

An important—but, sadly, little-used—manuscript collection was also useful in the preparation of this chapter: The Owen D. Young papers (privately held, Van Hornesville, New York). The over 700 boxes of papers composing this collection are particularly strong in materials dealing with Owen D. Young's public and private career as General Electric's resident business statesman. (The phrase is not used only ironically.) The collection, however, is weak in internal company memoranda and directives issued after approximately 1924. Approximately 20 file boxes concerning such matters were shipped to General Electric by Young's family some years ago for review—and have never been seen since. The Young papers were supplemented by the excellent holdings of the Columbia Oral History Project at Columbia University in New York. The oral history memoirs of Gerard Swope, Robert E. Wood (Sears, Roebuck), Cyrus Ching (U.S. Rubber), and Henry Bruere (Bowery Savings Bank) proved particularly valuable.

CHAPTER 4

Information concerning federal social welfare programs in the 1920s is difficult to come by: Many analysts continue to believe that federal programs began with the New Deal. Some historians, particularly Ellis W. Hawley and other Hoover scholars, know better and their books and articles cited in the footnotes and elsewhere in this essay affirm that fact. To gain a more complete understanding of the Hoover era the reader should turn to William Starr Myers and Walter H. Newton, *The Hoover Administration: A Documented Narrative* (New York, 1936), which contains revealing documents concerning Hoover's concern for the problems of children. This collection should be supplemented with Hoover's own writing, in particular *The Memoirs of Herbert Hoover* (New York, 1951-52), in which an unapologetic man defends his administration, and *Recent Social Trends in the United States: Report of the President's Research Committee on Social Trends* (New York, 1933), in which the former president explains his theory of social action.

The other sources for the chapter are mostly reports from the federal government. These reports require a great deal of patience, but, despite their dense, bureaucratic prose, they reveal a great deal about the early years of federally assisted public welfare. Most useful were the *Annual Report(s) of the Federal Board for Vocational Education*, which contains information about vocational education and vocational rehabilitation, and the *Bulletin* of the Federal Board for Vocational Education, which contains detailed studies of various aspects of those two programs.

Two scholarly studies on vocational rehabilitation have been published. Mary E. MacDonald, *Federal Grants for Vocational Rehabilitation* (Chicago, 1944) is a very painstaking analysis of the program, written in an era when social workers needed to know their history and to understand the institutions on which they reported. E. Esco Obermann has written a more casual and a more recent overview, *A History of Vocational Rehabilitation* (Minneapolis, 1965).

Books on women are becoming more numerous, and some of those books contain information on the Sheppard-Towner Act. A good starting point is William H. Chafe, *The American Woman: Her Changing Economic and Political Roles, 1920-1970* (New York, 1972)— good unpolemical history that does not overwhelm the reader with facts.

CHAPTER 5

Manuscript collections useful for determining welfare capitalist responses to the challenges posed by the Great Depression include the General Records of the Department of Commerce, Office of the Secretary, General Correspondence, National Archives, Washington, D.C. (especially boxes 783-787 and the contents of file # 102517/36); Record Group 9, Series 37, National Recovery Administration, Miscellaneous Reports and Documents Series, National Archives, Washington, D.C. (especially boxes 8336 and 8415-8416); and the Franklin D. Roosevelt papers, Official File, FDR Presidential Library, Hyde Park, New York (especially box 3-Q). The Edward N. Stettinius, Jr. Papers at the Alderman Library of the University of Virginia in Charlottesville and the Pierre S. DuPont Papers at the Eleutherian Mills-Hagley Foundation Library in Wilmington, Delaware are also good for determining how business leaders went about maintaining formal and informal ties with important federal officials during the New Deal period.

Specific citations illustrating the contents of these manuscript collections can be found in the footnotes to Edward Berkowitz and Kim McQuaid, "Businessman and Bureaucrat: The Evolution of the American Social Welfare System, 1900-1940," *Journal of Economic History* vol. 38 (March 1978); Kim McQuaid, "Corporate Liberalism in the American Business Community, 1920-1940," *Business History Review* vol. 52 (Autumn 1978; idem, "The Business Advisory Council of the Department of Commerce, 1933-1961: A Study in Corporate-Government Relations" in *Research in Economic History*, vol. 1, edited by Paul Uselding. (Greenwich, Conn., 1976); idem, "The Frustration of Corporate Revival During the Early New Deal," *The Historian* (August 1979).

Secondary sources for the period include Ellis W. Hawley, "Herbert Hoover, The Commerce Secretariat, and the Vision of an 'Associative State,' 1921-1928," *Journal of American History* vol. 61 (June 1974); Barry D. Karl, "Presidential Planning and Social Science Research: Mr. Hoover's Experts," *Perspectives in American History* vol. 3 (1969); J. J. Huthmacher, *Senator Robert F. Wagner and the Rise of Urban Liberalism* (New York, 1968); Albert U. Romasco, *The Poverty of Abundance* (New York, 1965)—all useful for the strategies and responses of the Hoover administration; Otis L. Graham, Jr., *An Encore for Reform: The Old Progressives and the New Deal* (New York, 1970); R. Alan Lawson, *The Failure of Independent*

Liberalism, 1930–1941 (New York, 1971); Theodore Rosenhof, *Dogma, Depression, and the New Deal: The Debate of Political Leaders over Economic Recovery* (Port Washington, New York, 1975)—for the reticence of key political and intellectual leaders to countenance the federal government as a direct provider of welfare services; Ellis W. Hawley, *The New Deal and the Problem of Monopoly: A Study in Economic Ambivalence* (Princeton, 1966); Bernard Bellush, *The Failure of the N.R.A.* (New York, 1975); James A. Gross, *The Making of the National Labor Relations Board: A Study in Economics, Politics, and the Law, vol. 1 (1933–1937)* (Albany, 1974); Lewis Lorwin and Charles Wubnig, *Labor Relations Boards* (Washington, D.C., 1935); Irving Bernstein, *The New Deal Collective Bargaining Policy* (Berkeley, 1950); Melvyn Dubofsky and Warren Van Tine, *John L. Lewis* (New York, 1977); and William Leuchtenburg, "The New Deal and the Analogue of War" in *Change and Continuity in Twentieth Century America*, edited by John Braeman. (Columbus, Ohio, 1964)—for the failure of the effort to improve welfare and employment standards via industrial "self-regulation."

CHAPTER 6

Most of this chapter concerns the development of the Social Security Act, a phenomenon on which historians have reported only in the most general terms. Social security for most historians is unambiguously good; progress can be measured by the degree to which Congress adopts the suggestions of the Social Security Administration for amending the act. This view of social welfare as a contest between good and evil forces ignores many questions concerning social security such as how this new program changed the federal government's bureaucratic structure. To answer this sort of question means going back to the sources stored in the National Archives. This task is complicated by the fact that Record Group 47, the Records of the Social Security Administration, are housed in the National Archives and in a big warehouse known as the Federal Records Center in Suitland, Maryland. As a general rule, materials dating from before 1940 are in the National Archives, and materials from after that date are in Suitland, but there are no simple rules.

Material in the National Archives can be supplemented by consulting the interviews of Eveline Burns, I. S. Falk, and others at the Columbia University Oral History Collection (New York). The interviews vary in quality, but they constitute a very complete attempt to talk with the prominent officials in the Social Security program. In addition, researchers should examine a remarkable book by two academics who observed the early years of the Social Security Board's operations, Charles McKinley and Robert W. Fraser, *Launching Social Security* (Madison, 1970).

Wisconsin's State Historical Society is another important center for information concerning social security. Particularly valuable collections are the Arthur Altmeyer Papers and the Wilbur Cohen Papers, both of which are well-indexed.

As for the secondary literature, no one has surpassed Arthur M. Schlesinger, *The Coming of the New Deal* (Boston, 1959) for descriptions of New Deal social reform. Schlesinger needs to be supplemented, however, by two more recent works. One is Roy Lubove, *The Struggle for Social Security* (Cambridge, 1968), a well-written account of contemporary reformers' approaches to the problems of social security, and the other is Daniel Nelson, *Unemployment Insurance: The American Experience, 1915–1935* (Madison, 1969), a monographic account of the origins of an American unemployment insurance law.

Two remarkable participant's memoirs also supply information about the passage and the early years of the Social Security Act. Arthur Altmeyer, *The Formative Years of Social Security* (Madison, 1968) tells of the trials and tribulations of administering America's most important social welfare law. Edwin Witte, *The Development of the Social Security Act* (Madison, 1962) is an aide de memoire that reveals the bitter infighting that preceded the passage of the act.

Finally, the Department of Labor's *Growth of Labor Law in the United States* (Washington, 1962) is the best single source of information on the Fair Labor Standards Act and other programs administered by the Department of Labor.

We might add that in the years since this book first appeared historians have begun to take a greater interest in social security. New books include W. Andrew Achenbaum, *Social Security: Visions and Revisions* (New York, 1986), an attempt to blend history with explicit policy recommendations. The bibliography of this book is astonishingly complete and provides the best single introduction to the new social security literature. Also noteworthy is Carolyn L. Weaver, *The Crisis in Social Security* (Durham, North Carolina, 1982), a very thorough look at the early years of the social security program. Weaver, who later served on the staff of the Senate Committee on Finance, looks at the program from what the economists call a "public choice" perspective. In her work, bureaucrats foil entrepreneurs from the private sector. Despite the heavy-handed analysis, the book does offer some durable insights, such as the notion of FDR offering Congress a "tie-in" deal. Jerry R. Cates, *Insuring Inequality: Administration Leadership in Social Security, 1935-1954* (Ann Arbor: 1983) looks at social security from the opposite point of view. In his book, social welfare bureaucrats turn the program to the right rather than to the left. Cates, like Weaver, has done some impressive primary research into Social Security records, yet his thesis asks readers to accept a great deal on faith. It is hard to make someone like Wilbur Cohen, the former Secretary of Health, Education, and Welfare, look like a conservative, yet Cates makes the attempt.

In 1985, the fiftieth anniversary of social security spawned a new wave of writing on social security. Of note is Edward D. Berkowitz's edited volume, *Social Security: Successes and Failures* (Westport, Connecticut, 1987) which contains essays on social security's history by Berkowitz, Mark Leff, Achenbaum, and Martha Derthick. Leff does a particularly good job in trying to make sense of the growing social security literature. Martha Derthick has written what is destined to become the single best book in the field, *Policymaking for Social Security* (Washington, D.C., 1979), which arrived too late for us to make use of in the first edition. It is masterful in examining how the bureaucrats, politicians, and interest groups have shaped the program.

Another essay deserves special mention. Jill Quadagno has written a solid historical piece on "Welfare Capitalism and the Social Security Act of 1935," which appeared in the October 1984 edition of the *American Sociological Review*. This piece proved helpful to us in assessing the importance of welfare capitalists in the creation and maintenance of social security. So did an early draft of Theda Skocpol's forthcoming work on the development of the welfare state.

Social security also figures prominently in some recently published general works on social welfare. These include Michael Katz, *In the Shadow of the Poorhouse: A Social History of Welfare in America* (New York, 1986) and James Patterson, *America's Struggle Against Poverty* (Cambridge, Massachusetts, 1981). Both do a good job relating the specifics of social policy to more general societal trends. Finally, William Graebner, *A History of Retirement* (New Haven, 1980) makes provocative points on the relationship between the social security program and the promotion of retirement.

As for primary sources, we have benefited from examining Murray Latimer's papers at George Washington University. This source remains almost completely untapped, as far as we know. For the Clark Amendment, the collection is particularly useful.

CHAPTER 7

The Edward N. Stettinius Jr. papers at the University of Virginia in Charlottesville are valuable for organized businessmen's activities in the early wartime mobilization drives. Other good sources for the wartime and immediate postwar years include the Paul Hoffman papers (especially Box 40), the Lou Holland papers (especially Boxes 76 and 77), the Will Clayton papers (especially Box 70), and the John W. Snyder papers—all at the Harry S. Truman Presidential Library, Independence, Missouri. Preliminary examination of two other collections make it appear that they, too, can yield important data. These collections are the Ralph Flanders papers at Syracuse University and the Marion B. Folsom papers at the University of Rochester.

Eliot Janeway, *The Struggle for Survival: A Chronicle of Economic Mobilization during World War II* (New Haven, 1951); Bruce Catton, *The Warlords of Washington* (New York, 1948); and H. M. Somers, *Presidential Agency: The Office of War Management and Reconversion* (Cambridge, 1950) are old standbys for the bureaucratic infighting accompanying the war mobilization and reconversion. Good recent sources include Barton J. Bernstein's articles "The Removal of War Production Board Controls on Business, 1944-1946," *Business History Review* vol. 39 (Summer 1965), "The Debate on Industrial Reconversion: The Protection of Oligopoly and Military Control of the Economy," *American Journal of Economics and Sociology* vol. 26 (April 1967); idem, "The Truman Administration and the Steel Strike of 1946," *Journal of American History* vol. 52 (March 1966).

Four recently-published studies illustrate the effects of the war experience on governmental, social, and industrial structure: Otis L. Graham, Jr., *Towards A Planned Society: From Roosevelt to Nixon* (New York, 1976); Richard W. Polenberg, *War and Society: The United States, 1941-1945* (Philadelphia, 1972); Geoffrey Perrett, *Days of Sadness, Years of Triumph: The American People, 1939-1945* (New York, 1973); and John Morton Blum, *'V' Was For Victory: Politics and American Culture during World War II* (New York, 1976).

The birth of the Committee for Economic Development and other businessmen's efforts to influence the formulation and implementation of social welfare legislation in the immediate postwar period are covered in Karl Schriftgeisser's semiofficial *Business Comes of Age: The Story of the C.E.D.* (New York, 1960) and *Business and Public Policy: The Role of the C.E.D., 1942-1967* (Englewood Cliffs, New Jersey, 1967). These volumes should be used in conjunction with Robert Brady, "The C.E.D.: What Is It and Why?", *Antioch Review* vol. 4 (Spring 1944); Robert Collins, "Positive Responses to the New Deal: The Roots of the C.E.D., 1932-1942," *Business History Review* vol. 52 (Autumn 1978); David Eakins, "Business Planners and America's Post-War Expansion," in *Corporations and the Cold War* edited by David Horowitz (New York, 1970); and David Eakins, "The Development of Corporate Liberal Policy Research in the United States, 1865-1965," (Ph.D. diss., University of Wisconsin, 1966). In recent years, following up on the work of C. Wright Mills and William Appleman Williams, business-backed organizations such as the CED have come under increased scrutiny from scholars of various Marxist and/or Libertarian persuasions. This has resulted in some shoddy work. But for a concise and readable example see G. Wiliam Domhoff, *The Powers That Be: Processes of Ruling-Class Domination in America* (New York, 1978). Such revisionist estimations, however, too often exist in a vacuum—a vacuum caused partly by the fact that mainstream investigations of organizations such as the CED have not been very numerous. It is possible that a forthcoming work by Leonard Silk of the New York *Times* (tentatively entitled *The American Establishment*) will do something to restore a balance.

Until fairly recently, good general treatments of the domestic politics of the Truman era have been sparse indeed. This situation now appears to be being improved. Of particular use to this study were Bert Cochran, *Harry S. Truman and the Crisis Presidency* (New York, 1973); Alonzo L. Hamby, *Beyond the New Deal: Harry S. Truman and American Liberalism* (New

York, 1973); Robert J. Donovan, *Conflict and Crisis: The Presidency of Harry S. Truman, 1945–1948* (New York, 1978); Richard S. Kirkendall, ed., *The Truman Period as a Research Field—A Reappraisal* (Columbia, Missouri, 1974); Susan Hartmann, *Truman and the 80th Congress* (Columbia, Missouri, 1971); Joseph Goulden, *The Best Years: 1945–1950* (New York, 1976); and Barton J. Bernstein and Allen J. Matusow, eds., *The Truman Era: A Documentary History* (New York, 1968).

Specialized monographs on domestic political and economic affairs during the Truman era are still, however, spotty. Those of particular use to this work include Stephen Bailey, *Congress Makes A Law* (New York, 1961) (for the Employment Act of 1946); Davis R. B. Ross, *Preparing for Ulysses: Politics and Veterans During World War II* (New York, 1969) (for the GI Bill of Rights); Monte Poen, "The Truman Administration and National Health Insurance," (Ph.D. diss., University of Missouri, 1967); J. R. and L. B. Lave, *The Hospital Construction Act: An Evaluation of the Hill-Burton Program, 1948–1973* (Washington, D.C., 1973); Joel Seidman, *American Labor From Defense to Reconversion* (Chicago, 1953), H. A. Millis, *From the Wagner Act to Taft-Hartley: A Study of National Labor Policy and Labor Relations* (Chicago, 1950); and Patrick G. Brady, "Toward Security: Post-War Economic and Social Planning in the Executive Office," (Ph.D. diss., Rutgers University, 1975).

CHAPTER 8

This literature concerning the Eisenhower years resembles the scholarship for the Hoover years. In both cases historians are rehabilitating a president's reputation, a process that produces a predictable shower of monographs in the historical journals. The 1950s will soon become the new 1920s in the peculiar world of historiography.

The best way to enter this field is to consult the collection of documents in Robert L. Branyan and Lawrence H. Larsen, *The Eisenhower Administration: A Documentary History* (New York, 1971). This book is a model for the proper way to make archival materials accessible to a wide audience. It should be supplemented by Robert J. Donovan, *Eisenhower: The Inside Story* (New York, 1956), an inside journalistic view of the administration; and by Charles C. Alexander, *Holding the Line: The Eisenhower Era, 1952–1961* (Bloomington, 1975), a general but scholarly treatment of the period.

To analyze social welfare events of the 1950s the researcher needs to go beyond the standard accounts of Eisenhower's presidency. The *Social Security Bulletin* will someday be cited as an invaluable source that chronicles the federal government's rising importance in American life. Less accessible, but still informative, are the memos and other musty papers in Record Groups 290 and 363, records of the vocational rehabilitation program, both stored in the Washington National Records Center.

The Wisconsin State Historical society holds two very informative sets of papers concerning the devleopment of Social Security and other social welfare programs in the 1950s. One is Nelson Cruikshank's papers, which provide a view of one lobbyist's efforts to get Congress to liberalize Social Security. The other is Wilbur Cohen's papers, which contain a very candid exchange of correspondence between Cohen and Arthur Altmeyer concerning the social welfare politics of the 1950s.

For a view from the other side, see Arthur Larson, *A Republican Looks At His Party* (New York, 1956), an articulate defense of the Eisenhower administration. More recent works on social welfare in the 1950s include Martha Derthick, *Uncontrollable Spending for Social Service Grants* (Washington, 1975), a book whose title reveals its theme. This book could be supplemented by Daniel P. Moynihan, *Maximum Feasible Misunderstanding: Community Action in the War on Poverty* (New York, 1970), which is witty and enjoyable even if the author takes too much credit for the formation of social policy.

Those who prefer a more conspiratorial view of events should see Francis Fox Piven and Richard A. Cloward, *Regulating the Poor: Functions of Public Welfare* (New York, 1971). This book makes Washington bureaucrats purposeful actors, and, in so doing, attributes more competence to these bureaucrats than some believe possible.

CHAPTER 9

The research for this paper directly reflects our recent writings. In particular, it draws upon Kim McQuaid's *Big Business and Presidential Power: Roosevelt to Reagan* (New York, 1982), which updates the story of business-government regulation. The chapter also draws upon studies made by Edward Berkowitz for the President's Commission for a National Agenda for the Eighties, the American Enterprise Institute, the Twentieth Century Fund, the Committee for Economic Development, and the Group Health Association. In addition, the chapter relies on the archival records of the Department of Health, Education, and Welfare, which are housed in the Washington National Records Center. It should be noted that these records are chaotic and very difficult to use.

Health care has received considerable scrutiny from scholars in recent years. This note provides us with an opportunity to acknowledge with admiration Paul Starr's *The Social Transformation of American Medicine* (New York, 1982), as fine a piece of policy history as one is likely to find. We also made use of Dan Fox's *Health Politics, Health Policies* (Princeton, 1986) which provides a very useful overview.

A final note: This chapter, more than the rest, relies on personal observation and interviews. Until someone come along who takes contemporary history seriously and who can synthesize from many sources, we suppose that this is inevitable.

INDEX

About the Authors

EDWARD D. BERKOWITZ is Associate Professor of History and the director of the Program in History and Public Policy at George Washington University. In 1987 he was a Robert Wood Johnson Foundation Faculty Fellow in Health Care Finance at Johns Hopkins University. In 1980 he served as a senior staff member of the President's Commission for a National Agenda for the Eighties. Widely published in social welfare history and policy, Berkowitz is the author most recently of *Disabled Policy: America's Programs for the Handicapped* and *Group Health Association: A Biography of a Health Maintenance Organization,* and the editor of *Social Security After Fifty: Successes and Failures.*

KIM McQUAID is Associate Professor of History at Lake Erie College. He is the author of *Big Business and Presidential Power: From Roosevelt to Reagan* and of the forthcoming *A Rip in Time: America During the Vietnam-Watergate Era.* He has also written numerous articles on business-government relations and on various aspects of American history that have appeared in the *Harvard Business Review,* the *New England Quarterly,* and other journals. In 1985-86, he served as the Mary Ball Washington Visiting Professor of U.S. History at University College, Dublin, Ireland.

DATE DUE